Victory at Midway

Victory at Midway

The Battle That Changed the Course of World War II

James M. D'Angelo

Foreword by William S. Dudley

McFarland & Company, Inc., Publishers
Jefferson, North Carolina

LIBRARY OF CONGRESS CATALOGUING-IN-PUBLICATION DATA

Names: D'Angelo, James M., 1937– author.
Title: Victory at Midway : the battle that changed the course of World War II / James M. D'Angelo ; foreword by William S. Dudley.
Description: Jefferson, North Carolina : McFarland & Company, Inc., Publishers, 2018. | Includes bibliographical references and index.
Identifiers: LCCN 2017053065 | ISBN 9781476670713 (softcover : acid free paper) ∞
Subjects: LCSH: Midway, Battle of, 1942.
Classification: LCC D774.M5 D36 2018 | DDC 940.54/26699—dc23
LC record available at https://lccn.loc.gov/2017053065

BRITISH LIBRARY CATALOGUING DATA ARE AVAILABLE

ISBN (print) 978-1-4766-7071-3
ISBN (ebook) 978-1-4766-2995-7

© 2018 James M. D'Angelo. All rights reserved

No part of this book may be reproduced or transmitted in any form or by any means, electronic or mechanical, including photocopying or recording, or by any information storage and retrieval system, without permission in writing from the publisher.

Front cover: the flight deck of USS *Yorktown* (CV-5) shortly after she was hit by two Japanese aerial torpedoes, June 4, 1942 (official U.S. Navy photograph, U.S. National Archives)

Printed in the United States of America

McFarland & Company, Inc., Publishers
Box 611, Jefferson, North Carolina 28640
www.mcfarlandpub.com

To the veterans of the Battle of Midway, whose valiant efforts resulted in a victory for America at a pivotal moment in our history and saved democracy for the Western world. The decisive battle fought by the United States at Midway ranks among those fought at Salamis, Marathon, and Trafalgar.

Their sacrifice of life and limb to the cause of freedom can never be repaid. This book is written to tell their story and the profound impact it had on altering the course of World War II, which even today has not been fully appreciated. Hopefully, it will give the battle and the men who fought it the recognition they deserve.

Acknowledgments

I want to thank my wife Christine Sims for her support and effort in editing this manuscript. Her diligence, literary sense and commitment contributed immensely to the quality of this work.

I also want to acknowledge the support and suggestions offered by Dr. William S. Dudley, former director of the Naval Historic Center (now the Naval History and Heritage Command) throughout this process. His depth of knowledge as a historian and his experience as an author has been invaluable, and I thank him for providing guidance in these areas. I owe a debt of gratitude to Captain John W. Crawford, USN (Ret.) (CV-5), for encouraging me to write the script on new perspectives about the Battle of Midway. His firsthand knowledge, as well as his analytical skill, brought focus and gave purpose to the conclusions herein. I also want to express my appreciation for the assistance of John Deluca of the Naval History and Heritage Command Center in obtaining images, illustrations and maps for this book. In addition, I want to thank Jonathan Parshall for providing me with illustrations from his co-authored book *Shattered Sword*. Lastly, I want to acknowledge the assistance of Susan Brook from the U.S. Naval Institute for providing an image of the Japanese search plan.

Table of Contents

Acknowledgments	vi
Foreword by William S. Dudley	1
Preface	4
Introduction	5
1. Japan Keeps Its Vow	9
2. The First Carrier-to-Carrier Warfare	16
3. Aftermath	28
4. Prelude to Midway	48
5. The Battle of Midway Begins	66
6. The Turning Point	113
7. June 5–7, 1942	141
8. Analysis of the Defeat	154
9. The Significance of the Battle	168
Appendix I: U.S. Vessels and Aircraft	177
Appendix II: Japanese Vessels and Aircraft	183
Chapter Notes	188
Bibliography	192
Index	195

Foreword
by William S. Dudley

Historians and laypersons alike have long been fascinating by the earliest battles of World War II in the Pacific, commencing with the Japanese Imperial Navy's surprise attack on the U.S. naval base at Pearl Harbor, the U.S. carrier raids in the South Pacific, the Battle of the Coral Sea, and, ultimately, the Battle of Midway. The deeper one probes the actions of the Japanese and the reactions of the United States, the more questions are raised. Why did the Pearl Harbor attack occur? Why were the Americans in the Hawaiian Islands not ready to repel the enemy despite warnings from Washington? What role did naval intelligence play in developing strategy in the Pacific? What was the significance of the Battle of the Coral Sea for both the Japanese and the American navies? Why did Admiral Yamamoto use only four carriers at Midway when he sent six to attack Pearl Harbor? And, especially, how did it happen that only six months after the Pearl Harbor attack the United States was able to pull off a devastating surprise of its own on the Japanese fleet 200 miles from Midway Atoll? These and many other questions have triggered a great deal of scholarly investigation. As with most historic puzzles, there were many interlocking pieces that had to be assembled before the answers became clear. Literally thousands of books and articles have been written about these events that occurred over three quarters of a century ago, and because of conflicting opinions it has taken nearly that long for a deep understanding to spread in the scholarly community as well as the wider American public.

Such debates among historians as well as veteran participants in these historic events fascinated Dr. James D'Angelo, the author of this book, from an early age. He graduated from Fordham University, attended Georgetown University Medical School, served in the U.S. Air Force, and had a successful career as an oncologist. All the while, the study of the Battle of Midway was an avocational pursuit for Jim D'Angelo. He brings to this present historical study a particular cast of mind. He is a medical man, a scientist by training, who analyzes historic events in a disciplined scientific way. Readers will also notice that the author is always thinking about the "what-ifs" of the past, alternate ways in which events might have or could have worked out had a different path been followed by key personalities and institutions, whether they were American or Japanese. Some historians would call this a "counterfactual" approach which enlivens the reading of this book.

The principal theme of *Victory at Midway* is Dr. D'Angelo's belief that the Battle of Midway marked a turning point not only for the Pacific War, but also for World War II as a whole. In a global war, major victories and defeats change strategies among allies and their enemies, requiring a shift of assets and changing of priorities as to where those assets must be applied.

For this reason, D'Angelo stresses the need for a broader-than-usual historical perspective, taking into account the progress of World War II in Europe as of 1942, the Battle of the Atlantic, the Soviet-German Battle for Stalingrad, and the race for overwhelming technological superiority between the Allies and Axis powers. This sets the scene of the key question: What was the role of the Battle of Midway in a global context? To assess the answer one must deal with the hypothetical counterfactual argument: What would have happened had the Japanese outfoxed the U.S. task forces at Midway, sinking all three American carriers, followed by the invasion and occupation of Midway? Given this possible outcome, one considers the fate of the Allied "Europe First" strategy, a possible Japanese shift of its forces to attack Russia, and a German victory at Stalingrad. This could have created a major shift in the fortunes of war for the Allies as well as the Axis powers. This points to the validity of an assessment pronounced in 2002 by former Secretary of Defense James Schlesinger:

> There are too few of us who understand Midway's world-historic significance. And, as I will develop, it is essential for us to go forth and proselytize.... Why is not Midway recognized as the crucial battle for the West of World War II, just as Stalingrad is recognized as a crucial battle for the Soviet Union? The comparative neglect of Midway is a great historic puzzle, and, in a sense, a great injustice.... Midway was far more than a decisive naval victory. It was far more than the turning of the tide in the Pacific war. In a strategic sense, Midway represents one of the turning points of world history—and in that role it remains under-appreciated.

Dr. D'Angelo's deep interest in the U.S. Navy's victory at Midway made him sensitive to the fact that many outside of and even within the navy itself were unaware of the significance of the Battle of Midway. It became his self-appointed mission to stir others of like mind to do something to awaken public interest about the time of the fiftieth anniversary of the battle in the early 1990s. I recall being introduced to Jim at a meeting of naval aviators and naval historians in 1992, where we discussed what could be done. The decision was made to promote a conference in which historians and veterans would speak on their studies and experiences in order to inform each other and to get a mixture of viewpoints. One of the goals of this meeting was to stimulate the Navy itself to spread awareness of the Battle of Midway among active-duty officers and enlisted personnel. The conference was such a success that several non-profit associations as well as navy flag officers and civilian officials took note. Dr. D'Angelo, on his own account, established the non-profit International Midway Memorial Foundation, which counted several high-ranking officers and veterans of Midway among its board of directors. In June 1999, Chief of Naval Operations Jay L. Johnson released an administrative message that called on all commands to observe two major commemorations, the Battle of Midway on June 4 and the Navy's birthday, October 13, of each year. Admiral Johnson remarked that he considered Midway "one of the most decisive sea battles in world history. Midway was won, not by superior numbers or daunting technology, but by the courage and tenacity of sailors who fought a vicious air and sea battle against overwhelming odds. Their victory helped us win the world we have today, and it is appropriate that we remember it and those who participated in it." From these beginnings, it has become a tradition that all major commands commemorate these events, and several non-profit associations across the nation have undertaken to sponsor annual Midway Night Dinners, often favorably compared with the Royal Navy's Trafalgar Night Dinners.

Having already done so much to contribute to a new appreciation of the U.S. Navy's role in the Battle of Midway, Dr. James D'Angelo now brings forward his own penetrating interpretation of the significance of Midway and adds a thoughtful book to the existing body of World War II literature.

William S. Dudley was Director of Naval History from 1995 to 2004; he lives in Easton, Maryland.

Preface

The Battle of Midway is among the most decisive naval battles in world history, with far-reaching global effects. This book focuses on new historical perspectives on the Battle of Midway, one of the most important of which is that the victory at Midway changed the course of World War II. Other new perspectives on the battle settle ongoing controversies about decisions made during the battle, and different conclusions are drawn as to why Japan lost the battle.

I became interested in the battle at age eighteen when I read Mitsuo Fuchida and Masatake Okumiya's book *Midway*. The story line inspired me to admire and respect the men who participated in the battle. Over the years, as I learned more details about the battle, I wanted to bring public attention to the widespread heroism, courage and determination of those men who fought the battle. I had a great desire to find out and tell the truth of one of history's most important and decisive naval battles. I have attempted to do so in the work that follows.

Many important works on the Battle of Midway have been written, among them *Incredible Victory*; *Shattered Sword*; *Return to Midway*; *Joe Rochefort's War*; *A Glorious Page in Our History*; *What If?*; *Codebreakers*; *The First Team*; *Battle of Midway*; and *Fading Victory*. This work is different from other works because it focuses on new historical perspectives and new information regarding the battle, including the following: (1) That the Battle of Midway was not only the turning point of the war in the Pacific but of World War II in its entirety. (2) Although prior naval intelligence was available to the United States before both the battles of the Coral Sea and Midway, the outcomes of both battles were very dissimilar. (3) The 75-year history of criticism by historians of Admiral Nagumo's decision not to immediately launch all of his available aircraft on June 4, 1942, to attack the American fleet presents an irony that hasn't been fully appreciated. (4) The role of the submarine *Nautilus* in winning the battle. (5) The nearly 75-year-old controversy as to the nature of Admiral Halsey's rash. (6) The fact that one of only two pilots who had two direct hits on two different Japanese carriers that day, Lieutenant Richard Best, USN, was flying with active tuberculosis.

I have researched the medical records of Admiral Bill Halsey and Lieutenant Richard Best; interviewed many Midway veterans, including one Japanese pilot and one Japanese observer; reviewed significant books on the battle; reviewed documentary films on the battle; and interviewed the late Walter Lord, author of *Incredible Victory*, and the late Admiral Thomas Moorer, USN (Ret.), former Chairman of the Joint Chiefs of Staff.

Introduction

There have been a number of excellent books written on the Battle of Midway that describe the fascinating details of this battle, in which a numerically superior—but tactically poorly positioned—Japanese Navy was defeated by a smaller but tactically superiorly positioned U.S. fleet. The bravery of the men who fought at Midway contributed enormously to its successful outcome, and Americans owe them a great debt of gratitude for the freedom we enjoy today.

My purpose in writing this book is to present the Battle of Midway from a broader historical perspective than has been customary. The value of this approach is that it allows us to gain greater insight into the Battle of Midway's significance in a way that one is not able to do when one studies it in the context of the Pacific war alone. In addition, the impact of seemingly remote occurrences on future events—the essence of historical perspective—will be demonstrated by an examination of the interwoven relationship between the Battle of the Coral Sea and that of Midway. The decisive American victory at the Battle of Midway in June 1942 had profound effects on the outcome of World War II in its entirety, having both short- and long-term global consequences. The well-documented short-term consequence was that the battle ended a series of consecutive offensive successes by Japan in the Pacific. Much less appreciated is the long-term consequence that the decisive victory by the United States at Midway permitted both America and Great Britain to continue to focus the majority of their World War II military resources on Europe rather than the Pacific.

In the aftermath of the Japanese attack on Pearl Harbor on December 7, 1941, and of Germany's and Italy's declaration of war against the United States four days later, the United States was faced with a dilemma in its military response to these events. Should its main focus of military action be in the Atlantic or the Pacific? America was not fully prepared for war in 1941 and did not have the capability of fighting a two-ocean war. Efforts in one theater of operation would automatically limit effort in the other; attempts by the United States to bolster its military strength in the Atlantic would result in a diminution of its efforts in the Pacific. Weighing the circumstances, America, along with Great Britain, committed to its "Europe First" policy on December 22, 1941. This decision had significant military implications for the U.S. efforts to constrain Japanese successes in the Pacific. During this time, America would have to forego its attempts to take back its territories captured by Japan: the Philippine Islands, Wake Island, Guam, and the western Aleutian Islands. There were several reasons for this

Air strips on Midway, 1941 (photo 80-G-451086, courtesy Naval History and Heritage Command).

strategic decision implemented jointly by the United States and Great Britain which gave the conflict in Europe precedence over the war in the Pacific. First, Great Britain was the only country remaining in Europe that was free of German domination and, as such, it represented the last bastion of democracy in western Europe; second, Britain was the only country in Europe that America could count on as a military base; third, German submarine attacks against U.S. Merchant Marine vessels in the Atlantic were raging, and the Allies were losing these battles; and fourth, Britain's colonies in Southeast Asia, namely Hong Kong, Singapore, and Malaya, had fallen to the Japanese military by June 1942, and neither the United States nor Great Britain were in a military position to recapture the colonies at that time.

Introduction

During the summer of 1942, the military situation in Europe was precarious at best. Germany was winning the Battle of the Atlantic; during June, tons of Allied shipping were lost to German submarines at sea, the worst losses of that year to date. In addition, the military outcome in North Africa was in doubt; Tobruk had fallen into German hands ten days before the Battle of Midway; the German army was at the doorsteps of Stalingrad and the Caucasus oil fields in southeast Russia; and, most importantly, Germany was ahead of the United States in the development and implementation of jet and rocket technology. Although this latter scientific achievement was in the early stages of its development, the Germans were rapidly closing in on realizing the full potential of the science, so as to produce a potent and superior military weapon in its fight against the Allies. Time was of the essence if the Allies were to prevent the Germans from gaining air superiority over the skies of Europe as well as the capability of reaching Britain and the United States with intercontinental ballistic missiles.

Germany had also begun research on nuclear fission in 1938–1939. This was the subject of a letter to Franklin Roosevelt written by Leo Szilard and signed by Albert Einstein in 1939, advising the president to begin research on nuclear weaponry.

If the United States had lost all three of its carriers at Midway and Japan's carrier strength had remained intact, President Roosevelt would have been faced with a difficult military and political decision because Hawaii and the entire West Coast of the United States would have been vulnerable to Japanese attack. In addition, Australia, a significant ally in the Pacific and a critical base for American military operations, would have been isolated by Japan's control of the sea-lanes to and from Australia. Japan would have had the ability to bomb our oil reserves in Hawaii, which, even without an invasion, would have successfully forced the U.S. Navy to withdraw to San Diego. This in turn would have necessitated a significant movement of naval forces from the Atlantic to the Pacific, with no certainty of victory assured by these deployments.

This change of tactical superiority in favor of Japan in the short term would have seriously affected the timeline of our offensive assault on North Africa and our decision to invade Normandy in 1944. Furthermore, these circumstances would have provided Germany with the time needed to develop its superior weapons in its fight against the Allies, which could have tipped the outcome of the war in Germany's favor or—at the very least—left the conclusion of the war uncertain.

In addition to the events taking place in Europe, the Soviet Union would have faced a dilemma if Japan had won at Midway; they would either have to expose the Manchurian border to attack by the Japanese or weaken their position at Stalingrad by not reinforcing the city with much-needed troops from eastern Russia. Therefore, a decisive victory by Japan at Midway would have given Japan the opportunity to invade the Soviet Union on its eastern border. The Soviet Union would then have been compelled to fight the war in Europe and enter the war against Japan.

Now, facing a war on two fronts, Russia's ability to resist the German army in the west would have been weakened further. These events would have clearly delayed the timetable for the Allies to take the offensive in Africa and on the beaches of Normandy.

The foregoing reveals how precarious the balance of victory was for the Allies in the early part of World War II and how events in the Pacific clearly influenced events in the Atlantic and their ultimate outcomes. It describes how the decisive victory of the U.S. Navy at Midway influenced the whole of World War II, affecting the outcomes not only in the Pacific but in the Atlantic as well, and paved the way for the ultimate victory by the United States and its allies over Japan and Germany.

1

Japan Keeps Its Vow

It had been eighty-eight years (1853) since Commodore Matthew C. Perry entered Yedo Bay (Tokyo Bay) and demanded that Japan open its doors to world trade. Realizing that the Samurai had become weak and soft, the Japanese government decided that the country would capitulate to U.S. demands, but with the caveat that it would mimic the West in every way. When it was strong enough, it would attack the United States. Thus, the seeds were sown for Japan's attack on Pearl Harbor on December 7, 1941.

Since the attack on America's main naval base in the Pacific, Japan improved its defensive perimeter to include territory as far west as Burma, as far east as the Gilbert Islands, as far north as Manchuria and as far south as New Guinea. During the first six months of the war in the Pacific, U.S. naval policy was defensive in nature, with the one exception of the Doolittle Raid on the Japanese Islands on April 17, 1942 (U.S. date).

Tactically, the United States changed its naval policy following the attack on Pearl

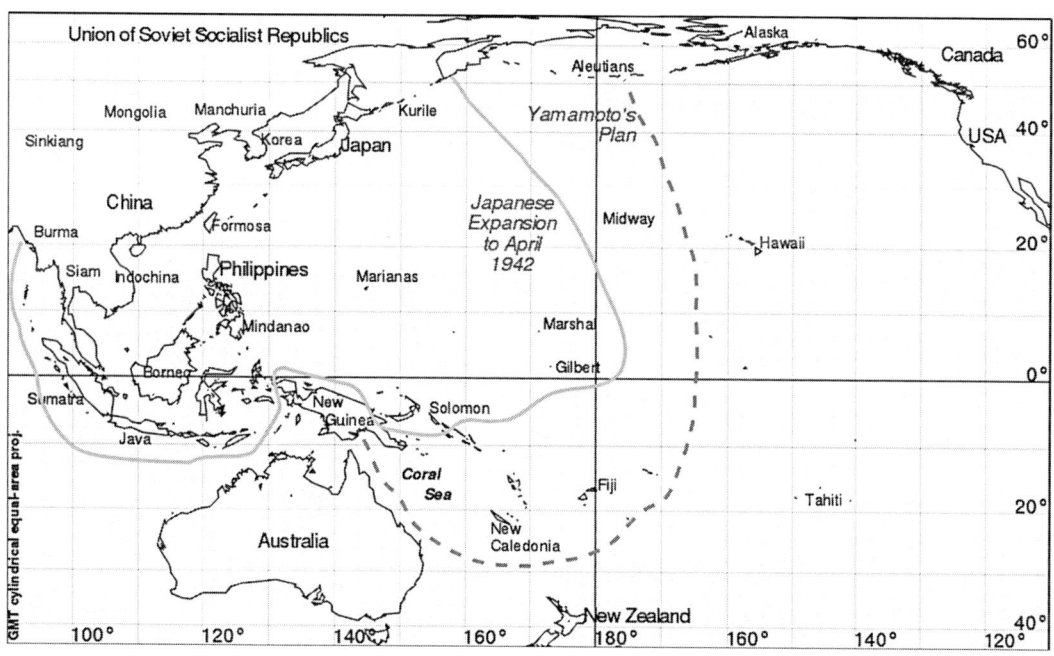

Japanese expansion through 1942.

Harbor. In the aftermath of the surprise attack, with its old battleships damaged or sunk and the remaining battleships too slow to keep up with carriers, the U.S. Navy decided to form a task force with the carrier in the center surrounded by cruisers and destroyers. This decision to change its naval policy was a major departure from the concept that prevailed, that is, that the battleship was the supreme ship in U.S. naval tactics. The golden age of the carrier and naval aviation was on the horizon.

As of April 1942, with the Japanese Army and Navy gaining territory with every military offensive, the United States needed a psychological victory to boost morale back in the States. Prior to the Doolittle Raid, the United States had only two carriers in the Pacific: *Enterprise* and *Lexington*. On April 3, 1942, *Hornet* entered the Pacific carrying sixteen B-25 twin-engine bombers.

It was to meet *Enterprise* on April 12 and together with *Hornet* head west to a point about 400–500 miles east of the coast of Japan. On April 18 (Japanese date) at 0738, the voyage was interrupted by the sight of the No. 23 *Nitto Maru*, a converted seventy-ton whale catcher, which had reported the task force sighting back to Japan. The *Nitto Maru* was subsequently sunk by cruiser *Nashville* and *Enterprise*'s SBD dive-bombers thirty minutes later. The pilots of the B-25s were immediately given the order to man their planes. All the B-25s were aloft by 0920 in spite of the inclement weather and thirty-foot waves.[1]

The sixteen B-25s reached their Japanese targets at 1220 (Japanese time) and dropped their bombs on Tokyo, Yokohama, Kobe, Osaka, Nagoya and Yokosuka. A tailwind allowed fifteen of the U.S. bombers to reach the eastern coast of China (Japanese-occupied territory) where, running out of fuel, they either bailed out or crash-landed their planes. Eight

Leaving deck as part of the Doolittle Raid, April 18, 1942 (photo 80-G-41196, courtesy Naval History and Heritage Command).

men were captured by the Japanese, while the rest safely reached Chunking. The other B-25 flew safely to Vladivostok, Russia, where the crew was promptly imprisoned by the Russians, who had not yet entered the war against Japan. The Chinese paid a heavy price for the raid, as over 250,000 Chinese soldiers and civilians were killed in a campaign of revenge by the Japanese.[2]

Prior to the Doolittle Raid, the Japanese Navy was in a heated debate as to what direction the military should take to improve the defense perimeter of Japan. The Japanese military had been successful in its Phase One operations, which had focused on securing oil and other materials it needed to fight the war, but had not designed a plan for future operations. Thus, military leaders began to ask questions such as whether Japan should unite with Germany on the African continent, consider invading Australia, or possibly attack Hawaii for a second time. The answer revolved around which military direction would most enhance the security of the Japanese Islands and promote Japan's spheres of influence over the continent of Asia.

Japan's strategic policy was supposed to be formulated by the Army and Navy General Staffs operating as sections of the Imperial Headquarters. The Chief of the General Staff was assigned to be the Chief of the Navy Section of Imperial Headquarters, but in fact it was the Chief of the Combined Fleet, Admiral Yamamoto Isoroku, who dictated Navy policy. Therefore, Rear Admiral Ugaki Matome, Combined Chief of Staff, was asked to study the second phase of naval operations for Japan in the war in the Pacific. He ultimately decided that Japan should stay on the offensive because within a year, the United States could eliminate Japan's naval supremacy over America. By late 1943, Japan's leaders were aware of America's industrial capacity and its ability to greatly surpass Japan's initial carrier advantage.[3]

Ugaki's plan was for Japan to first seize and occupy the Midway and Palmyra Islands, and when these islands' air strength was sufficient, the Combined Fleet would then invade the Hawaiian Islands. He reasoned that an attack on Hawaii was feasible because Japan had a 3:1 superiority over the United States in aircraft carriers; in addition, an attack on Midway or Hawaii would certainly draw out the American aircraft carrier fleet. The destruction of the American carrier fleet would result in a devastating blow to the efforts of the United States both strategically and tactically in the war in the Pacific. However, his plan to invade Hawaii was rejected by his subordinate staff as surprise could no longer be achieved because the United States had been on high alert since the war began; the Japanese could not provide enough aircraft to control the skies over Hawaii, and the U.S. shore batteries would have a clear advantage in destroying or damaging the invading Japanese ships.[4]

With the foregoing criticisms, Admiral Ugaki withdrew his plan to invade Hawaii and focused on an offensive to the west, as recommended by Captain Kuroshima Kamato, senior fleet operations officer. The plan would involve a joint Axis offensive, with Germany moving its army east from western Africa and Japan moving its forces west from the Indian Ocean to the Suez Canal, where the armies would unite. Germany, however, had no interest in this concept, so this plan was also discarded. Thus, Japan's new objective became the destruction of the British fleet, the conquest of Ceylon, and air superiority over the Indian Ocean. This objective was accomplished by April 1942.[5]

During this time, the Japanese Naval General Staff had been looking at the possibility of invading Australia. Captain Tomioka Sadatoshi of the Plans Division of the First (Operations) Section spearheaded this concept and studied its strategy. His thinking was that Australia, due to its size and location on Japan's defense perimeter, would be the place where the United States would launch its counteroffensive against Japan. If the subcontinent remained in the Allies' hands it would pose a definite threat to the security of Japan. This plan, however, was also rejected because the Japanese Army could not provide the necessary ten divisions required to invade Australia. The Navy suspected the real reason why the army would not provide troops was that it expected Germany to be successful in its invasion of the Caucasus region of southeastern Russia. The victory would alter the course of the war in favor of Germany and require Russia to reinforce its armies in the west by moving troops from the Manchurian border to the east. This occurrence would allow the Japanese army to invade eastern Russia.

The focus of the Naval General Staff now turned to less formidable objectives such as invading New Guinea, the Solomon Islands or the New Caledonia/Fiji Islands areas. The conquest of these islands would effectively cut off Australia from the United States. Lae and Salamaua in eastern New Guinea had already been occupied by Japanese troops, and the army had agreed to the use of the South Seas Detachment for the invasion of Port Moresby on the southeast border of New Guinea and for Tulagi in the Solomons. The plan would force the United States to send all of its carriers in the Pacific to Australia, because America needed the subcontinent in order to carry out future offensive operations against Japan. Proof of this premise lies in the fact that not only were *Lexington* and *Yorktown* assigned to the upcoming Battle of the Coral Sea, but *Enterprise* and *Hornet*, having returned from the Doolittle Raid, were also sent on their way to the Coral Sea when Task Force 16 learned the battle was over.

By the middle of March, Admiral Yamamoto had already made up his mind that Midway should be the focus of a Japanese offensive against the United States. He sent Commander Watanabe Yasuji, the operations officer on his staff, to represent him in the meetings in Tokyo with the Naval General Staff. Yamamoto realized that getting the approval of the adoption of his Midway plan would not be easy.

On April 2, 1942, a debate began between Commander Watanabe and Commander Miyo Tatsukichi, the First Section Air Officer who represented the Naval General Staff. Miyo pleaded that Midway presented an unfavorable tactical situation for Japan, and its strategic value was questionable even if it was successfully occupied because of the logistics in supplying the vast amount of material and aircraft needed to support Midway. He argued that owing to the short supply of Japanese aircraft and material it would be next to impossible to meet the June deadline. The shortage of aircraft was becoming very serious for Japan. Every air unit was supposed to have been backed up with reserve planes equal to one-third of the operational complement. In fact, the vast majority of units not only did not have any reserve aircraft, but the air fleet was operating under normal operating strength. His objections to the Midway plan were that since Midway was close to Hawaii, U.S. submarines could more easily observe Japanese fleet movements, so that surprise was not likely to be achieved. In addition, Japanese forces would have to proceed against Midway without land-based air support. This would reduce the effective striking power of the carriers because some of the aircraft would have to be diverted for scouting reconnaissance. Miyo had doubts that an attack on Midway would bring out the U.S. carrier fleet. Once Midway was seized, there would be a difficulty in defending the atoll against counterattacks by the U.S. Navy. Midway's value as an advance base for air patrols was questionable because the patrol planes could only cover a 600–700-mile radius, and—lastly—Miyo believed it was overly optimistic that the loss of the Midway Atoll would greatly affect America's morale.[6]

Miyo therefore presented his arguments in favor of the New Caledonia, Fiji and Samoa campaign. He pointed out that although the islands were further away from Japan than Midway, they also were equally distant for the United States. The assault by Japan on the islands would almost certainly draw out the U.S. fleet because seizure of these islands would threaten Australia with being cut off from the United States, and America needed the subcontinent as a base for a counteroffensive against Japan. Miyo failed to point out another advantage to the Japanese in attacking the three-island group. Unlike the situation at Midway, where the Japanese fleet would be faced with the tactical dilemma of being wedded to a fixed schedule in attacking Midway and alternatively destroying the U.S. fleet, the Japanese fleet in seizing New Caledonia, Fiji and Samoa would not be concerned in attacking a fixed target—a U.S. airstrip. At Midway, the Japanese fleet would violate one of the basic tenets of ships at sea engaged in battle; that is: *the fluidity of a fleet's movement* is paramount in ensuring a successful naval outcome. Thus, an operation on the foregoing islands would surely enhance the chance of success over that offered at Midway.

On April 5, Admiral Yamamoto, through his representative Commander Watanabe, voiced his objections that he opposed any offensive plan except the one that involved an operation against Midway. The Japanese Naval General Staff reluctantly agreed with Yamamoto, but the date of invasion was still in contention. The Naval General Staff wanted to postpone the date until late June in order to allow more time for preparations for the invasion. The Combined Fleet argued that a full moon was necessary for the night landings, and delay would impair the chance of success for the operation. Vice Admiral Inouye Shigeyoshi, Commander of the Fourth Fleet, who was responsible for operations in the Southwest Pacific, declared that seizing Midway would overextend the area to be defended by Japan. In addition, he stated that he had no confidence in the Fourth Fleet's ability to supply the atoll. Vice Admiral Nagumo Chuichi, Commander of the First Air Fleet, and Vice Admiral Kondo Nobutake, Commander of the Second Fleet, were not consulted in the plans for the Midway invasion as they were involved in Japan's southern operations until mid–April. Therefore, the status of the operational capacity of these two forces was lacking in the discussion of the plan for the invasion of Midway. Although the Naval General Staff gave its consent to the Midway plan, it continued to be highly skeptical of the operation. In April 1942, and in spite of the incredible success of the Japanese Navy in the first five months of the war, Navy leaders were very concerned about a sneak attack on Tokyo, Japan's capitol and the city of residence of the Imperial Emperor. If such a raid were to occur, Japanese leaders knew the damage would be light, but the psychological effects on the Japanese people would be profound, as the emperor's safety would come into question. The responsibility for the defense of the Japanese Islands was in the hands of the Army, but if an air attack were to come from the sea, the Navy would bear the brunt of the blame for the consequences.

Yamamoto was obsessed with keeping the emperor free from any sea-based air attack. Japanese history during the Russo-Japanese War demonstrated that such an attack would result in violence and chaos in the streets of Japan.[7]

After the Doolittle Raid on April 18, 1942 (Japan date), Japan concluded that minimum damage had been done by the U.S. raid and little advantage was gained by the Americans as a result of the attack. Contrary to Japanese assessment, the Doolittle Raid sped up the course of the war in the Pacific because it created a sense of urgency that the U.S. threat needed to be contained. The raid ensured that the controversy regarding the proposed invasion on Midway was over and that Midway would be attacked. Although the Naval General Staff had reluctantly agreed to the plan, other vital points in the execution of the mission were in doubt. Yamamoto was more determined than ever to attack Midway at any cost and as soon as possible. The initial opponents of the Midway operation now had to agree that the threat from U.S. carriers was more immediate than any attack to isolate Australia. The opponents failed to realize that Japan's attempt to isolate Australia would also present an opportunity for Japan to destroy all four U.S. carriers, as has been previously discussed. The plan's creation was expedited to meet the early June deadline for the Japanese attack on Midway. By the end of April, the complete plan was finished by Combined Fleet Headquarters and submitted to the Naval General Staff for approval. On May 5, Admiral Nagano Osami, Chief of the Naval General Staff, acting in the name of the emperor, issued Imperial General Headquarters Order No. 18, which directed the Commander in Chief of the Combined Fleet to execute the order to occupy Midway and the western Aleutian Islands in cooperation with the Army. The Army was to provide one infantry regiment for the Midway landing operation, but the troops were to be withdrawn as soon as the atoll was secured, leaving the defense of Midway to the Japanese Navy.[8]

Japanese military leaders appear to have made the decision to attack Midway and the Aleutians in a vacuum, without proper consideration being given to the tactical and logistical disadvantages involved in the Midway operation. It seems more than probable that the upcoming Port Moresby operation or the New Caledonia, Fiji and Samoa plan would have obtained the same results without accepting the risks inherent in the plan for the Midway operation. The destruction of the U.S. carrier fleet was the main objective of any future Japanese operation, not the occupation of Midway and the Aleutian Islands. If all 11 of Japan's aircraft carriers had come to bear on the four U.S. carriers available in the upcoming Battle of the Coral Sea, it would have given the Japanese an 11:4 advantage in aircraft carriers, with a strong possibility that all four U.S. carriers would be sunk or damaged in a head-to-head naval engagement. The United States had already committed two carriers (*Lexington* and *Yorktown*) in the upcoming Battle of the Coral Sea, and Nimitz had directed *Enterprise* and *Hornet* back from the Doolittle Raid to proceed from Pearl Harbor to the Coral Sea.

The knowledge by the United States that eleven Japanese carriers would be present in the Coral Sea might have caused the United States to abort the Doolittle Raid so that all four U.S. carriers would be available in the ensuing battle. In that event, the emotional impact on the Japanese leaders resulting from the raid would not have existed. On the other hand, if *Lexington* and *Yorktown* entered the Coral Sea alone (as actually happened), both carriers would certainly have been sunk by the overwhelming force of the

Japanese expansion through 1942.

11 Japanese carriers. In addition, the Port Moresby invasion would have been successful and Australia would have become one step closer to being effectively cut off from the United States. At the very least, if America declined to engage the Japanese in the Coral Sea operation, Australia would have been in danger of being cut off from the United States.

Yamamoto's decision to invade Midway was based on the concept that Japan needed to be immunized against further U.S. air attacks and Midway was the best place to draw out and destroy the U.S. fleet. The irony of that thinking is that independent of the outcome of the Battle of Midway, the United States did not again attempt an air raid on Japan until October 1944, when the United States, having captured the Mariana Islands, began to bomb Japan. In late 1944, there was little doubt as to the outcome of the war in the Pacific.

2

The First Carrier-to-Carrier Warfare

One of the most significant errors in judgment by Japan during the war in the Pacific was the failure to seriously consider that the United States would commit all of its available carriers to the defense of Australia. Yamamoto was fixated on Midway regardless of the strategic and tactical disadvantages it offered, rather than taking advantage of the huge opportunity to destroy the existing U.S. Navy operational carrier fleet in the Pacific that the Battle of the Coral Sea offered to Japan.

On April 3, Lieutenant Commander Joseph Rochefort, head of the Communications Unit at Pearl Harbor (Station Hypo), had deciphered enough of the JN-25B Japanese naval code to discover that the military operation known to the Japanese as the "RZP Campaign" was applicable to the invasion of Port Moresby in southeastern New Guinea and the occupation of the island of Tulagi in the Solomon Islands. British intelligence also learned that Carrier Division Five (*Zuikaku* and *Shokaku*) was to sortie from Japan and arrive in Truk on April 28.[1]

The United States was not able to pinpoint where the two large carriers would be once they reached the Coral Sea because the carriers were not assigned to a fixed target as would be the case at Midway, where the U.S. carriers waited in ambush of Japan's Kido Butai (mobile force) during the Battle of Midway. In the Battle of the Coral Sea, the two carriers were released from their primary mission to protect the MO (code name for the Port Moresby's invasion) Invasion Force and were given the flexibility to roam the Coral Sea looking for the American carriers. Therefore, U.S. intelligence could not alert Admiral Frank Fletcher, Commander of Task Force 17, as to the location of the Japanese carriers.

Admiral Chester W. Nimitz, Commander in Chief of the U.S. Fleet, was determined to prevent Japan from gaining control of Port Moresby which would interrupt the lines of communication between Australia and the United States. On April 25, he discussed the issue with Admiral Ernest King, Chief of Naval Operations, who took the unprecedented step of requesting the opinion of Rochefort in the matter. Rochefort pointed out that the Indian Ocean operations by the Japanese were over; that Japan was planning an offensive on eastern New Guinea, while there was no evidence that Japan would invade Australia; and, finally, that another operation in the Pacific was planned but the details of this operation were not yet clear. King was very impressed with Rochefort's assessment and without conferring with Commander John Redman, the head of OP-20-G in Washington, D.C., granted Rochefort the authority to focus on the decryption and interpretation of Pacific intelligence. As a result Redman, now more than ever, became determined to centralize control of radio intelligence in Washington, setting up a rivalry between Rochefort and himself as to which intelligence unit best evaluated intelligence.[2]

During the meeting between Nimitz and King, King expressed concerns over Admiral Frank Fletcher being the assigned leader of Task Force 17. The Chief of Naval Operations was worried over Fletcher's lack of aggressiveness at Wake Island and in the raid on the Marshall Islands. Nimitz reassured him that Fletcher was capable and the right person to lead Task Force 17.

Nimitz realized he was taking a monumental risk by assigning all four U.S. carriers to the Coral Sea operation. He appreciated that his primary responsibility was the protection of the Hawaiian Islands, but the loss of Australia would have profound effects on the balance of power in the Pacific. He ordered *Lexington* from Pearl Harbor to join *Yorktown* in the Coral Sea. Task Force 17 was also to be joined by Admiral John Crace, RN, and his ANZAC (Australian and New Zealand Army Corps) cruisers, which were designed as Task Force 44 for the upcoming battle. He hoped but doubted that *Enterprise* and *Hornet* could return to Pearl Harbor from the Doolittle Raid in time to make the 1,000-mile voyage to the Coral Sea, but the plan was to send these two carriers if possible into the Coral Sea.[3]

In Japan, Admiral Yamamoto continued to be obsessed with the early June deadline for the Battle of Midway and that Midway was the only military target that would definitely draw out the U.S. carriers. This reasoning was clearly a fatal error in judgment. As we have seen, the United States was ready to commit all four of its carriers to the Coral Sea operation. One of the significant results of the Doolittle Raid was that it focused Yamamoto so much on Midway that it caused him to move up the entire timetable for the invasion of Port Moresby (from late to early May) in order to meet the June 4 deadline for the Battle of Midway. This action resulted in Japan not only losing the inclusion of *Kaga* for the Coral Sea operation (which was being repaired in early May, but would be available in late May) but also *Akagi*, *Hiryu* and *Soryu*, which were returning from the Indian Ocian operation. In addition, *Kaga* alone would have provided the necessary experienced pilots that were lacking in the pilots of the *Zuikaku* and *Shokaku*. Thus, Japan lost a golden opportunity to achieve a clear tactical victory in the Battle of the Coral Sea to destroy all four U.S. carriers (*Enterprise* and *Hornet* would have been available in late May).

Yamamoto's preoccupation with Midway set in motion a series of events in the Coral Sea that primed Japan for failure not only in the Battle of the Coral Sea, but also in the upcoming battle at Midway. The inextricable link between the Battle of the Coral Sea and the Battle of Midway is that in both conflicts, Japan squandered its opportunity to achieve numerical superiority, and in so doing lost its chance to destroy all or part of the existing U.S. Pacific Fleet. If Yamamoto had committed all eleven of his carriers to the Battle of the Coral Sea (six fleet carriers, two light carriers and three small carriers), the United States would have faced a numerically superior ratio (11:4 in favor of Japan), though the number of aircraft on the carriers would have made the ratio closer to 8:4 in favor of Japan and almost certainly would have resulted in damage to—or loss of—all four U.S. carriers. If the Battle of the Coral Sea had taken place in mid- to late May, all four American carriers would have been available for the Battle of the Coral

Sea, as that would have allowed time for *Enterprise* and *Hornet*, then stationed in Pearl Harbor, to reach the battle. Importantly, Australia would have effectively been cut off from the United States and its allies.

Japan would have gained other tactical advantages by making the Coral Sea operation the arena in which to engage the United States in a decisive carrier battle. These advantages included that (1) unlike Midway, the Coral Sea area of conflict was equally distant from Japan and the United States, so that the logistical difficulties, as a result of the distance would be the same for both countries; (2) the Japanese would not have faced the land-based aircraft that were based on Midway; (3) Japan would have had the support of 135 land-based bombers and 135 land-based fighters at the Coral Sea; and, very importantly, (4) at the Coral Sea, at least 100 search aircraft stationed in Rabaul, Lae, Shortland and Tulagi would be available. The foregoing supports the contention that Yamamoto did not use sound military judgment in the planning and execution of either battle—that of the Coral Sea or of Midway.

On April 29, the invasion plan by the Japanese began when the Tulagi force left Rabaul, and the Main Body, including the small carrier *Shoho*, sailed from Truk. Four days later, Japan made its first move in the Battle of the Coral Sea when, unopposed, the Third Kure Special Naval Landing Force occupied Tulagi (a small Australian base in the mid–Solomon Islands) and Gavutu.[4] The landing was supported by the light carrier *Shoho* which sailed to within 180 miles of Tulagi and then sailed northwest to support the Port Moresby Invasion Force.[5] Carrier Division Five (*Shokaku* and *Zuikaku*) stayed close to Rabaul because they were waiting to ferry nine Zero fighters to Rabaul's air base to supplement its depleted fighter reserves. As a result, the carriers were not available to support the Tulagi invasion, leaving that seaplane base vulnerable to U.S. carrier counterattack. The chronic shortage of Japanese reserve aircraft and pilots for the front lines, despite relatively few aircraft losses in the early part of the war, would significantly haunt the Japanese throughout the War in the Pacific.[6]

On May 4, *Yorktown*'s aircraft began the first of its four strikes on Tulagi. Japan lost 87 men, and 124 were wounded in the attacks. Had *Shokaku* and *Zuikaku* not been needed to facilitate the replenishment of Rabaul's depleted aircraft reserve and instead supported the Tulagi landings, Fletcher's decision not to unite first with *Lexington* would have placed *Yorktown* in harm's way. The two Japanese carriers would have outnumbered *Yorktown*'s aircraft by a margin of 2:1, clearly favoring the Japanese in a naval confrontation.

On May 5, Task Force 17 (without *Lexington*), after its strikes on Tulagi, united with Rear Admiral Audrey Fitch's Task Forces 11 and 44, which were 325 miles south of Guadalcanal.

Fletcher received intelligence that the Japanese convoy would sail south from Rabaul across the reef-studded waters of the Louisiade Archipelago and invade Port Moresby on May 10. This information provided Fletcher with not only the day on which the Japanese invasion force and carrier *Shoho* would arrive at Port Moresby but also the course they would take. U.S. intelligence assumed that *Shokaku* and *Zuikaku* would be in close proximity to the invasion force. This position would have allowed the two Japanese carriers not only to protect the Japanese invasion force but also to make air attacks on Port Moresby. However, Carrier Division Five did not behave as U.S. intelligence expected, and for the moment, the Americans did not know where the Japanese carriers were, unlike the situation at Midway where Japan's tactical plan had the Kido Butai (with little flexibility of movement) on a fixed course for Midway.[7]

At 1015 on May 6, a Japanese Kawanishi flying boat discovered that both U.S. carriers (Task Force 17, united with *Lexington*) were now also united with Admiral Fitch's Task Forces 11 and 44.

Zuikaku and *Shokaku*, under the command of Rear Admiral Hara Chuichi, were 300 miles to the north but were still in the process of refueling. Finally, at 1200, the two large Japanese carriers were ready to depart (without its cruisers) to the location of the sighted U.S. carrier fleet. The Japanese carriers then ran into a band of bad weather causing Hara to decide to cancel the mission. At one point in the voyage, unbeknownst to the Japanese, they were only 70 miles from the U.S. fleet. Thus, Japan lost a great opportunity to strike the U.S. force first and inflict heavy damage in the process. Hara, unaware of how close they were to the American fleet, turned his fleet to the north to a point 280 miles south of Tulagi (Hara did not learn until the end of the war that the U.S. fleet had been only 70 miles south).[8]

The failure of Hara to attack the American carriers first on May 6 allowed Fletcher to move his fleet into a tactical position to attack the carrier *Shoho* and the Port Moresby Invasion Force.

Task Force 17 cut through the Jomard Pass in the Louisiades on May 7 and sailed 170 miles southeast of Deboyne Island poised to strike the Japanese Invasion Force's carrier *Shoho* off Misima Island in the central Louisiades.

On May 7, 1942, the first confrontation between two opposing carrier forces was about to take place in the Coral Sea. This battle ushered in the era of the carrier as the predominant factor in deciding naval engagements and the end of the battleship as a major force in the outcome of naval battles.

None of the U.S. carriers in the Pacific were anchored in Pearl Harbor at the time of the Japanese attack on December 7, 1941. The number of U.S. fleet carriers in the Pacific in May 1942 was five (including *Saratoga*, which was being repaired in Bremerton, Washington, due to a torpedo hit in January 1942). Japan, however, had six fleet carriers and five small carriers, giving Japan the advantage by a margin of over 2.5:1. Due to the timing of the Battle of the Coral Sea, *Enterprise* and *Hornet*, en route from the Doolittle Raid, were not able to reach the area in time to participate.

Task Force 17, now steaming northwest from its position 150 miles south of Rossel Island, arrived near the Louisiades (a group of islands located southeast of New Guinea), which would place the U.S. fleet in perfect position to attack the Japanese invasion convoy. Fletcher then decided to send Rear Admiral J. G. Crace's Task Force 17.3 with two heavy cruisers, one light cruiser and three destroyers westward to guard the Jomard Passage in the Louisiades. This decision removed one-third of Fletcher's carrier screen and left Crace's task force open to air attacks by Japanese land-based aircraft with no air cover from the U.S. carriers. Unwittingly, his decision resulted in Crace's task force being misidentified by Japanese search planes as Fletcher's fleet carrier task force, which was actually hundreds of miles to the east.[9]

While Crace sailed west, Fletcher kept the remainder of Task Force 17 (36 fighters, 70 dive-bombers, and 22 torpedo bombers, a total of 128 aircraft) south of Rossel Island (located at the eastern end of the Louisiades) ready for combat. Japan's Carrier Division Five, located 280 miles west of Tulagi, was also poised for battle. Rear Admiral Hara recommended to Rear Admiral Takagi Takeo, Commander of the MO Carrier Striking Force, that he head south after launching his search planes. This decision would have catastrophic results for the Japanese. While Japanese land-based commands were searching the western area of the Coral Sea, the Japanese MO Main Force, which was reinforced with the light carrier *Shoho*, was operating northeast of Misima Island, located near the southeastern end of the Louisiades. At 0727, on the morning of May 7, two search planes launched from *Shokaku* erroneously reported an American carrier 150 miles south of the Japanese Striking Force. At 0800, Hara impulsively launched 78 aircraft to the site reported by the search planes. At 0900, both reconnaissance planes, realizing their mistake, confirmed that only a destroyer and an oiler were present. At 1100, Hara recalled all the aircraft except the thirty-two-plane dive-bomber group. By noon, the dive-bombers sank the one destroyer, *Sims*, and damaged the oiler tanker *Neosho*, which eventually sank. Again, the Japanese blundered by sending a large contingent of aircraft against two relatively insignificant targets instead of striking the first blow against the U.S. carrier fleet.[10]

While Japan was attacking *Sims* and *Neosho*, at 0820, Japanese search planes discovered the actual site of Task Force 17 which was located southeast of Rossel Island. Now Hara realized that the American task force was only 200 miles southeast of Carrier Division Five.[11]

At 0815, American search planes discovered that two Japanese carriers and four cruisers were located 200 miles northwest of Task Force 17. One hour later, Fletcher launched his entire strike force against the Japanese task force with the anticipation of destroying *Zuikaku* and *Shokaku*. At 1040, aircraft from *Lexington* spotted a task force that contained only one carrier.

The Americans had actually come upon the MO Main Force which provided escort for the nearby convoy force, but the two large Japanese fleet carriers were nowhere to be found.

At 1050, the MO Main Force was now just northeast of Misima Island in the Central Louisiades when the Americans attacked.[12] At 1118, fifteen aircraft of Bombing Two dove down on *Shoho* with the first 1,000-pound bomb landing on the center of the carrier's flight deck.

The second 1,000-pound bomb struck the carrier forward of the first hit, igniting intense fires on the carrier. Six torpedo planes from Torpedo Two attacked, with five of the six planes' torpedoes hitting the ailing carrier. This was the first successful torpedo attack by the United States against an enemy carrier in U.S. naval history.

At 1125, seventeen dive-bombers from *Yorktown* arrived and inflicted nine direct and two near misses on *Shoho*. The carrier was now ablaze from bow to stern. At 1129, the carrier sustained two more torpedo hits from Torpedo Five, and *Shoho* began to sink. At 1210, Lieutenant Commander Robert Dixon, upon returning to Task Force 17, radioed back to the fleet in the Coral Sea, "Scratch one flat top."[13] With the sinking of *Shoho*, 800 men were lost; only 200 Japanese sailors survived the attack. Rear Admiral Goto Aritomo, Commander of the MO Main Force, ordered the fleet to retreat at high speed to the north.[14]

2. The First Carrier-to-Carrier Warfare

On May 7, twenty Japanese land attack planes from Rabaul armed with torpedoes and bombs, failing to find the U.S. fleet in the area reported by the Rabaul search plane, returned to Rabaul. At 1430, they inadvertently found Crace's fleet and attacked. Crace's fleet not only avoided being hit by the twenty Japanese aircraft but also avoided being hit by three U.S. Army bombers from Australia, which mistook the American fleet for the enemy. After this encounter, Crace's fleet turned south out of harm's way.[15]

At 1515, the Japanese dive-bombers returned from bombing *Sims* and *Neosho*—a flight of seven hours. The Japanese task force was now steaming west, closing the distance between the two enemy carriers. At 1615, twelve dive-bombers and fifteen torpedo planes (equipped with a homing device that was vital for navigation after dark) were launched and headed toward the American carriers. The aircraft were to fly west 280 miles, but the pilots observed no evidence of the U.S. carriers. In actuality, the American task force was only 150 miles away and hidden by heavy clouds. Unable to find the Americans, the Japanese planes dropped their ordnance and headed home.

At 1747, *Lexington* spotted on its radar the first group of nine torpedo bombers forty-eight miles away from the carrier. Five of the torpedo bombers were shot down by *Lexington*'s Combat Air Patrol (CAP). At 1808, the second group of six Japanese torpedo bombers arrived, and two of the aircraft were shot down. A few minutes later, a third group of Japanese aircraft reached *Lexington*, composed of twelve dive-bombers. One of the Japanese dive-bombers was shot down by a CAP "Wildcat" fighter. In the end, the U.S. CAP destroyed eight Japanese torpedo planes (one torpedo plane later ditched into the sea) and one Japanese dive-bomber. Only three U.S. fighters were lost in the ordeal.[16]

The melee lasted twenty minutes, and when it was over, the surviving Japanese planes retreated. They had to face the dark and worsening weather as they flew back. They tuned their radio directional finders to a medium-high frequency, but one that was exactly the same frequency used by the American CAP radio transmissions.

A 1840, the Japanese broke through the American CAP and radioed back their position to the fleet. Flying on, the Japanese pilots observed for the first time an American carrier. The Japanese, however, had already dropped their ordnance, and there was nothing they could do. The American task force was completely unaware of their presence. Several minutes later, U.S. destroyer *Dewey* spotted the six aircraft circling above in preparation to land on *Lexington*. (John Lundstrom stated in *The First Team*, published in 1984, that the Japanese pilots were confused and were trying to get the carriers below them to turn on their lights; the Japanese assumed they were over *Zuikaku* and *Shokaku*.) Initially, the ships in Task Force 17 did not open fire on the incoming planes because U.S. fighters were also in the process of landing. Shortly thereafter, *Yorktown*, the heavy cruisers, and destroyers began to fire on both the Japanese and U.S. aircraft. At this time, the Japanese carriers, which were turning into the wind, had turned on their homing transmissions and awaited the landing of their aircraft by turning on their landing lights, a courageous decision considering this made the task force vulnerable to U.S. attack. At 2000, the Japanese aircraft finally returned, the last plane landing at 2200. Fletcher was continuing to move his task force further west toward the Jomard Passage and nearer to Crace's fleet. Carrier Division Five was now steaming north to close the distance between itself and the two cruisers from the Port Moresby Main Force and the Japanese Striking Force.

Only eleven torpedo bombers and seven dive-bombers landed on *Zuikaku* and *Shokaku* that night. Overall the Japanese had lost ten torpedo bombers and one dive-bomber. This drastic loss of Type 97 torpedo bombers would have a significant effect on Japan's inability to sink the *Yorktown* the next day. The prospective loss of *Yorktown* as well as *Lexington* would have had a profound effect on the outcome of the Battle of Midway, leaving the United States with only two available carriers for that battle.

On May 8 at 0820, U.S. scout planes discovered the Japanese Striking Force, and its location was radioed back to *Lexington*. The Japanese had only ninety-six operational aircraft available (thirty-eight fighters, thirty-three dive-bombers and twenty-five torpedo bombers) after sustaining heavy losses the day before.

At 0807, a *Shokaku* search plane found the American task force some 230 miles away. At 0901, eighteen fighters, thirty-three dive-bombers and eighteen torpedo bombers launched from *Zuikaku* and *Shokaku* turned south toward the American task force.[17]

At 0900, *Yorktown* was first to launch its planes, which at 0915 departed for the Japanese Striking Force, now only 210 miles away. The U.S. fleet now turned northeast to close the distance to the enemy, shortening the distance that the return flight of aircraft would have to travel to reach the carriers. At 1032, the U.S. planes spotted the Japanese task force only thirty miles away. While the U.S. aircraft were heading for a coordinated an attack on *Zuikaku*, the carrier slipped out of sight under a rainstorm, and *Shokaku* headed for heavy cloud cover.[18]

Seven SBD dive-bombers from Scouting Five dove down on *Shokaku*, but all seven of the 1,000-pound bombs released missed the carrier. The seventeen SBD dive-bombers from Bombing Five now dove down on *Shokaku* registering two direct hits. At 1108, nine TBD Devastators from Torpedo Five closed in on *Shokaku*, but all nine torpedoes missed. At 1115, all of *Yorktown*'s planes had left the battle area to return to their carrier.

After having trouble finding the Japanese Striking Force, *Lexington*'s aircraft finally located the Japanese carriers, and at 1130, *Lexington*'s four dive-bombers, eleven torpedo bombers and six fighters began their attack on *Shokaku*. Only one of the four dive-bombers had a direct hit on *Shokaku*, the bomb having landed on the starboard side of the carrier's island. All eleven torpedo bombers from *Lexington*, upon release of their torpedoes, missed their mark. In the attack on *Shokaku*, two U.S. dive-bombers and three fighters were lost, while the Japanese lost four Zero fighters. Although the *Shokaku* was left in flames after receiving a total of three direct hits, the carrier was still operational. One hundred nine Japanese on *Shokaku* were killed and one hundred fourteen wounded.[19]

At 1055, *Yorktown* and *Lexington*'s radar detected a large group of aircraft sixty-eight miles from the carriers and closing in fast. The task force's CAP were alerted and were immediately launched. At 1109, the sixty-nine Japanese planes broke formation to get into their tactical positions to attack the U.S. carriers. Eighteen Japanese torpedo bombers approached *Yorktown* and *Lexington* in a shallow dive. Fourteen of the bombers were directed to attack *Lexington*, and the other four torpedo planes headed toward *Yorktown*.

The reason why only four Japanese torpedo planes attacked *Yorktown* was that nine torpedo planes (all with elite crews) were lost by the Japanese in the mistake-ridden course of events that occurred the day before. Since the Japanese depended on the superiority of its torpedo as its major effective offensive weapon, the loss of aircraft the day before precluded an excellent opportunity for the Japanese to significantly damage or sink the *Yorktown*.[20]

At 1118, as the fourteen torpedo bombers headed toward *Lexington*, they split up into two groups so that they could attack the carrier from both the starboard and port sides. A torpedo struck the carrier on its port side at the forward gun gallery. A second torpedo hit opposite the carrier's island. These results left the carrier leaking oil, and the main water line and three other water lines were severely damaged, causing the water pressure to drop and the boilers to shut down.

The Japanese attack on *Yorktown* was not as effective, as all four torpedo bombers missed with their torpedoes. The results of the torpedo attack were inconsequential. One of the four aircraft was shot down by antiaircraft fire after it released its torpedo, and another was shot down by the CAP.

Thirty-three Japanese dive-bombers headed southeast toward *Lexington* and *Yorktown*. The formation divided up into two groups with nineteen dive-bombers from *Shokaku* flying toward *Lexington* and fourteen dive-bombers from *Zuikaku* relegated to attack *Yorktown*. The Japanese dive-bombers that attacked *Lexington* succeeded in obtaining one direct hit. The U.S. carrier was only mildly damaged by this Japanese assault.

At 1124, the fourteen Japanese dive-bombers dove down on *Yorktown*, but only one 242-kilogram high-explosive bomb was a direct hit, landing in the center of the flight deck. The bomb descended four decks before detonating in an aviation storeroom. The explosion damaged the carrier's bulkheads. Further damage was inflicted by near misses which created holes in four places in the carrier and severed a seam under the armored deck that caused oil to leak out into the sea. However, the carrier was still able to maintain a speed of twenty-eight knots. The result of the total aerial engagement was that the Japanese lost ten planes (four dive-bombers and six torpedo aircraft) and the Americans lost eight aircraft (three fighters and five dive-bombers).[21]

At 1233, *Yorktown*, now traveling at 25 knots, was still capable of accepting the returning U.S. aircraft strike and the CAP. *Lexington* was able to get all of its major fires out, but fumes from small leaks in the port stowage gasoline tanks seeped into the IC motor generator room. Sparks from the electric motors of the generator ignited the gasoline fumes, and a huge explosion followed, killing twenty-five men. Subsequent low pressure in the water hoses resulted in the spread of existing fires. At 1442, a second huge explosion shook the carrier, and now *Lexington* was in serious trouble. At 1525, a third major explosion occurred on the carrier, sealing its fate by severing the pressure in its water hoses, which resulted in its inability to control the fires throughout the ship. By 1600 the carrier speed slowed, and the ship was going around in circles due to the loss of the steering mechanism. Shortly thereafter, *Lexington* came to a stop, so Fletcher decided to separate the two carriers, with *Yorktown* moving south. At 1707, the order was given to abandon *Lexington* because the torpedo ordnance could go off at any moment, endangering 2,500 sailors on board. At 1800, a final fourth explosion occurred, spreading the fires, so that now the entire carrier was ablaze.[22]

At 1841, the destroyer *Phelps* was given the order to sink the carrier. The destroyer fired five torpedoes at point-blank range, and *Lexington* rolled over to port and slid under the waves at about 1952. Of the total crew of 3,011, 92 percent (2,770) of the sailors were saved. Rear Admiral Thomas Kinkaid's group (Task Force 17.2) consisting of four heavy cruisers and four destroyers reunited with Fletcher, and the two fleets headed southwest.[23]

Admirals Hara and Takagi were left with only one operational carrier, *Zuikaku*, now that *Shokaku* was heading home. Before *Shokaku* left, the carrier transferred all of its operational aircraft to *Zuikaku*. With all of its aircraft having returned from its strike on the U.S. task force, *Zuikaku* headed north to regroup and access the situation. The losses sustained by the Japanese carrier aircraft in the Battle of the Coral Sea and the number of operational aircraft available caused Takagi not to strike again and to retire to the north for refueling. On May 8, when Vice Admiral Inoue Shigeyoshi, Commander of the Fourth Fleet received news that *Enterprise* and *Hornet* were 445 miles away from Tulagi, he canceled the entire MO Operation. Thus ended the Battle of the Coral Sea and the prelude to the Battle of Midway began.[24]

In the final analysis of the Battle of the Coral Sea, one must view the conflict in a historical perspective, not as an isolated battle. The confrontation by the Japanese with the Americans in the Coral Sea is intimately interwoven into the fabric of the Battle of Midway, so that each battle influenced the outcome of the other. First, one must take a step back and appreciate that it was the Doolittle Raid that aligned the Imperial General Headquarters behind the Combined Fleet's Midway-Aleutian operation and Yamamoto's decision to set the date for the assault on June 4, 1942. Even though the Battle of Midway had not taken place yet, it profoundly affected the Battle of the Coral Sea, and as we shall see the Battle of the Coral Sea had a critical effect on the outcome of the Battle of Midway. When Admiral Yamamoto became obsessed with the decision that Midway was the only military target that would bring out the U.S. carriers, he made a critical error in judgment. We now know that Nimitz was willing and did send all of his available carriers into the Coral Sea operation. Yamamoto had the opportunity to concentrate all eleven (six fleet carriers, two light carriers and three small carriers) of his aircraft carriers into the Coral Sea operation as opposed to the four fleet carriers for the United States, a ratio of almost 3:1 in Japan's favor, and the loss of two or more of the American carriers was a real possibility. At the very least, if the United States did not engage the Japanese fleet in the Coral Sea, Australia would have been isolated from the United States and the lines of communication severed with the Allies.

To compound the situation, Yamamoto was fixated on a June 4 deadline for the attack on Midway. This decision to move the date for the Port Moresby invasion from mid- to late May to early May 1942 resulted in the following: (1) *Kaga* (with its experienced pilots, in contrast to the inexperienced pilots of Carrier Division Five), which was being repaired in Japan, was not available for the Coral Sea battle; (2) the movement of the date also did not allow enough time for land-based aircraft to arrive in New Guinea to provide air cover for the invasion of Port Moresby; and (3) *Shokaku* and

Zuikaku had to cover both the invasions of Tulagi in the mid–Solomon Islands and Port Moresby in southeast New Guinea.

The Battle of the Coral Sea was not technically a tactical victory for Japan, but its outcome was both a tactical and strategic victory for the United States (the Port Moresby invasion was canceled). Even though *Lexington* was lost in the battle, *Zuikaku* and *Shokaku*, although not fatally damaged, were not available for the Battle of Midway on June 4 due to repairs of *Shokaku* and the loss of personnel and aircraft for *Zuikaku*. Thus, the Battle of the Coral Sea actually resulted in the loss of *Shoho* and the functional losses of *Zuikaku* and *Shokaku* (a total of three carriers), compared to one U.S. carrier (*Lexington*) for the upcoming Battle of Midway.

Observed in this context, the Battle of the Coral Sea was a clear tactical as well as a strategic victory for the United States. Unwittingly, Yamamoto not only faced the United States in the Coral Sea without using his carrier superiority but would repeat the same mistake at the Battle of Midway.

Thus, Yamamoto lost his two greatest opportunities (the Battles of the Coral Sea and Midway) to decisively crush the existing U.S. carrier fleet in the Pacific in late spring of 1942.

On May 1, Japan began the first of a series of war games preparing for the Battle of Midway on board the battleship *Yamato* in Hashirajima Bay. The war games lasted five days, concluding on May 5. The intent of the games was to have an honest appraisal of the outcome of the Midway plan and to make adjustments to the plan where flaws existed so that contingency plans could then be drawn up. A series of map exercises were laid out on a large table in the presence of the command staffs of the different task forces involved in the operation. It was at these games that the weakness of Admiral Yamamoto's military judgment was clearly demonstrated, because he did not allow the conclusion of the games to play out. Instead, he instructed the table judge as well as Rear Admiral Ugaki Matome, the Combined Fleet Chief of Staff, who oversaw the proceedings, to overrule and disregard the outcomes of the war games that were unfavorable to Japan, so that he could gain the approval of the Midway operation plan without dissent and without change.[25]

There are two examples of Yamamoto's flawed judgment during the Midway war games. First, when Japan's fleet was attacked on its flank by American forces, three Japanese carriers were severely damaged, and the invasion of Midway was placed in jeopardy. The table judge casually stated that this outcome could not occur in the actual battle and reversed the damage done to the three carriers. Thus, the events unfolding in the war games were restructured to fit Yamamoto's vision that U.S. forces would not surprise the Japanese by attacking the Kido Butai on its flank.

In the second example, Lieutenant Commander Okumiya Masatake rolled the dice which indicated that nine bombs would strike the Japanese carriers and result in the loss of *Akagi* and *Kaga*. Ugaki then imposed his will on the game by reducing the bomb hits on the Japanese carriers to three and declaring that only *Kaga* had been sunk. Later in the same exercise, *Kaga* suddenly was resurrected and participated in the subsequent Japanese operations against the Fiji and New Caledonia Islands. Following the war games on May 5, there were two additional days devoted to studying the Midway plan, and various recommendations were made for changing the operational plan; but none were adopted by the Japanese high command.[26] Almost all of the participating fleet commanders, including Vice Admiral Kondo Nobutake, recommended postponement of the operation, but he later changed his mind because this would result in the operation being delayed for a month due to inadequate moonlight for night maneuvering, needed in order for them to succeed off the beaches of Midway.

At the end of the exercises, Yamamoto himself asked Nagumo what he would do if U.S. forces appeared on his flank while he was staging his operation against Midway. Air Officer Captain Genda Minoru instead responded to the question, not by stating a cogent contingency plan but rather with an emotional response, which was, "We'll wipe them out!"[27] Captain Miwa Yoshitake, member of the Combined Fleet Staff, also replied with an inexplicable statement when he expressed his opinion that it was a matter of small concern.

These emotional responses, rather than rational ones, were forthcoming in spite of the outcomes that the war games had produced. One point that has not been stressed by previous historians is that on May 1, Japan's high command did not know that the *Shokaku* and *Zuikaku* would not be available for the upcoming Battle of Midway. Thus, the deleterious results of the first war games were presumably based on Japan having six, not four, carriers at Midway. This observation further emphasizes the flaws in Yamamoto's plan. In addition, in the final series of war games held by Japan on May 25, it was presumed by Japan that the United States would have only two carriers present at Midway, giving Japan a 2:1 ratio of superiority in carriers over the Americans. Yet, in spite of these presumed odds in favor of Japan, the Japanese lost one carrier and had two carriers damaged in the war games. When Yamamoto again asked the question of what Nagumo would do if U.S. forces appeared unexpectedly off Midway, Nagumo and his subordinates responded that he had a contingency plan in mind but did not specify what the plan was. In spite of all these shortcomings, Yamamoto did not alter his plan or the timetable of the attack on Midway.

The reason for his refusal to alter the plan or postpone the Midway operation has been attributed by historians to overconfidence (victory disease), but this author would like to submit an additional rationale, that is, that Yamamoto was so emotionally obsessed with removing the threat posed by the Doolittle Raid to the Japanese emperor and the homeland that he lost his objectivity, thus being unable to reason. This opinion is best supported by the fact that while he insisted on making a surprise attack on Pearl Harbor with six carriers, he was now willing to confront the remaining U.S. carrier force (two to three carriers plus the aircraft on Midway) on an equal footing with only four Japanese carriers, rather than insisting that small carriers *Junyo* and *Ryujo*—delegated to the Aleutian campaign—be included in the Midway First Carrier Striking Force. Yamamoto could have waited for *Shokaku* and *Zuikaku* to be ready. The shortage of pilots for *Zuikaku* existed because Japan never implemented a program that took its most experienced pilots and transferred them to the naval air stations to act as instructors of new flying recruits. The repairs on *Shokaku* were delayed because the Japanese were not as efficient as the United States in repairing their ships, but even if they had been, the replacement pilots for both carriers would not have been available to participate in the Battle of Midway.

In fairness to the admiral, delaying the Midway operation for a month or two while

2. The First Carrier-to-Carrier Warfare

waiting for *Shokaku* to be repaired and *Zuikaku* to have its flying personnel replaced would have reduced Japan's carrier advantage from a ratio of 3.5:1 to a ratio of 2:1. This conclusion is based on the fact that the addition of *Shokaku* and *Zuikaku* to the Japanese Midway Carrier Striking Force would have been counterbalanced by the addition of *Saratoga* and *Wasp* to the U.S. fleet, which would have been available to participate in the Battle of Midway. However, the point here is that Yamamoto never seriously considered utilizing his carrier advantage in the Battle of Midway.

3

Aftermath

On May 9, with the Battle of the Coral Sea over (May 3 to May 8), U.S. Task Force 17 was retreating in a southerly direction into the vastness of the Coral Sea. Trailing behind *Yorktown* was the persistent leakage of oil into the sea. With the loss of its oiler *Neosho*, the fleet now found it imperative to refuel in Tongatapu in the Tonga Islands, south of the Fiji Islands. That afternoon, Fitch's Task Force 11 was ordered to unite with Task Force 16 as soon as possible.

On May 11, cruisers *Minneapolis* and *New Orleans* were detached from Task Force 17 to join Halsey's Task Force 16, which was now entering the South Pacific.[1]

Late on May 8, the Combined Fleet in Japan received word that Admiral Inouye had canceled Operation MO. They were furious that Inouye had not pursued *Yorktown* to the south. At 2200, Admiral Yamamoto gave the order for Inouye to pursue and destroy the enemy. Thus, at midnight, Inouye directed Takagi's MO Striking Force, centered now around carrier *Zuikaku*, to seek out the enemy after they refueled. On May 9, however, Takagi spent the whole day refueling. In addition, Hara discovered that *Zuikaku* had only forty-five operational aircraft: twenty-four Zero fighters, thirteen carrier dive-bombers and eight carrier torpedo planes. On May 10, Takagi finally sent out his search planes to locate *Yorktown* but only found the drifting oiler *Neosho*. There was no trace of the enemy, as the Americans had been retreating to the south and were out of range of the pursuing Japanese search aircraft. On this date, the Japanese head command officially canceled the MO Operation, and with that directive, Japan suffered its first major strategic setback of the war in the Pacific.[2]

Meanwhile, on April 25, Vice Admiral William F. Halsey, Jr., Commander of Task Force 16, who had returned from the Doolittle Raid, was now ordered to take over tactical command of all the carriers in the Pacific. Five days later, Task Force 16 left Pearl Harbor and headed toward the Coral Sea. On May 5, Halsey learned of the events unfolding in that area of the South Pacific, so he increased the speed of the carriers in Task Force 16. He subsequently became informed of the loss of *Lexington* and the damage to *Yorktown*, as well as the intention of the Japanese to invade the islands of Ocean and Nauru. On May 10, Halsey learned that *Yorktown* had left the area of battle and was now safe. With that information, he slowed down the accelerated speed of his task force. Halsey was now focused on the fact that the *Zuikaku*-led Striking Force would support the invasion of Ocean and Nauru, so he waited out of range of the Japanese flying boats for Japan to make the first move.[3]

On May 12, Halsey learned that the Japanese Ocean/Nauru invasion force had left Rabaul, and it was estimated that May 14 was the probable date of the landings. Task Force 16 responded to this intelligence by heading northwest to intercept *Zuikaku* and the invasion force it was covering.

U.S. submarine S-42, however, sank the large minelayer *Okinoshima*, flagship of the Japanese invasion force, which led to the postponement of the invasion of Ocean and Nauru until May 17.

Thus, Halsey canceled his thrust to the northwest and remained south of Efate. He then received word that *Zuikaku* was ordered back home to Japan.[4]

On the evening of May 14, Halsey received the first of two messages from Nimitz who insisted that Halsey not sail beyond the range of Allied land-based aircraft. The second communication, which was marked secret and only for Halsey himself, reversed the former directive. The tactical commander of Task Force 16 was now ordered to make sure his fleet was spotted by Japanese search aircraft and then to withdraw immediately from the area. Halsey turned northwest at fifteen knots toward the Tulagi Japanese search zone. The next day (May 15) at 1015, Task Force 16 was spotted by a Japanese flying boat. Cryptanalysis on board *Enterprise* confirmed that the search plane had radioed back its finding to its air base.[5]

Halsey's appearance east of Tulagi caused Inouye to now cancel the Ocean and Nauru Island operation. At 1424, Halsey ordered Task Force 16 to retreat to the east at twenty knots. Three hours later, he turned the fleet south toward Efate. On May 16, Task Force 17.2 consisting of *Minneapolis* and *New Orleans* and three destroyers united with Task Force 16. That same day, Halsey received a directive that he should immediately return to Pearl Harbor.[6]

On May 13, Admirals King and Nimitz were involved in a critical debate. King felt that Japan soon would resume their military actions in the South Pacific. His position was to leave some of the carrier's aircraft and its pilots behind on New Caledonia and the Fiji Islands. King felt that the carriers should then operate in the rear and let the air groups left behind on the islands defend the threatened shore bases. Nimitz strongly opposed this view and with good reason. On April 27, Rudy Fabain in Melbourne intelligence deciphered a Japanese communication that requested charts whose map coordinates were consistent with the Aleutian Islands. At the same time, Rochefort's unit on Oahu intercepted a Japanese message that requested information as to the number of U.S. planes at Dutch Harbor and Kodiak in Alaska. These decrypts clearly indicated that Japan was considering an attack on the Aleutian Islands in the near future.[7]

On May 4, Rochefort learned that the Japanese battleship *Kirishima* was undergoing repairs and that the ship would not be ready by May 21. Two days later, Hypo picked up a message from the Japanese Navy's Fourth Air Attack Force, based at Kwajalein in the Marshall Islands, requesting ten radio crystals for frequencies 4990 and 8990 kilocycles from their base at Yokosuka in Japan.

They were to be placed in aircraft for the second King campaign. The target was Affirm King (Pearl Harbor). Rochefort hand delivered the urgent dispatch to Admiral Nimitz, Commander in Chief, Pacific Fleet (CINCPAC), and sent the communication to Station Negat (OP-20-GY) in Washington, D.C., and Belconnen (the U.S. intelligence unit now stationed in Belconnen, Australia). Rochefort commented that Affirm King was also the target of a message sent on March 4 prior to a Japanese flying boat attack on Pearl Harbor. He emphasized that Affirm King, or AK, was the Japanese navy's geographic designation for Pearl Harbor, which was attacked on March 4. The Japanese attack on Pearl Harbor occurring on March 4 was code-named Operation K, and its mission was successful. It consisted of two flying boats taking off from Wotje in the Marshalls and refueling by submarine at French Frigate Shoals, which was located 500 miles northwest of Hawaii. The planes then flew to Pearl Harbor and arrived there at night to gain intelligence regarding the ships in the harbor. After obtaining the information they needed, they released a few bombs for a psychological effect before heading back to Wotje. When Hypo learned that the crystals requested were primarily used for communication between aircraft and submarines, it concluded that Pearl Harbor was going to be attacked again by a coordinated air-submarine attack on or about May 17.[8]

Questions were being asked in Hypo as to the location of the formidable Japanese Second Fleet (Midway Invasion Force). This fleet was a mobile unit made up of small carrier *Zuiho* accompanied by two battleships, eight heavy cruisers, one light cruiser, nine destroyers, six oilers, one repair ship, twelve transport ships and three patrol boats carrying troops. There were no radio transmissions being sent by the Second Fleet; therefore, U.S. intelligence did not know where this force was located. On May 8, Thomas Huckins and John Williams, Rochefort's top traffic analysts, were able to place Nagumo's First Air Fleet, which now included the four carriers *Akagi*, *Kaga*, *Soryu* and *Hiryu*, with the fast battleships *Hiei* and *Kongo* and the heavy cruisers *Tone* and *Chikuma* of Kondo's Second Fleet in the home waters of Japan. These two fleets represented the most prodigious show of force ever assembled by the Imperial Japanese Navy.[9]

On May 9, Hypo deciphered a Japanese message revealing that a Japanese destroyer force would leave Yokosuka in Tokyo Bay on May 15 and unite with unidentified ships on May 18 and then proceed to Sasebo on the southern coast of Kyusho in the Japanese Islands. From that southern base, the entire surface striking force would depart for an unknown destination. Rochefort was certain it was not headed south toward the Coral Sea. His conviction was based on the fact that there was no radio traffic or ship activity intelligence that indicated any movement to that area.

In addition, he was now aware that the Japanese destroyer group had been assigned to the mid–Pacific area. The only two geographical areas targeted by the Japanese that Rochefort and Lieutenant Commander Edwin T. Layton, Nimitz's fleet intelligence officer, were certain of were the raid on Pearl Harbor in about ten days and an incursion into the Aleutian Islands scheduled for late May. However, the available intelligence indicated that Japan's intentions were much greater than these two military targets.[10]

Hypo discovered that a Yokosuka landing force would be training on Guam. This intelligence clearly indicated that a landing was going to take place on some island in the Pacific. Now that Rochefort had ruled out the South Pacific, he concluded that it would be somewhere else. On May 11, Hypo learned that Admiral Kondo's Second Fleet would sail to Saipan in the Mariana Islands and wait for the campaign to unfold. The significance of this information, however, did not point to Japan's main objective, and thus, as of May 12, the main target of the Japanese campaign remained unclear to the analysts at Hypo.

3. Aftermath

During the first two weeks of May, the Japanese transmitted some 500 to 1,000 messages, which were far more than Hypo could decipher. As a result, the intelligence unit on Oahu deciphered only twenty-five per cent of all the Imperial Japanese Navy intercepts received by Station H (intercepting unit in Hawaii) on Oahu. Fortunately, this proportion of intercepts deciphered turned out to be sufficient for U.S. intelligence to gain the necessary information for its analysts to discover Japan's true mission. The effort to decipher even this percentage of intercepts received required that the men at Hypo stay up an average of twenty hours a day.[11]

On May 13, Nimitz, armed with the foregoing intelligence, was able to cleverly work around King's insistence to keep Task Force 16 in the South Pacific. His reasoning for having Halsey's task force spotted by the Japanese was not only to have Japan's high command think that there were two U.S. carriers stationed in the South Pacific but also that Nimitz was aware that *Zuikaku* was ordered to return to the home islands and that this decision would leave the Ocean and Nauru invasion force isolated and without carrier support. Nimitz knew that the recall of the only supporting Japanese carrier would result in the Ocean/Nauru operation being canceled in the face of two unopposed American carriers. As a result, Nimitz was able to persuade King to bring *Enterprise* and *Hornet* back to Pearl Harbor. Nimitz felt that Japan would not invade Port Moresby until Rabaul was reinforced with ships and aircraft for the invasion. Since there was no intelligence that this reinforcement was about to happen, Nimitz was convinced that Japan instead would attack somewhere in the mid–Pacific.[12]

On that same day, intelligence gained from Station Negat (OP-20-GY) revealed that someone in the Japanese military was requesting that they be resupplied with maps of Oahu, Pearl Harbor, Seward Anchorage and the Western Hawaii Group. This new information caused King (for the moment) to change his mind about Japan's intentions and to agree with Nimitz. The commander in chief of the Pacific Fleet was more worried about Japan's massive offensive into the mid–Pacific; however, he was also concerned that Japanese flying boats could attack Pearl Harbor as they did before. To prevent this from happening, Nimitz ordered that the waters around French Frigate Shoals be mined and that a seaplane tender accompanied by a destroyer be sent to guard the area. In addition, a seaplane base was established on French Frigate Shoals. Nimitz then placed the shore facilities and warships on high alert in the areas of the maps requested by the Japanese intercept.[13]

On May 13, the tide turned for the intelligence team at Hypo regarding the direction that Japan would take on its next mission. Hypo received and decrypted a Japanese communication which, on the surface, was not particularly meaningful. The message revealed that an ordinary supply ship called *Goshu Maru* anchored at Wotje Atoll in the Marshall Islands was ordered to Imieji, a small Japanese base near Jaluit. The ship was to transport air-base equipment and munitions for the K operation and proceed to Saipan. Once the ship arrived, it would join the occupation force that had gathered there. More importantly, the letters AF were mentioned in the message, and Rochefort, after an unknown period of time, recalled that AF was in a communication that had been decrypted on March 9. Hypo's translators had concluded that AF was the coded designation for Midway. Whether Rochefort made this deduction from pure memory or from a list of geographic designators is not certain, but he now had the confirmation he needed to conclude that Midway was the main target of the Japanese navy in the Pacific. This conclusion by Station Cast was their assessment on March 23.[14]

Rochefort passed the Midway intelligence to Layton, who in turn spoke to Admiral Nimitz. The commander in chief was interested, but he had a meeting scheduled so he could not discuss the issue further with Layton. Instead, Nimitz scheduled Captain Lynde McCormack, who was the new and experienced war officer, to meet with Rochefort the next day. Rochefort, after he and his translators had again carefully reviewed the decrypted messages, sent the intelligence package to his superiors in OP-20-G in Washington on May 14.

That same day, Captain McCormick visited the basement in Pearl Harbor where Hypo's men worked. The essence of the case that Rochefort presented to McCormick was the proof that they had concluded that AF in the decrypted code represented Midway. Rochefort pointed out that the Japanese used two or three Roman letters in their messages to represent American geographical locations. For example, AH stood for Hawaii, AO represented the Aleutian Islands, and AK (Operation K was named after the code letters) were the code letters for Pearl Harbor. In the March 1942 decrypt, the Japanese stated that the Americans operated an extensive air search base from AF, which was important information for the Japanese participants in the K Operation.

The unknown location (AF) would have to have a seaplane base or an airstrip on its premises. The only naval base in the area that fit that description was the Midway Islands. The two facts that Rochefort could say with certainty were that the Japanese Second Fleet would gather in Saipan and that at least four Japanese carriers would leave Hashirajima Bay on May 21 and head for the main thrust of the operation: Midway.[15]

McCormick, having seen the evidence firsthand, became convinced that Rochefort and his staff were correct and returned to Admiral Nimitz's headquarters to meet with him. He was able to convince Nimitz that Midway was the main objective of Japan's excursion into the mid–Pacific on the basis of the evidence and on his reputation as an experienced naval officer. On May 14, Nimitz embraced Hypo's analysis that Midway was going to be attacked by the Japanese.

Admiral Nimitz now had to convince Admiral King of Hypo's analysis. Nimitz had already broken with King's orders not to place Task Force 16 in harm's way as the carriers neared the Ocean/Nauru Islands, ordering Halsey to close within 500 miles of Tulagi, which was well within the range of the 700 miles of Japan's search-plane radius. The directive to Halsey was executed without Nimitz notifying the Commander in Chief (COMINCH) Admiral King that he was taking this action. Nimitz gambled that this order would cause Japan to cancel the invasion of Ocean/Nauru and withdraw its forces from the area because the removal of *Zuikaku* from the task force had left the invasion force vulnerable to a U.S. carrier attack. As a result, Nimitz was able to bring Task Force 16 back to Pearl Harbor. The admiral's gamble paid off, as Japan canceled its invasion of the Ocean/Nauru Islands exactly as Nimitz had predicted. On May 16, Halsey received orders from Nimitz to return to Pearl Harbor, but first he had to gather his oilers and other detached ships. Finally, on the morning of May 18, he set a course directly for Pearl Harbor. That night, Halsey received another message from Nimitz: "Expedite return." Halsey knew something big was in the making, but he did not know at this time what it was.[16]

On May 15, Task Force 17 arrived in Tongatapu's Nukualofa anchorage to refuel and refurbish its depleted supplies. The next day, cruiser *Astoria* joined the group after a brief stopover in Noumea. *Lexington*'s survivors and its pilots were then transferred to the two transports, which would take them to San Diego. On May 19, Fletcher ordered the cruiser *Chester* to become the flagship of the small Task Force 17.6 and escort the transports back to the California coast. On the same day, Fletcher received orders from CINCPAC to return to Pearl Harbor, so he ordered Fitch to go back to San Diego to reform Task Force 11 with *Saratoga* as its centerpiece. Also on May 19, *Yorktown*, leaking oil, departed from Nukualofa anchorage and headed out to sea with Task Force 17.6, until May 21, when the task forces departed to go their separate ways.[17]

Five days earlier, the Japanese Naval Staff in Tokyo learned that *Shokaku* and *Zuikaku* would not be ready for the next operation. *Shokaku* arrived in Japan on May 17, and it was estimated that repairs would take up to three months to complete. The carrier also needed replacement pilots. When *Zuikaku* arrived at Kure four days later, undamaged but with her air group totally depleted, it was realized that there were no replacement air groups available for either carrier.

Young replacement pilots would eventually come from fresh out of training and needed more time to gain experience before they would be ready for carrier aviation. It was estimated that this process would take from two to three months. The decision by Yamamoto to allocate these two carriers to the Coral Sea operation was one of his most critical errors in judgment in the war in the Pacific as it deprived Japan of one-third of its carrier strength for the Battle of Midway and was a significant factor in the outcome of that battle, pointing out that the United States not only won a strategic victory at the Coral Sea but also a critical tactical victory as it related to the upcoming Battle of Midway.

On May 16, Hypo learned from decrypted messages that the Japanese carriers would attack their target from fifty miles away and out of the northwest. This communication appeared to support the concept that AF stood for Midway because tactically it would be more appropriate that an enemy would attack from that direction. However, skepticism persisted, not only in OP-20-G but also in OP-20-GZ (the Japanese-language unit of OP-20-G) and its sister unit, OP-20-GY (NEGAT), which specialized in cryptology. Commander Redfield Mason, a highly respected Japanese linguist, vehemently disagreed that AF stood for Midway, and he felt the target was somewhere else in the Pacific. Thus, the intelligence units in Washington did not accept that AF stood for Midway, but they were not sure what area in the Pacific it did represent. In the middle of this dispute, Rear Admiral Richmond Turner, Director of the War Plans Division, felt that all of the evaluation of naval intelligence should fall under the auspices of his department and not the Office of Naval Intelligence (ONI). Though exceedingly intelligent, his credentials were questionable, being based on a ten-day stay he had in Japan in 1939. Turner was displeased with the intelligence evaluations submitted both by Hypo and OP-20-G. He was resolute that the Japanese AF and K missions were unrelated. He circulated a memo to OP-20-G to that effect, believing that the attack most likely would come in the South Pacific between June 15 and June 20.[18]

On May 17, Admiral King suddenly changed his mind and supported Nimitz's point of view that Japan's next major thrust was into the mid–Pacific.[19] This action by

King was unexpected, since Jack Redman held the strong opinion that the Japanese would next attack in the South Pacific. Jack Redman had replaced Captain Laurence Stafford as head of OP-G-20 in an unceremonious political coup by U.S. Naval Communications in early 1942. Stafford had been called the father of U.S. Navy cryptology, while Commander Jack Redman was not even a trained cryptologist and probably owed his position to his brother, Captain Joseph Redman, director of Naval Communications. By March, Jack Redman decided that OP-G-20 would join Hypo and Cast in working on the JN-25B code, and in so doing take control of the operation. Rochefort retaliated in April by requesting that COMINCH direct Hypo to take over primary control of the JN-25B radio traffic. Thus, a major conflict began between OP-G-20 and Hypo.[20]

Redman and his staff did not believe that AF represented Midway and voiced their opinion to King. In spite of Redman's objections, King sided with Hypo on this critical issue. However, King was known to be mercurial in his decision making, so Rochefort knew that Hypo's opinion regarding Japan's next critical move in the Pacific could easily still be discounted by King. To add to the confusion, Belconnen (Cast), now situated in Melbourne, Australia, which usually agreed with Hypo, disagreed on this point. It would not be until May 21 (Hawaii date) that Belconnen would concede that AF was Midway. The Office of Naval Intelligence, on the other hand, supported Hypo's contention that AF stood for Midway. The ONI reasoned that the Japanese naval forces were assembling in the Saipan-Guam area as a prelude to attacking Hawaii and invading Midway.[21]

Redman rejected that AF stood for Midway because he felt that the abbreviations stood for a communication zone designation and not a geographical destination. OP-20-G was adamant in their resistance to Hypo's interpretation of the meaning of AF. As a result, OP-20-G began to distrust Hypo's additives—key numbers, added to the original code number—and refused to use them. Without the additives, the underlying code groups in the JN-25B could not be read. Redman's group felt that an attack on Midway was out of the realm of possibility in contrast to Hypo, which felt that an attack on Midway was a certainty.

Rochefort's group was so certain that it placed its evidence in the A category, which meant the data had been confirmed by more than one source and detected by radio traffic a number of times.[22] Rochefort began to hear outside rumors that OP-20-G was of the opinion that he was misleading the U.S. Navy into a making an egregious tactical error which would have serious consequences for the U.S. carrier fleet. On May 18, feeling the pressure, Admiral Nimitz requested confirmation of Rochefort's analysis. He wanted Rochefort to affirm or deny that AF stood for Midway by any means possible. The next morning, on May 19, Rochefort began a meeting with a small group of his analysts, seeking their input on how to validate their belief. Lieutenant Wilfred Jasper Holmes, in charge of the newly created Combat Intelligence Unit (CIU), an intelligence arm of the Hypo Unit, came up with a solution that pleased Rochefort but required Nimitz's approval. The plan was simple but ingenious. Jasper Holmes, an engineer on the faculty of the University of Hawaii, was studying the possibility of using saltwater and coral for mixing concrete on Midway. This study was being conducted because the freshwater supply on Midway was limited, and any interruption of the freshwater distillation process would be of serious concern to those on Midway.[23]

Since fresh water was necessary for making concrete on Midway, Captain Cyril

Simard, Naval Commander of the Midway Atoll, was made aware of the ruse and instructed by Nimitz to send out an urgent message in the clear (communication not coded) about the problem. To enhance the deception, Rear Admiral David Bagley, commandant of the Fourteenth Naval District, notified Simard, again in the clear, that a water barge was on its way to Midway. On May 19, the Japanese gave the first sign that had fallen for the ploy when they sent a message from Wake Island that "AF" was out of water. This radio communication confirmed that AF stood for Midway and was the intelligence that Rochefort's team was waiting for.

The initial contact between CINCPAC and Simard that explained the plan to Simard was made in secret by using the undersea telegraph cable between Midway and Hawaii.[24] The Pacific Commercial Cable Company completed the construction of an underwater telegraph cable linking Midway to Honolulu on July 3, 1903, at which time the entire length of the cable stretched from San Francisco to the Philippines, and by 1906 to China and Japan. After the outbreak of war in the Pacific on December 7, 1941, the telegraph cable that was laid westward from Midway was closed down, and only that portion of the cable from Midway to Hawaii remained operational. As a result, the communications between Nimitz and Simard were kept secret since the discussion did not rely on the airwaves as a means of transmission.

On May 18, COMINCH received news that Britain was concerned about the U.S. carriers leaving the South Pacific. Former Chief of Naval Operations Harold Stark, the Navy's special representative in London, was instructed to go to the First Sea Lord to relay to him that the United States had intelligence indicating that, since Japanese attacks on Midway, the Aleutians and possibly Hawaii were imminent, it would be necessary for the United States to remove all of its carriers in the South Pacific. Stark, therefore, suggested to the British that they send a carrier from its Eastern Fleet to cover the South Pacific, a request that was denied by Britain because it was necessary to keep their carriers off the coast of eastern Africa, which was being threatened by the Japanese.[25]

It is a little known fact that the United States, prior to the Battle of Midway, requested that the British send one of its carriers into the South Pacific and not to Midway. Without knowledge of this information, the opinion arose that the United States had actually asked Britain to send a carrier to Midway. Britain did have two carriers (HMS *Illustrious* and *Indomitable*) in Madagascar, an island off the coast of eastern Africa. However, since the United States had not gained the Midway intelligence until May 13, the carrier would have no more than twenty-one days to reach Midway.

The distance from Madagascar to Midway is about 9,784 miles. Even if the carriers and its escorts were to steam at seventeen knots, it would take at least twenty days (not accounting for refueling time along the way) to reach Midway. The huge distance would make the carrier's arrival time problematic at best. In addition, both British carriers at Madagascar were equipped with obsolete Swordfish bi-winged torpedo bombers on their decks, making their aircraft's effectiveness against the more modern Japanese Zero in Japan's CAP questionable. Therefore, it is unlikely that the U.S. high command would have requested a carrier from Britain to be sent to Midway, but rather that Stark suggested to the British that they send a carrier to the South Pacific to cover that area.

On May 21, Belconnen picked up the message that the Japanese sent from Wake

Island to Tokyo that AF had enough water for only two weeks. After Cast (the U.S. intelligence unit in Corregidor) abandoned the Philippines in early 1942, they migrated to Belconnen, Australia, a district of Canberra, the capital city of Australia. There a composite of American and Australian code breakers formed a new intelligence unit known as Belconnen, code-named after its associated Australian radio site. Belconnen then passed the translated form of the Japanese radio communication to OP-20-G. At the same time, Lieutenant Rudy Fabian, Director of Naval Intelligence at Belconnen, informed Washington that if the Fourteenth Naval District at Pearl Harbor confirmed the information, then AF would be confirmed as representing Midway. Three days later, Nimitz ordered Midway to carry out air reconnaissance out to a range of seven hundred miles northwest of Midway.[26]

In spite of the confirmation, doubts lingered among the army's top leaders and in the Roosevelt administration that Midway was the prime objective of Japan. General George Marshall, Chief of Staff, felt the Japanese were deceiving the United States into believing their target was Midway, when in reality it was somewhere else. Secretary of War Henry Stimson thought the attack would come as a strike on Panama, Alaska, or the West Coast in revenge for the Doolittle Raid. OP-20-G, for their part, resented that Hypo had devised the water ruse on Midway without first consulting them.

Redman felt that Navy intelligence in Washington, D.C., should have the final say, even though OP-20-G's opinion of Japan's next mission was at variance with Hypo, and were it not for the independent thinking of Hypo, Japan would have been victorious at Midway. Rochefort's position was that he alone brought to the table the most experience in all facets of intelligence, and as such, he was not interested in being relegated to merely passing on information to Washington for their analysis.[27]

On May 21, Task Force 16 (*Enterprise* and *Hornet*) was continuing on its way back to Pearl Harbor. *Yorktown*, after refueling at Tongatapu Island, was now steaming northeast toward Oahu. Admiral King wanted the carrier *Yorktown* to return to Bremerton, Washington, to complete its repairs, but Nimitz, who needed the carrier in the Battle of Midway, tactfully got King's permission to have *Yorktown* return first to Pearl Harbor for repairs, and then, if the repair base was inadequate, to send the carrier to Puget Sound for restoration. *Enterprise* and *Hornet* would arrive at Pearl Harbor on May 26, while *Yorktown* was anticipated to return on May 27.

The Japanese continued to believe that the most likely location of Task Force 16 was still in the Coral Sea rather than in Pearl Harbor. To add to the deception by the United States, Nimitz ordered the seaplane tender *Tangier* to begin radio transmissions characteristic of a carrier force on the prowl in the South Pacific. Nimitz then ordered PBY flying boats to bomb Tulagi. With these results, Japan radioed back to Yamamoto that Halsey's carriers were still in the South Pacific, and it appeared that the United States would provide minimal carrier opposition at Midway.[28]

By May 25, King and Nimitz were on the same page in that Midway was the prime target of the Japanese mission in the central Pacific, but now the date had to be agreed upon. King felt that the date for the invasion of Midway was May 30, while Nimitz thought it would be during the first week of June. Naval intelligence at this juncture had come of age, for now the United States would know every move Yamamoto made as he made it. In late May, due to heavy radio traffic, Hypo could decipher over one-third of the code groups it received, compared to one-fifth in April. The intelligence derived from this percentage of the decoded messages was enough for the United States to know exactly what Japan's intentions were.[29]

On May 20, Hypo noted a marked increase in the volume of Japanese messages. One of the messages in particular drew the interest of Alva Lasswell, one of the analysts on duty that day.

By May 25, the final translation of the operational battle order for the Battle of Midway was completed by Hypo. This account was denied by Layton, who stated he had never heard of it. Layton pointed out that if the message about the Japanese battle plan had been deciphered, it would have mentioned that Yamamoto was on the battleship *Yamato*, which was part of a formidable thirty-four-ship fleet (Main Body) and included Battleship Divisions One and Two. Nimitz claimed he was unaware that the Main Body existed 600 miles to the west. After the war, Rochefort refuted Layton's and Nimitz's accounts and stated that he had told Nimitz about the battle plan.

The issue is unresolved to this day. The supposed translation of the battle order has never been found in Hypo's or CINCPAC's files, nor were they found in the files of OP-20-G or Belconnen.

The controversy persists today as questions remain as to how solid Rochefort's evidence was that Midway was the target of the Japanese in the mid–Pacific. Were the Japanese using trickery to fool the United States into believing Midway was their target? Certainly Lasswell and his colleagues spent a great deal of time in decrypting the message of May 20, and even if the intercept did not include the actual battle plan, the intelligence derived from this communication allowed Hypo and Belconnen to provide an accurate assessment of Yamamoto's battle plan.[30]

On May 26, Nimitz produced a document in which he wrote an "Estimate of the Situation, Attack on Hawaiian and Alaska Bases," which was held by Hypo, Belconnen and Negat and included a statement that the Japanese might be deceiving the United States regarding Midway. He also acknowledged that uncertainty persisted in the U.S. Navy's high command regarding Hypo's conclusion that Midway was the main target of the Japanese in the Pacific.

This difference of opinion with Hypo would persist for another week. Nimitz then requested that Rochefort come to his office the next morning to discuss not only the controversy that existed between the Navy's high command and Hypo but also the date that Hypo believed Japan would attack Midway. Rochefort felt that the answer to the date of the attack must lie in a super-enciphered code within a code as it did with the Battle of the Coral Sea. On May 25, one such message came in to Belconnen in Melbourne from a box of garbled traffic. The analyst could get only so far with the decryption, so he referred the message to Hypo and Negat. Hypo immediately went to work on the baffling message. Joe Finnegan, Hypo's Japanese-language analyst, was able to decipher two of the three katakana code groups, but not the third. He showed the problem to Rochefort and Ham Wright, a Hypo cryptologist. Wright agreed to work on the problem with Finnegan. They worked on the third kana until 0530, when Wright solved the code and remarkably concluded that Dutch Harbor in the Aleutian Islands would be attacked on June 3 and Midway on June 4.[31]

Rochefort, now armed with the foregoing intelligence, headed to the meeting

Nimitz requested but showed up thirty minutes late. In addition to Nimitz, Major General Robert Richardson, General Marshall's personal representative; Rear Admiral Raymond Spruance, who replaced Vice Admiral William Halsey, who became ill on his long tour of duty in the Pacific, as Commander of Task Force 16; Captain Lynde McCormick, Head of CINCPAC's war plans staff; Rear Admiral Milo Walter Draemel, Nimitz's Chief of Staff; and Captain Delany, Fleet Operations Officer, were there. Conspicuously absent was Fleet Intelligence Officer Lieutenant Commander Edwin Layton, possibly because of his lower naval rank.[32]

Historians and biographers alike strive to present the most accurate information when writing about their subjects. Literature on the Battle of Midway, which took place June 3–7, 1942, is no exception. Many books have been written which expound on every facet of the battle, its leaders, and how those leaders shaped the outcome of the battle. Invariably, however, details may become misconstrued over time or misstated altogether. These misshapen details in turn may result in a misunderstanding of the context in which situations exist, and how they affect the interpretation of historical data. One detail about the Battle of Midway that has been described differently by various authors is the affliction with which Vice Admiral William "Bull" Halsey was affected as early as May 1942.

Task Force 16 (*Enterprise* and *Hornet*) was just returning from the Doolittle Raid and its aborted attempt to reach the Battle of the Coral Sea. When carriers *Enterprise* and *Hornet* entered Pearl Harbor on May 26, 1942, Halsey reported directly to Admiral Chester Nimitz's office in CINCPAC headquarters. Immediately upon seeing Halsey, who at that time was visibly affected by some type of illness, Nimitz ordered him to be hospitalized. When asked by Nimitz who his replacement should be, Halsey responded by recommending Rear Admiral Raymond Spruance.

While the outcome of the battle which was to ensue may (or may not) have been different had Halsey been available for service, there is no doubt that Spruance's leadership was paramount in how the battle played out.

Despite the fact that some authors have described Halsey's rash as "dermatitis," there still is a prevailing thought that Halsey had shingles. As a physician, this author has noticed that there has been no real attempt to exclude shingles as the reason for Admiral Halsey's removal from duty prior to the Battle of Midway. Although shingles could be considered a form of dermatitis, not all dermatitis is shingles.

Over the years, it has been reported that, at the time of the Battle of Midway, Admiral Halsey had "shingles," "dermatitis" and "psoriasis," and it has been described by various authors as "very painful lesions," "extremely pruritic" (i.e., with extreme itching) and most importantly involving "most of his body."

The following is a partial compilation of previous authors' descriptions of Halsey's malady:

- In 1967, Walter Lord, in *Incredible Victory*, states, "The itch was driving him crazy. He tried everything even oatmeal baths—nothing helped."
- In 1990, John Lundstrom in *The First Team* writes, "A skin disease had made his life miserable for a month."
- Also in 1990, Robert Cressman et al., in *A Glorious Page in Our History*, tells

us, "Vice Admiral Halsey suffering from painful worries of his own—dermatitis."
- In 2005, Jonathan Parshall and Anthony Tully, in *Shattered Sword*, actually state that "Halsey had recently contracted shingles."
- In 2007, Evan Thomas, author of *Sea of Thunder*, writes that Halsey was "covered with blisters (Halsey could not stop himself from scratching)."
- John Wukovits, in his book *Admiral Bill Halsey: The Life and Wars of the Navy's Most Controversial Commander*, states in 2010, "The rash so assailed the admiral's entire body that Lieutenant Ashford tried to conjure ways to alleviate the exasperating itching."
- In 2011, Elliot Carlson writes, in *Joe Rochefort's War*, "He [Halsey] had contracted dermatitis, a painful disease."
- Craig Symonds, in *The Battle of Midway*, published in 2011, writes that Halsey had "a severe form of dermatitis—aggravated by the sun and very painful. He had lost 20 pounds."
- In 2012, Ian W. Toll writes of Halsey's condition in *Pacific Crucible*, "[His] skin had erupted into scaly patches of red and white."

In addition to these descriptions of the rash, some authors have mentioned that Halsey's sleep was disrupted by his problem. Another clinical feature of Halsey's condition was a twenty-pound weight loss, which, in the absence of any serious organic illness, could have been stress induced. (This latter point gives credence to the importance of the intense pressure that wartime military leaders endure and the subsequent implications it has on the health and well-being of those leaders.)

This author has obtained the medical records of Admiral Halsey in their entirety. The following are excerpts from the "Report of Medical Survey," a summary of his admission to the U.S. Naval Hospital, Pearl Harbor, on May 26, 1942, written on June 2, 1942, by three members of the Board of Medical Survey, Commander E. J. Best, MC-V(S), USNR; Lieutenant Commander C. McKenney, MC-V(S), USNR; and Lieutenant Commander J. D. Viecelli, MC-V(G), USNR[33]:

> This officer was admitted complaining of a severe, burning rash of the body and extremities.
> He states that he has had for many years a chronic dermatitis of the inguinal region which was considered to be a fungus infection and which was relieved several years ago by the administration of a fungus extract. The dermatitis recurred several months ago with the additional involvement of the hands and feet. These areas were treated with local applications, x-ray, and the injection of fungus extract, the latter being discontinued when he began to notice redness and itchiness on both sides of his chest....
> ... On admittance, his skin was dry, moderately scaly, and brightly erythematous (reddened). The skin about the neck, of the [inner-elbow] and [behind the knees] was thickened and [leathery].
> ... The treatment has been ... sedatives, [oatmeal] bath, and the application of a cold cream made of wax, mineral oil, sodium perborate and water.
> Lab results were significant in that he had a 26 percent increase in the number of circulating eosinophils (normal is 1–6 percent). An increase in eosinophils has been known to occur in neurodermatitis, allergic dermatitis and psoriasis, but not shingles.
> It is interesting to note that, according to his medical records, Halsey had a previous medical history of "neurasthenia" in 1915 which resulted in a 3-month medical leave from his naval service. Neurasthenia (literally a "weakness of the nerves") is defined by the Merriam-Webster dictionary as

"a psychological disorder marked especially by easy fatigability and often by lack of motivation, feelings of inadequacy, and psychosomatic symptoms—compare chronic fatigue syndrome."

The Report of Medical Survey on June 2 continues:

"It is the opinion of the dermatologist that this officer has ... acute generalized eczematous dermatitis caused by a sensitization to either local use of drugs, the use of fungus extract, or fungus products from an original and probably still active fungus infection of the feet and inguinal region. The strenuous duty and mental strain that he has undergone has probably been a contributing factor. The generalized acute condition as well as the sensitivity of the skin manifested by flare-up upon the use of but the mildest and weakest medications precluded testing for specific irritants. Further observation and study is required to exclude a possible but not probable malignant erythroderma such as mycosis fungoides.
  Present condition: Unfit for duty
  Probably future duration: Indefinite
Recommendation: That he be transferred to a naval hospital on the mainland for further treatment and disposition.[34]

As we can see, with no improvement in Halsey's symptoms despite treatment at the Pearl Harbor Naval Hospital, on June 14, 1942, Halsey was transferred to the care of Dr. Warren W. Vaughan, a leading U.S. allergist at Johnston-Willis Hospital in Richmond, Virginia. Within a week, Halsey began to improve and was subsequently discharged on July 21 on the premise that he continue to rest for six weeks. By August 5, he was nearly fully recovered, and on August 31, he gave a speech at the U.S. Naval Academy vowing to return to the Pacific theater of the war.[35]

With this description of Admiral Halsey's condition, there were three possible causes of his rash: neuro-dermatitis (itching and rash brought on by stress and/or other psychological factors), allergic dermatitis (caused by allergies to external substances) and psoriasis (an autoimmune condition in which the body "attacks" its own skin cells). Shingles was never entertained as a diagnosis in the medical record, nor does Halsey's clinical picture described in the record support that diagnosis.

Shingles is caused by the varicella zoster (chicken pox) virus. If one is infected with the chicken pox virus as a child, the virus remains dormant in nerve tissue in the spinal cord and brain.

Many years later, the virus may reactivate and cause a rash known as "shingles" or "herpes zoster." The disease manifests itself almost exclusively as a localized area (on one side of the body) of fluid-filled blisters along a single nerve which break open and form a crust. The disease rarely occurs as a generalized rash, which can happen only when one is immunologically suppressed by medications or by a genetic defect. Symptoms of shingles—whether localized to one area or, rarely, spread throughout the body— are pain, burning, numbness or tingling, sensitivity to touch, and itching. Halsey's rash has been clearly described as generalized, which virtually excludes the diagnosis of shingles. The possibility that Halsey was on immunosuppressive drugs (which would allow shingles to become widespread over the body) is excluded by the fact that those medications did not exist at the time of his diagnosis (they were not available until 1948). The diagnosis of genetically induced immunosuppression in Halsey is very unlikely due to its rarity, and because there is the absence of repeated bacterial infections in Halsey's medical history. In addition, eosinophilia rarely, if at all, occurs in shingles. Other than shingles, there are a number of other possible diagnoses which resemble the symptoms that Admiral Halsey had: allergic dermatitis, psoriasis, and neuro-dermatitis.

Psoriasis, a chronic (i.e., recurring) disease, is characterized by patches of skin covered by silvery scales, itching, and dry cracked skin that may bleed. The clinical diagnosis of psoriasis at presentation is usually straightforward, and was well known at the time of Halsey's illness.

However, there is an inverse type of psoriasis that involves the inguinal (groin) area whose lesions appear as smooth and inflamed patches of skin. However, this presentation occurs in less than 10 percent of cases of psoriasis. Notably, weight loss is not a feature of psoriasis, and Halsey never had a reoccurrence of his extensive skin disorder, which makes psoriasis, a chronic condition, unlikely. The fact that the medical staff wrote in the medical chart that it was "a generalized allergic dermatitis" gives testimony to the fact that it was not thought to be either shingles or psoriasis.[36]

With psoriasis and shingles ruled out, and given the fact that no one knows with certainty the extent of his disease, the most likely condition from which Halsey suffered was a form of neuro-dermatitis, complicated by an allergic reaction, possibly related to the fungal extract he was receiving. Typically, neuro-dermatitis is a dermatological disorder which occurs in individuals who are under intense emotional stress—as was Halsey. The skin lesions are leathery or scaly in texture and occur on any or all parts of the body. It can cause intense itching and burning, which can interfere with sleep. In combination with extreme stress the disease can be accompanied by weight loss.

So what did Admiral Halsey actually have? In an effort to define Halsey's illness, Dr. Vaughan provided Halsey's medical evaluation and treatment to—and sought the opinion of—Dr. Marion B. Sulzberger, a leading immunological dermatologist at that time who was practicing in New York City (Sulzberger later became Chairman of the Department of Dermatology, New York University School of Medicine, and held other prestigious positions throughout his sixty-two-year career in medicine).[37] In a letter to Admiral Halsey from Dr. Vaughan dated September 9, 1942, Dr. Vaughan summarized Dr. Sulzberger's opinion thus:

> The technical diagnosis of your condition is "generalized non-exudative dermatitis associated with focal infection and bacterial allergy, fungus infection, probably drug allergy and possibly food allergy." I had asked Sulzberger to abbreviate this, selecting a term that would fit in with the Navy medical nomenclature and I feel that he has done very well in suggesting the term "toxic dermatitis." While it possesses the disadvantage that it is just a generalization and does not adequately describe what you had, it possesses the advantage that when friends get inquisitive, you can shut them up with just the two words (how I have enjoyed your elephant story!).[38]

(The reference to the "elephant story" gives us interesting insight into the personalities of both Admiral Halsey and Dr. Vaughan.)

In conclusion, it is most likely that Admiral Halsey had a form of neuro-dermatitis—not shingles—that had both allergic and infectious components and could very well have been brought on or aggravated by stress, given his previous history of neurasthenia and the disposition of the Board of Medical Survey. While the role that stress may have played in Halsey's illness was not included in the final diagnosis, there is enough evidence to suggest that it contributed to his condition. Halsey's misfortune demonstrates the role that stress can play in the development of physical illness and the incapacitating effect it can have on the well-being of an individual and his ability to provide effective leadership. Thus, eliminating shingles as his diagnosis has far more profound implications than just getting his diagnosis correct. It implies that Halsey, an outstanding, experienced and proven Navy admiral, suffered from one of the fragilities of humanity: that of having a physical condition, most likely related to the level of stress he had endured over time, and severe enough to render him unfit for duty during one of the most significant naval battles in world history.

Following Halsey's admission to the hospital, Rochefort was called to a meeting to give credence to Nimitz's plan to counteract Japan's attempt to invade Midway. Rochefort presented his case to the high-ranking officials in the room. He stated that within a week Japan would be approaching Midway with four Japanese carriers—*Akagi*, *Kaga*, *Soryu* and *Hiryu*—and possibly a fifth carrier, *Zuikaku*, with an escort screen of three battleships, four to five cruisers and a destroyer squadron. They would converge on Midway out of the northwest at a bearing of 315 degrees, close the distance to Midway to within fifty miles and launch their aircraft against the atoll at about 0700. He then reported that two days later, the Japanese Occupation Force, having sailed west from Saipan, would begin landing its forces on Eastern and Sand Islands. The date of the attack given by Rochefort and supported by Ham was reportedly June 4 (U.S. date); but at that time, Yamamoto had originally set the date for June 3 (U.S. date), and days later, Yamamoto decided to change the date to June 4 (U.S. date), presumably to give the Midway Invasion Force time to reach Midway. Nimitz and King were also working on the premise that June 3 was the date of the attack. Whether Rochefort and Wright forgot or misrepresented the date (June 4) to fit the actual date of the attack will never be known.[39]

Rochefort estimated that the Northern Force, consisting of one fleet carrier, one light carrier, two cruisers, three destroyer divisions and a submarine squadron, had already left the northern Japanese island of Ominato. The force would then divide, and one segment would head for Kiska and Attu in the western Aleutians and the other would attack Dutch Harbor to the east.

Questions among the doubters in the meeting still remained as to why the Japanese Navy would put their entire plan on the radio airwaves where it could be detected. Could Japan be so guileless, or were they cunning and deceiving the United States into believing that they would muster almost their entire Navy on two small islands in the Pacific? Nimitz interjected that the purpose of Japan's large force was to destroy the remaining U.S. carrier force in the Pacific with the expectation that, by attacking Midway, such an opportunity would arise. As far as the second Operation K was concerned, Rochefort could not offer any help. Its purpose was still a mystery, and its significance as it related to Oahu remained unknown. It is significant to point out that at the meeting and prior to the Battle of Midway, the United States did not know about Yamamoto's Main Body of ships lingering behind the First Striking Force. If the U.S. high command were aware of its existence, Nimitz may well have altered his decision to engage the Japanese Navy at Midway.[40]

Nimitz devised a scheme known as Operation Plan No. 29–42 based on his belief that Hypo's estimates were correct. In addition to his directive to Midway for the PBYs to search out to a range of 700 miles southwest to an arc due north from Midway. Nimitz also ordered thirteen fleet submarines to patrol the same arc out to a distance of 200 miles from Midway and ordered a destroyer, in addition to the seaplane tender *Thornton*, to reinforce the area around French Frigate Shoals to prevent another successful Operation K. His plan directed Task Force 16 (consisting of *Enterprise* and *Hornet* under the command of Admiral Raymond Spruance, with an escort of five heavy cruisers, *New Orleans*, *Minneapolis*, *Vincennes*, *Northampton* and *Pensacola*; one light cruiser, *Atlanta*; and nine destroyers, *Phelps*, *Worden*, *Monaghan*, *Aylwin*, *Balch*, *Conyngham*, *Benham*, *Ellet* and *Maury*, with oilers *Cimarron* and *Platt* and destroyers *Dewey* and *Monssen*) to leave Pearl Harbor on May 28 and sail to a point 350 miles northeast of Midway (Point Luck). *Enterprise* had twenty-seven fighters, thirty-two dive-bombers and fourteen torpedo bombers operational, and *Hornet* had twenty-seven fighters, thirty-four dive-bombers and fifteen torpedo bombers operational, for a total of 150 operational aircraft (Task Force 16). *Yorktown* (Task Force 17), which arrived in Pearl Harbor on May 27 and was under the command of Admiral Frank Jack Fletcher, consisted of two heavy cruisers, *Astoria* and *Portland*; six destroyers, *Hammann*, *Hughes*, *Morris*, *Anderson*, *Russell* and *Gwin* were to depart Pearl Harbor three days later. *Yorktown* carried twenty-five fighters, thirty-four dive-bombers and twelve torpedo bombers, for a total of seventy-one operational aircraft. Thus, the combined total of operational aircraft from both task forces was 221 planes. The total number of vessels in Task Force 16 (minus the Oiler Group) was seventeen ships, and the total number of

CV-5 *Yorktown* entering Pearl Harbor, May 27, 1942 (photo 80-G-21931, courtesy Naval History and Heritage Command).

vessels in Task Force 17 was nine ships, for a total number of twenty-six U.S. ships facing off against the twenty Japanese ships in the battle to come.[41]

In comparison to Nimitz's plan, Yamamoto's was vastly more complex and an interwoven scheme of multiple forces on various timetables and distances from the Kido Butai. The prime mission of the Japanese Navy was the occupation of Midway Atoll and the destruction of the remaining American carriers in the Pacific. The carrier attack on the Aleutians at Dutch Harbor and the occupation of Attu and Kiska was a mission unto itself. It was felt by the Japanese that these incursions in the Aleutians would probably be unopposed by the U.S. forces because America would be preoccupied with events unfolding at Midway.

It is now known that the long-held belief that Japan's decision to attack the Aleutian Islands as a diversion to lure the Americans away from Midway is not true. The Japanese excursion into the Aleutians was an operation in its own right and not intended to draw American forces from Midway. Parshall and Tully present new evidence indicating that on April 5, 1942, Yamamoto and Admiral Nagano Osami, Head of the Naval General Staff, compromised on a plan in which the independent invasion of the Aleutian Islands was incorporated into the overall operational Midway plan. Thus, the invasion of the Aleutian Islands was not originally conceived as part of the Midway operation plan but one that was adapted to it later.[42]

The Japanese operation plan for the Aleutian Islands consisted basically of the Northern Force (Fifth Fleet) and was composed of four groups: (1) the Northern Force Main Body, which was under the command of Vice Admiral Hosogaya Moshiro and was composed of heavy cruiser *Nachi* (flagship) and two destroyers; (2) the Second Carrier Striking Force, which was under the command of Rear Admiral Kakuta Kakuji, consisting of light carrier *Ryujo* (sixteen fighters and twenty-one torpedo bombers) and carrier *Junyo* (twenty-four fighters and twenty-one dive-bombers) and escorted by heavy cruisers *Maya* and *Takao* and three destroyers; (3) the Attu Invasion Force, which was under the command of Rear Admiral Omori Sentaro and was composed of light cruiser *Abukuma* (flagship) and accompanied by four destroyers, one minelayer and a transport which carried the Army Landing Force (1,200 troops); and (4) the Kiska Invasion Force, which was under the command of Captain Ono Takeji and consisted of light cruisers *Kiso* (flagship) and *Tama*, auxiliary cruiser *Asaka Maru*, three destroyers, three minesweepers and two transports carrying the Naval Landing Force (1,250 troops). Five submarines (I-9, I-15, I-17, I-19 and I-26) were assigned to escort the ships into the Aleutian area.

On May 26, the Northern Force was to depart from Ominato Naval Base, which was located on the northern part of the Japanese island of Honshu. The Kiska Invasion Force would sail independently to Kiska, while the Attu Invasion Force would parallel the Second Carrier Striking Force eastward until it reached Adak, where it would turn north toward Adak, landing troops there, and then turn west to invade Attu. The Second Carrier Striking Force would continue east until it reached Dutch Harbor, where it would turn north to attack the American bases on that island. The Japanese felt that the destruction of U.S. bases on these islands would protect the northern flank of the main Japanese offensive at Midway.[43]

The main body of ships directed at Midway was divided into four main forces:

3. Aftermath

(1a) The First Carrier Striking Force departed from Hashirajima Bay on May 27, under the overall command of Vice Admiral Nagumo Chuichi, and was composed of Carrier Division One (*Akagi* [flagship] and *Kaga*) and Carrier Division Two (*Soryu* and *Hiryu*), which was under the command of Rear Admiral Yamaguchi Tamon. *Akagi* had eighteen fighters, eighteen dive-bombers and eighteen torpedo bombers on board, and *Kaga* carried eighteen fighters, twenty dive-bombers and twenty-seven torpedo bombers. *Soryu* had eighteen fighters, eighteen dive-bombers and eighteen torpedo bombers on its deck, while *Hiryu* carried eighteen fighters, eighteen dive-bombers and eighteen torpedo bombers. The Kido Butai was also ferrying twenty Zero fighters to Midway: *Akagi* carried six, *Kaga* nine and *Soryu* and *Hiryu* each carried three, for a total of twenty-one aircraft. The total operational aircraft aboard all four carriers was 227 planes, which when added to the twenty-one aircraft being ferried to Midway totaled 248. This number of aircraft represented a reduction in the full capacity of all four carriers, as compared to the attack on Pearl Harbor in which 355 operational aircraft were on board all six carriers. Thus, when compared to the attack on Pearl Harbor, not only was the number of Japanese carriers reduced at Midway but also the number of aircraft. The four carriers in the First Carrier Striking Force were escorted by seventeen escort vessels, giving a total number of only twenty-one Japanese ships that would be present to engage the Americans at the forefront of the battle at Midway.

(1b) The Supply Group consisting of five oilers, *Kyokuto Maru*, *Shinkoku Maru*, *Toho Maru*, *Nippon Maru* and *Kokuyo Maru*, were escorted by destroyer *Akigumo*. These ships would depart from the First Air Fleet on the morning of June 3 (Midway date), one day prior to the attack on Midway.

(1c) The Support Group, which escorted the First Carrier Striking Force, was under the command of Rear Admiral Abe Hiroaki and consisted of battleships *Haruna* and *Kirishima*, heavy cruisers *Tone* (flagship) and *Chikuma* and a Screening Group under the command of Rear Admiral Kimura Susumu, which were composed of light cruiser *Nagara* (flagship) and eleven destroyers. The First Carrier Striking Force assisted by the Support Force would attack Midway and oppose any U.S. carriers by itself, without any immediate assistance from the remaining support forces that were kept in the rear from 300 to 500 miles due west of Midway.

(2a) The Main Body Force, which was the last contingency of ships to leave Japan, would leave Hashirajima Bay on May 29 under the command of Admiral Yamamoto Isoroku. The Main Force consisting of light carrier *Hosho* (carrying eight Type 96 bombers, which were bi-winged aircraft) was escorted by destroyer *Yukaze*; battleships *Yamato* (Combined Fleet flagship), *Nagato*, and *Mutsu*, escorted by light cruiser *Sendai*; and destroyers *Fubuki*, *Shirayuki*, *Hatsuyuki*, *Murakumo*, *Isonami*, *Uranami*, *Shikinami* and *Ayanami*, which on June 4 (U.S. date) were located 300 miles west of the Kido Butai.

(2b) An Aleutian Guard Force under the command of Vice Admiral Takasu Shiro, which included battleships *Hyuga* (flagship), *Ise*, *Fuso* and *Yamashiro*, and light cruisers *Kitakami* (flagship) and *Oi*, escorted by destroyers *Asagiri*, *Yugiri*, *Shirakumo*, *Amagiri*, *Umikaze*, *Yamakaze*, *Kawakaze*, *Suzukaze*, *Ariake*, *Yugure*, *Shigure* and *Shiratsuyu*. The Guard Force would sail with the Main Body until it was about 700 miles northwest of Midway, at which time it would head northeast toward the Aleutian Islands.

(3a) The Midway Invasion Force Main Body was composed of three groups. The First Group, referred to as the Invasion Force Main Body, under the command of Vice Admiral Kondo Nobutake would leave Hashirajima Bay on May 29 just before the Main Force departed. This force consisted of light carrier *Zuiho* (carrying twelve fighters and twelve torpedo bombers) escorted by destroyer *Mikazuki*; battleships *Kongo* and *Hiei*; heavy cruisers *Atago* (flagship), *Chokai*, and *Haguro*; light cruiser *Yura*; and destroyers *Murasame*, *Samidare*, *Harusame*, *Yudachi*, *Asagumo*, *Minegumo* and *Natsugumo*. This force would sail south and then east on a direct path to Midway.

(3b) The Second Group, called the Transport Force, sailed from Saipan in the Marianna Islands on the evening of May 28 under the command of Rear Admiral Tanaka Raizo. This force was composed of light cruiser *Jintsu* (flagship), ten destroyers and twelve transports and three destroyer-transports carrying the Midway Landing Force (Army personnel). The invasion would be made up of both army and naval units. Fifteen hundred naval sailors were scheduled to disembark on the southern shore of Sand Island, and 1,000 soldiers would land on the southern shore of Eastern Island. The invaders would be brought in by barge to the reef from which the men would wade until they reached the beaches. Two construction battalions would bring the total Japanese ground forces on Midway to over 5,000 men and turn Midway into a frontline airbase. The Transport Group sailed from Saipan directly northwest and then mostly east to Midway.

(3c) On the evening of May 28, the Third Group, called the Close Support Force, commanded by Vice Admiral Kurita Takeo and consisting of heavy cruisers *Kumano* (flagship), *Suzuya*, *Mikuma* and *Mogami* and two destroyers, left Guam in the Marianna Islands en route to Midway. It would take a parallel course about forty miles southwest of the Transport Group where it would escort the Transport Group to Midway Atoll.

(4) The Advance Submarine Force was under the overall command of Vice Admiral Komatsu Teruhisa, who remained on board light cruiser *Katori* (flagship) at Kwajalein in the Marshall Islands. The Submarine Force was composed of three components: (1) Submarine Squadron Three commanded by Rear Admiral Kono Chimaki, who stayed on board submarine tender *Yasakuni Maru* (flagship) at Kwajalein, and which included submarines I-168, I-169, I-171, I-174 and I-175; (2) Submarine Squadron Five commanded by Rear Admiral Daigo Tadashige, who remained on board submarine tender *Rio de Janeiro Maru* (flagship) at Kwajalein, and which included submarines I-156, I-157, I-158, I-159, I-162, I-165 and I-166; (3) Submarine Division Thirteen commanded by Captain Miyazaki Takeharu

and composed of submarines I-121, I-122 and I-123. Each of these three squadrons was designated to cover Cordons A, B and C. Squadron Three was positioned at Cordon A and was to be located west of Hawaii; Squadron Five covered the area known as Cordon B, which was to be situated northwest of Hawaii. Cordon A and B were located about halfway between Hawaii and Midway. Squadron Thirteen was stationed at Cordon C and covered the area that was more to the northwest of Hawaii than Cordons A and B and nearer to the Aleutian Islands. These three cordons were to be in place by June 2 so that the submarines could intercept any American carriers that may have left Pearl Harbor and were heading northeast of Midway and where they would occupy a position on Japan's left flank.

4

Prelude to Midway

Admiral Nimitz had been involved in building up the defenses of Midway Atoll. On May 3, he notified COMINCH that he was planning to send twelve three-inch anti-aircraft guns, eight 37mm antiaircraft guns and twelve twin 20mm mounts to Midway from the Third Defense Battalion, as well as troop reinforcements. There were only 1,300 men to defend Midway against the invasion force of 5,000 men Japan was planning to hurl against the atoll. The Sixth Marine Defense Battalion on Midway had five five-inch/.51-caliber guns, four three-inch anti-boat guns, twelve three-inch antiaircraft guns, and forty-eight .50-caliber and thirty-six .30-caliber machine guns.[1]

On May 15, four VP-23 Consolidated PBY-5 Catalinas (twin-engine search seaplanes) under Lieutenant Howard Ady landed in the waters off Sand Island. Three days later, Nimitz directed the Second Marine Raider Battalion (Carlson's Raiders) to reinforce Midway. He also placed four submarines off Midway and ordered Army bombers to the atoll. On May 19, a catastrophic event occurred on Midway when an electrical wiring error resulted in an explosion, in which over 375,000 gallons of gasoline were lost. Nimitz urgently ordered gasoline drums to be sent to the atoll. On that same day, six PBY-5As (which had the ability to land on both land and water) from VP-44 landed in the waters off Eastern Island and complemented VP-23 in its air search missions and increased the search radius capability from 400 to 600 miles northwest by southwest of Midway.[2]

The Marine Air Group (MAG) was already stationed on Midway and consisted of VMF-221. VMF-221, which was under the command of Major Floyd Parks, consisted of five divisions. The first four divisions were comprised of nineteen Brewster F2A-3 Buffalo fighters. The fifth division consisted of six Grumman F4F-3 Wildcat fighters.

On May 25, the light cruiser *Saint Louis*, accompanied by destroyer *Case*, delivered Companies C and D of the Second Marine Raider Battalion to Midway. On the same day, a squadron of PT boats arrived at the atoll with four district patrol craft, with a converted yacht scheduled to arrive on the next day. On May 26, the aircraft ferry *Kitty Hawk*, accompanied by destroyer *Gwin*, arrived from Oahu carrying nineteen Dauntless dive-bomber SBD-2s to update the quality of aircraft in VMSB-241. The dive-bomber squadron was under the command of Major Lofton Henderson, USMC. These aircraft would replace the older SB2U-3 dive-bombers in the unit. The SBD-2 was almost equal to the SBD-3 in performance. However, the Marine pilots on the island would have only ten days to learn how to fly the new planes. In addition, seven F4F-3 Grumman Wildcat

A crowded scene as Nimitz visits Midway, March 10, 1942 (photo 80-G-6170, courtesy Naval History and Heritage Command).

fighters were also delivered to reinforce VMF-221 along with twenty-one new pilots (most just recently out of flight training) to fly the newly arrived aircraft. Also stationed on Midway was the VMSB-241 SB2U-3 Unit composed of eleven operational—but outdated— dive-bombers. One of the newly arrived pilots, Captain Benjamin Norris, was assigned to become the executive commander of the SB2U-3 Unit. The unit had eleven operational aircraft (the twelfth had engine trouble after takeoff on the morning of June 4). The group was divided into sections; the first group consisted of five SB2U-3 Vindicator dive-bombers, and the second group consisted of six SB2U-3 Vindicator dive-bombers. The Vindicator was a fabric-covered aircraft that lacked effective dive brakes and performed poorly when carrying a 1,000-pound bomb. The plane could only shallow-angle glide-bomb on its approach to an enemy ship, which made the plane vulnerable to a ship's antiaircraft fire. On the other hand, the pilots of the SB2U-3 aircraft, whose planes were replaced by the SBD-2 aircraft, found a vastly superior plane to fly when compared to the SB2U-3 dive-bomber.[3]

On May 27 at 1352, disabled *Yorktown* arrived from the Coral Sea and sailed into Pearl Harbor, the carrier's forty-two flyable aircraft having been sent aloft at 1026 prior to the ship's entry into the harbor. The carrier was sent immediately to the dry dock at

Berth 16 to evaluate the damage done to the ship. The repair area was in excellent condition to service the carrier due to the Japanese failure to destroy the repair areas in their attack on Pearl Harbor on December 7, 1941.

While *Yorktown* was being inspected, *Saratoga*, under the command of Rear Admiral Audrey Fitch, was ordered to leave the West Coast by June 5 and steam toward Oahu. However, when Fitch did not arrive to take over his new command in San Diego by June 1, Task Force 11.1 (*Saratoga*) left San Diego without him and headed toward Pearl Harbor. Fitch did not reach San Diego until June 4, where he boarded destroyer *Chester* and headed toward Hawaii. He was still en route to Pearl Harbor when *Saratoga* set sail from Pearl Harbor for Midway on June 7.[4]

It was determined that *Yorktown*'s underwater damage was minimal, so it would not be necessary to send the carrier to Bremerton, Washington, for repairs. It was estimated at first that the repairs would take up to ninety days, but Nimitz insisted the work be completed in seventy-two hours.

The carrier had lost its radar and refrigerator system. The seams from the carrier's hull had separated from the concussions of the bombs that were near misses. The damage extended to the fuel oil compartments, which were still leaking upon *Yorktown*'s arrival into dry dock. However, the main power plant and all of the carrier's elevators were still operational. Fourteen hundred shipwrights, machinists, welders, and electricians, both civilian and military personnel, were called in to make the ship battle worthy. It is important to note that the civilians played a critical role in ensuring that *Yorktown* was repaired and ready on time. The men worked continuously day and night during those three days to repair the ship, including making the bulkhead stanchions and deck plates necessary to restore the carrier's structural integrity and repairing the wiring, instruments and fixtures damaged by the bomb explosions. Steel plates were placed over holes in the flight deck and welded down. Temperatures in some of the carrier's compartments rose to 120 degrees due to the use of so many acetylene torches. Honolulu sustained voluntary power outages to ensure enough electrical power for Dry Dock 1 in Pearl Harbor. On May 30, the carrier was inspected and deemed sea and battle worthy. Admiral Nimitz came on board and told the crews that after this mission, *Yorktown* would be sent to Bremerton and the crew would get a well-deserved rest.[5]

During this time, the submarine force under the command of Rear Admiral Robert English, stationed at Pearl Harbor, was sent out to sea to take up its designated patrols. The Submarine Task Force (TG-7) was composed of three units: (1) the Midway Patrol Group (TG-7.1), which consisted of submarines *Cachalot*, *Flying Fish*, *Tambor*, *Trout*, *Grayling*, *Nautilus*, *Grouper*, *Dolphin*, *Gato*, *Cuttlefish*, *Gudgeon* and *Grenadier*; (2) the Roving Short-Stops (TG-7.2), which consisted of submarines *Narwhal*, *Plunger* and *Trigger*; and (3) the North of Oahu Patrol (TG-7.3) composed of submarines *Tarpon*, *Pike*, *Finback* and *Growler*.[6]

On May 18, a directive was given by Admiral Nimitz that the Northern Pacific Force (TF-8) head toward the Aleutian Islands to engage the Japanese forces expected in the region. However, it would take until a few hours after Japan struck Dutch Harbor on the morning of June 3 before the main body of Task Force 8 would be able to unite because the ships to be assigned to Task Force 8 were scattered over all parts of the Pacific. Task Force 8 was composed of a Main Body under the command of Rear Admiral

Robert Theobald and was composed of cruisers *Nashville* (flagship), *Indianapolis*, *Louisville*, *Saint Louis* and *Honolulu*, accompanied by destroyers *Gridley*, *McCall*, *Gilmer* and *Humphreys* and a destroyer striking force of destroyers *Case*, *Reid*, *Brooks*, *Sands*, *Kane*, *Dent*, *Talbot*, *King* and *Waters*. Submarines S-18, S-23, S-27, S-28, S-34 and S-35 were also assigned to the area.[7]

Admiral Yamamoto, in order to obtain the Japanese Naval Staff's approval for Midway as Japan's next major objective, had to give in to the demands of Admiral Nagano Osami, Chief of Japan's Naval General Staff, and agree to incorporate the invasion of the Aleutian Islands as part of his Midway plan. In addition, Yamamoto also had to accept sending two of his carriers to support the Port Moresby invasion in the Coral Sea prior to Midway. Initially, the Aleutians were to be attacked prior to any major operation, but in a fiery debate on April 5, 1942, both Yamamoto and Nagano agreed that the Aleutian invasion would become part of the Midway operational plan. In contrast to Yamamoto's insistence that six carriers be available in the operational plan for the attack on Pearl Harbor, where he was ready to resign his position as chief of the Combined Fleet if his plan was not adopted, he offered little resistance to placing *Zuikaku* and *Shokaku* in harm's way in the Battle of the Coral Sea or to not having small carriers *Junyo* and *Ryujo* present in his task force at Midway.

The inclusion of the Aleutian campaign in the Midway plan was questionable at best. It deprived the Japanese at Midway of at least forty-five first-line ships, including the addition of light carriers *Ryujo* and *Junyo* to the campaign, and unequivocally altered its outcome. The Aleutian force represented about 20 percent of the entire Japanese forces utilized in the Midway operational plan. The inclusion of the Aleutian invasion in the Midway plan is important in a negative way: (1) it deprived the Japanese of a significant portion of the available fleet (particularly the carriers) at Midway; (2) the plan widened the scope of operation between the two objectives—Midway and the Aleutian Islands—to nearly four million square miles, which resulted in neither operation supporting the other in case the situation warranted it (the distance between Dutch Harbor and Midway is 1,854 miles); and (3) the process created a strategic operational plan that lacked a single unified objective but rather was two independent plans that were mutually exclusive.[8]

The critical question to be asked is whether the attack on the Aleutian Islands at this time was of such importance that it warranted the diversion of over forty-five surface ships away from the Midway operation and more importantly deprived Yamamoto of two of its operational small carriers. On the surface, the answer may appear to be in the affirmative. Attu was just 650 miles from Paramushiro, a volcanic island in the northernmost area of the Kurile Islands, which Japan developed into a significant air and naval base. Japan also feared air attacks launched from U.S. bomber air bases that could be built in the Aleutian Islands. On closer inspection, one realizes that Japan's industrial centers were almost 2,000 miles away from Attu. In addition, any air attack on Japan from U.S. bases would have to confront the bad weather in the Aleutians. The warm Japanese current colliding with the extreme cold air coming down from the Bering Strait led to the skies being continuously overcast over the entire region during most of the year. These difficult weather conditions precluded any serious threat by the United States in establishing a significant base of operations in the Aleutians for attacking

Japan. Thus, the entire Aleutian operation was flawed from the beginning, and with the Aleutian campaign being included in the Midway operational plan, it deprived Yamamoto of two carriers (though small) at Midway, reducing that number to four instead of six. Neither the designation of *Shokaku* and *Zuikaku* to the Coral Sea operation nor the implementation of the Aleutian campaign by the Naval General Staff caused Yamamoto to pause in his goal to gain approval for his Midway plan from the Naval General Staff.[9]

On May 25, the seaplane tender *Ballard* left Pearl Harbor and was heading toward Midway. On board was Commander John Ford, USN, who directed such motion-picture films as *Stagecoach, The Searchers, The Grapes of Wrath* and *How Green Was My Valley*. Ford was given permission by Admiral Nimitz to go to Midway and film the upcoming battle. *Ballard* was accompanied by ten patrol torpedo (PT) boats. PT-20, PT-21, PT-22, PT-24, PT-25, PT-26, PT-27 and PT-28 were assigned to Midway, and PT-29 and PT-30 were sent to Kure Island, the last island in the Hawaiian chain, located just northwest of Midway. PT-25 had engine trouble on its way to Midway and had to be taken into tow by *Ballard*. This group arrived at Midway on May 29. The boats were on average eighty feet long and weighed fifty-five tons. The PT boats were powered by three Packard engines, which produced a top speed of forty knots. The craft was armed by two .50-caliber machine-gun turrets and manned with two twenty-one-inch-diameter torpedo tubes, which fired four Mark-8 torpedoes.[10]

On May 25, four Martin B-26 twin-engine bombers arrived at Midway from Ford Island. Their pilots had been given a crash course in torpedo bombing by airmen from *Enterprise*'s torpedo bomber crewmen. Shortly after the B-26s landed, four Catalina flying boats arrived from VP-11, and a little later, eight more PBYs reached Midway from VP-23, bringing VP-23 up to full strength at sixteen aircraft.

In Pearl Harbor, with *Yorktown* having passed the inspection that ascertained that its watertight compartments were sealed, arrangements were then made to restore its aircrews. Only Bombing Five (VB-5) was intact; the other three squadrons were depleted. Bombing Five was assigned now to become Scouting Five. Fighters (VF-3) and torpedo bombers (VT-3) from *Saratoga* replaced *Yorktown*'s VF-5 and VT-5 (the new TBF-1 torpedo bomber had not arrived in time to replace the TBD-1 torpedo bomber). In addition, VB-3 replaced *Yorktown*'s dive-bombing squadron. Thus, heading out to Midway, three of the four air squadrons on board *Yorktown* were replacements from *Saratoga*, which had just completed its repairs at Bremerton, Washington.[11]

On May 29, eight B-17Es landed on Midway's Eastern Island. These planes were taken from the 431st, 394th, 31st and 72nd Army Air Force Bombardment Squadrons. At 0730 on May 30, *Yorktown* eased out of Pearl Harbor, following six destroyers and two cruisers, to join *Enterprise* and *Hornet* at Point Luck, 350 miles northeast of Midway. *Enterprise* and *Hornet* had left Pearl Harbor before noon on May 28. All of its original aircraft came on board a few hours after the task force was out to sea. *Enterprise*'s planes came from Ford Island, while *Hornet*'s aircraft came from Ewa Mooring Mast Field.

Upon leaving Pearl Harbor, Task Force 16 headed northwest on a course of 340 degrees, steaming at a speed of sixteen knots. When Task Force 16 reached a position 350 miles northeast of Midway (Point Luck), it would wait on the arrival of *Yorktown*

4. Prelude to Midway

to unite with *Enterprise* and *Hornet*, which was expected on June 2. The barometric conditions were not good, with heavily overcast skies, occasional rain and cold temperatures. *Enterprise* (CV-6) was nicknamed *The Big E* and was the sixth carrier constructed by the United States, built in Newport News, Virginia. *Enterprise* was commissioned in May 1938. The carrier was one of the Yorktown class and was the only one of three carriers to survive the entirety of World War II (the others being *Saratoga* and *Ranger*).[12]

At 1600 on June 2, *Yorktown* was seen in the distance and joined Task Force 16, 325 miles northeast of Midway. Fletcher was in tactical command of the U.S. Striking Force, which consisted of three carriers, seven cruisers, one light cruiser and fifteen destroyers, for a total of twenty-six ships. His carrier air arm consisted of 221 operational aircraft. The United States was poised to spring its trap on the unsuspecting Japanese Kido Butai.

On May 31, nine more B-17E bombers arrived at Midway with two replacement PBY-5A aircraft for the PBY-5As that were damaged the day before. Fifteen of the now seventeen B-17 bombers were sent on patrol that day, searching out 700 miles to the west, but found no evidence of the Japanese fleet. During this time, Japanese submarine I-168 was keeping Midway under surveillance and was reporting the islands' activity back to the advancing Japanese fleet.

Lieutenant Commander Tanabe Yahachi, commanding I-168, specifically noted in his report the heavy reconnaissance missions being performed by the aircraft on the atoll. I-168 continued to scout Midway until June 3.[13]

On May 31, Lieutenant Langdon Fieberling was placed in charge of VT-8's detachment of six Grumman TBF-1 Avengers in Pearl Harbor. He led the squadron, whose pilots had never flown that distance before (1,140 miles), to Midway. The planes arrived at Midway on June 1, after an eight-hour flight. Midway was ready for the upcoming Battle of Midway, now having 127 operational aircraft, 10 PT boats, 5 tanks, 8 mortars, 14 shore-defense guns, 32 antiaircraft guns and 3,632 defenders. In addition, an SCR-270 radar system (Signal Corps Radio, the first operational early-warning system) was situated on the western part of Sand Island.[14]

On May 27, the Nagumo Force left Hashirajima Bay with twenty-one ships and headed through the Bungo Straits and out to the open sea of the Pacific Ocean. During this time, Commander Fuchida Mitsuo, leader of the Pearl Harbor attack, developed acute appendicitis on board *Akagi* and went immediately to surgery. The Japanese fleet was now 430 miles south of Tokyo and turned due east.

By May 29, the various Japanese forces were steaming toward their objectives without incident, except for the fog shrouding the Kakuta Forces. Two days later (May 31), the weather in the central Pacific worsened with high winds and seas, causing Yamamoto's Main Body and Kondo's Invasion Force to slow their speed down to fourteen knots. While en route, Yamamoto intercepted an urgent U.S. message that they could not totally decipher but which suggested that the enemy had discovered the Transport Group. If true, this fact would eliminate the element of surprise for Japan in the upcoming attack on Midway. In addition, Yamamoto's radio intelligence unit picked up American radio messages originating from Hawaii and the Aleutians that indicated that there was increased submarine and aircraft activity in these areas. Yamamoto and his staff were not concerned about the possible discovery of the transport fleet and concluded that Japan could now destroy the remaining U.S. carrier forces in the Pacific. The Hawaiian radio signals could be an indication that the enemy was aware of Japan's intentions to attack Midway and was sending a U.S. carrier task force to the area. As a result, Yamamoto eagerly awaited the results of Operation K, which would tell them whether or not the U.S. carriers were in Pearl Harbor. However, on May 27, when the Japanese submarine I-123 (refueling submarine) neared French Frigate Shoals, it found a seaplane tender *Thornton* and destroyer *Clark* guarding the area. (*Ballard*, which left Midway on May 29, had also been scheduled to be stationed at French Frigate Shoals but had not yet reached the area.)

The sighting was passed on from I-123 to I-121 (refueling submarine), which joined Japanese submarine I-123 in the area. The commanders of these submarines—I-123's Lieutenant Commander Ueno Toshitake and I-121's Lieutenant Commander Fujimori Yasuo, respectively—waited for seventy-two hours before radioing back to headquarters in Kwajalein, apprising them of the situation. The submarine commanders were then ordered to wait another twenty-four hours in the hope that the Americans would vacate the area. The next day, Ueno and Fujimori discovered that two U.S. flying boats (PBYs) were also present in the lagoon. With that information, Operation K was reluctantly canceled, depriving Yamamoto, now on board battleship *Yamato*, of vital information as to whether the U.S. carriers were in Pearl Harbor or not. He now had to depend on the three submarine cordons placed between Hawaii and Midway for the vital intelligence he needed regarding the disposition of the American carriers.[15]

It is ironic that had Operation K been successful in discovering that the U.S. carriers were not in Pearl Harbor, this finding may have actually reinforced in the minds of the Japanese navy the idea that the American carriers were still operating in the Southwest Pacific and not situated at Midway. This conclusion is drawn from the fact that it was the opinion of the Japanese Naval General Staff that the U.S. fleet was still steaming in the neighborhood of the Solomon Islands.

The commander of Japan's Sixth Fleet Submarine Forces was Vice Admiral Komatsu Marquis Teruhisa, the cousin of the Japanese empress and a close friend of Emperor Hirohito. His overconfidence of a Japanese victory in the Battle of Midway led him to have little regard for the operational planning of the submarine deployment against Midway. In actuality, the operational plan for the disposition of the submarine cordons west of Hawaii never included Captain Kuroshima Kameto, senior operations officer, who was responsible for the basic outline of the Midway operation plan. This task usually fell to Commander Arima Takayasu, Yamamoto's submarine officer, but Kuroshima curiously told him he did not have to write up such a plan. This left the entire submarine cordon disposition without a working operational plan.[16]

The submarines of Submarine Squadron Five (Cordon B), located to the northwest of Hawaii, were old and were being overhauled so that they could be relegated to training purposes when they were suddenly assigned to the Midway operation. Commander Iuru Shojiro of Naval General Headquarters complained that the submarines were too slow to arrive at their destinations on time and were unable to deal with air attacks, but his advice was rejected by Rear Admiral Fukudome Shigeru who presided over the Plans Division of the Naval General Staff.[17]

Commander Iuru was completely correct in his assessment of using the outdated submarines on such a vital mission. Not only had the submarines (Cordon B) left Japan two days late in heading for Kwajalein, causing them to leave the Marshall Islands between May 26 and May 30, but they were also limited in their daytime travels by American air patrols, which forced the boats to dive, limiting the speed at which they could travel. As a result, the submarines could only transit on the surface at night. These events resulted in the boats not arriving at their assigned positions between Midway and Hawaii on June 2. Instead, they were not in place until the morning of June 3, well after the U.S. carriers had sortied through the area and were northeast of Midway. In addition, the submarines of Submarine Squadron Three (Cordon A) located to the west of Hawaii were also tardy getting into position because of the delays in the execution of Operation K, and this squadron did not arrive until June 4. In retrospect, even if the submarines had arrived at their destinations on time, they were subject to fixed positions instead of sweeping the areas from the Hawaiian Islands to the waters northeast of Midway. This limitation would have reduced the possibility that the crews in the submarines could have detected the U.S. carriers heading for Midway.[18]

The failure of Operation K should have been reported to Admiral Yamamoto by Vice Admiral Komatsu on June 3, but Komatsu failed, intentionally or not, to report the delay of Submarine Squadron Five (Cordon B) in reaching their assigned positions on time. Thus, neither Admiral Yamamoto nor Nagumo knew of the tardiness of the submarines, nor the consequences of their delay, namely to observe whether or not the U.S. carriers were headed for Midway. The foregoing admirals naturally assumed the scouting arrangements were intact and that no American carriers had sortied from Pearl Harbor for Midway.

The Japanese committed only twenty major ships, including carriers *Akagi*, *Kaga*, *Soryu* and *Hiryu* (plus five oilers), from its vast navy to be in the forefront of battle in its confrontation with the U.S. Navy at Midway. It has been asserted by Fuchida and Okumiya in *Midway* and Walter Lord in *Incredible Victory* that America faced overwhelming odds at Midway. That may be true from a strategic viewpoint but certainly not from a tactical point of view, where the United States actually outnumbered the Japanese in naval vessels twenty-six to twenty ships. One of the reasons why the Kido Butai force was so small was that the Japanese still considered the battleship supreme and kept the battleships in the rear, out of harm's way. The second reason was that Yamamoto saw no need to cancel Japan's Aleutian campaign and assign that force (which included forty-five major ships) to the Midway operation.

There were at least seven major flaws in the operational planning that presented critical tactical disadvantages for the Japanese in the upcoming Battle of Midway. These shortcomings were largely ignored by the Japanese high command prior to its engagement with the Americans at Midway. The misjudgment begins with the duality of the Midway mission.

The objective of the Japanese carriers' mission was the cornerstone of Japan's misguided thinking regarding the operational plan for Midway. The first and perhaps most critical flaw in the Japanese Midway operational plan was the inability of Japan's high command to take seriously the idea that the Americans might be waiting on their right flank, ready to ambush their fleet. This viewpoint permitted the Japanese to have two missions in their planning, namely the assault on Midway and the destruction of the U.S. fleet. This naval policy was influenced by the fact that Admiral Yamamoto had the desire to eventually augment sea-based airpower with land-based aircraft on its island possessions and thus included the occupation of Midway in his planning. However, in fixating on Midway, the Japanese fleet lost flexibility of carrier movement, a prerequisite for victory in a naval engagement. The initial part of the Midway operational plan focused on neutralizing the airpower on Midway so that the Japanese carriers and the landings by the occupational forces would be successful. Tactically, the Japanese would divert half of its total striking force to attack Midway, while keeping the remainder of the aircraft in reserve in the event that the U.S. fleet was in the area. The air strike on Midway would be launched by aircraft from all four carriers. This meant that only half of the Japanese aircraft would be available to attack the U.S. carriers if they were discovered while Japan was attacking Midway. This circumstance would potentially create a dilemma for the Japanese high command at Midway. If the Japanese scouting aircraft discovered the American fleet before the Japanese planes returned from Midway, Nagumo would have to make a command decision, either to send aloft the weakened striking force to attack the American fleet or delay the launching until all of the planes returning from Midway had landed and were equipped with the proper ordnance for attacking surface ships. The latter option carried the risk that during the delay, the Japanese carriers would be vulnerable to attack by American aircraft. This was especially true because the only real defense the Japanese carriers had was their CAP, since they lacked radar and had minimum assistance from their carrier, cruiser and destroyer anti-aircraft guns.

The Japanese decision to attack Midway without first confirming the presence or absence of the American fleet precluded any possibility that Japan would strike the U.S. carrier fleet first. Yet it was imperative that Japan strike first if the Japanese were to maintain their carrier advantage in the war. A simultaneous exchange of air attacks by both sides would most likely result in a similar number of carrier losses on each side. Japan was aware that America had a much greater potential, as the war raged on, to produce large numbers of aircraft carriers than Japan. Naval battles that resulted in equal numbers of carrier losses for both sides would eventually benefit the United States.

On the other hand, the United States' ability to break the JN-25B code had profound effects on Japan's strategic and tactical plan for the Midway operation. The intelligence not only informed the United States of the date, time and location of the Japanese offensive, but it provided the means for the Americans to strike first and thus effectively destroy a significant number of the Japanese carriers. If the Japanese were able to simultaneously counterattack, the best they could expect with their present operational plan would be to lose an even number of carriers as the Americans. However, if Japan was unable to counterattack, they could expect to lose three carriers to the United States' one. The reasons for these assumptions are discussed below.

One important point that is not well appreciated in the historical literature is that, given the circumstances, the very moment Japan launched its planes to attack Midway, it lost the possibility of attacking the U.S. carrier fleet first with its full complement of aircraft on all four carriers. This fact makes irrelevant that seven scout planes launched from *Akagi*, *Kaga*, *Haruna*, *Chikuma* and *Tone* between 0430 and 0500 were sent to locate the U.S. carriers. This latter conclusion is drawn because once the first wave of Japanese aircraft left for Midway at 0500, Japan lost its chance to attack the Americans first with aircraft from all four of its carriers and thus lost its opportunity to destroy most or all of the U.S. carrier force. Even if the Japanese scout planes did locate the American fleet (Task Force 17) as early as 0630, the first Japanese wave of aircraft would still be attacking Midway and not on the Japanese carriers preparing to launch against the U.S. carriers. As a result, Nagumo was placed in a position to have to decide whether he should launch the remaining sixty-four operational aircraft on board all four carriers immediately or wait until the first wave of aircraft returning from Midway at 0830 had landed.

These planes would then have to be refueled and rearmed before Nagumo could launch all of his available planes against the American carrier fleet, which was now located in the waters northeast of Midway.

The Japanese were unaware that U.S. naval intelligence had deciphered the Japanese naval JN-25B code. That information would permit *Enterprise* and *Hornet* to launch their aircraft at 0700 and depart for the Japanese carriers at 0745. One hour later, *Yorktown* would lift off her aircraft and head for the Japanese carriers. If this scenario played out in the battle, Japan would have lost its opportunity to be the first ones to attack the American carriers.

The second critical flaw in Japan's Midway operational plan going into the battle was the ineffectiveness of its scouting intelligence and its inability to appreciate the nature of net striking power. In carrier operations, the crucial components for victory are scouting effectiveness and net striking power. The first component, scouting effectiveness, which included both scouting intelligence and cryptanalytical intelligence, would be judged by whether the scouting intelligence obtained would allow that carrier force to be the first one to strike. Regarding Japan's scouting intelligence, Genda assigned only seven aircraft to their search plan to locate the American carriers, and the operational plan permitted the Midway strike force to be launched before there was confirmation of the presence or absence of the American fleet. This oversight was particularly egregious since the early identification of the U.S. fleet would be a major factor in who would win the battle. As it has been previously stated, the side that strikes first will generally speaking inflict the most damage on its opponent's carrier fleet. Cryptanalytic capability was a crucial asset that resided only with the Americans, as the Japanese lacked the ability to significantly break the American code. In the Battle of Midway, the United States knew beforehand the exact date, location and time that Japan would attack Midway. This intelligence afforded the Americans an immense advantage, as it gave them an opportunity to strike the first blow at Midway.

The second component, net striking power, would be evaluated by the carrier damage inflicted upon one's opponent. In general, one carrier wing (CVW), defined as an operational naval aviation organization on a carrier, composed of several aircraft squadrons, would have the capability to sink or seriously damage one carrier, and the cumulative striking power was linear; that is, two carriers were twice as effective as one, and so forth. Thus, the greater the number of carriers on one side versus the other would significantly alter the results. Admiral Yamamoto, who had insisted on six carriers for the Pearl Harbor attack, now was comfortable with having only four carriers during Japan's confrontation with the United States at Midway. He acted on this decision even though Japanese war games had demonstrated the loss of two of Japan's carriers with his present operational plan.

In his 1986 book, *Fleet Tactics*, Captain Wayne P. Hughes, Jr., USN (Ret.), reveals that if Force A (U.S.) is the first one to attack an equal Force B (Japan) in the battle with a carrier ratio of 3:4 (U.S./Japanese), as existed in the Battle of Midway, the United States would lose one carrier and the Japanese three. This result is close to the scenario actually played out during the Japanese war games prior to the battle, but the results of the war games (discussed above) were largely discarded by the Japanese high command. If both opponents, Force A and Force B, were to attack each other simultaneously at Midway, then the United States would lose no carriers and Japan one.[19]

Unfortunately for Japan, Yamamoto was not able to appreciate the critical need for Japan not to be caught in a position where it was not the first one to attack the American carriers or at the very least to attack them simultaneously. The addition of the two small carriers from the Aleutians to the Kido Butai would have helped alter those statistical probabilities against Japan.

Yamamoto lost the opportunity in the Battle of the Coral Sea to have his best chance at fleet carrier superiority with an 11:4 ratio (*Akagi, Kaga, Soryu, Hiryu, Zuikaku, Shokaku, Shoho, Hosho* and *Zuiho* versus *Enterprise, Hornet, Yorktown* and *Lexington*). If Yamamoto had waited on the *Zuikaku* and *Shokaku* at Midway to be ready, *Saratoga* would have been available for Midway, giving the Japanese a carrier advantage of 11:5. Furthermore, if the Japanese had delayed its attack on Midway for sixty days, *Wasp* would have been present, and now the fleet carrier ratio (11:6) between Japan and the United States would still be in Japan's favor, though it would be less.[20]

Yamamoto's best chance for victory at Midway was to insist on carriers *Ryujo* and *Junyo* being part of his First Striking Force. The third flaw in Japan's Midway operational plan was that it was defensive in nature and was related to the lack of radar in all four carriers involved in the battle. Japan was many months to years behind the United States in the development of radar technology. Only two sets of radar equipment were available at the time of the Battle of Midway, and they were experimental models.

However, they were not placed in any of Midway's carriers but instead on battleships *Ise* and *Hyuga*, which were assigned to the Aleutian campaign. Japan's carriers entering the Battle of Midway not only lacked radar to detect and destroy any U.S. scouting aircraft before they could find the Japanese task force but also lacked the ability to have in place a significant early-warning system to detect any incoming U.S. aircraft heading in to attack the Japanese Striking Force. In its place, the Japanese used its cruisers and destroyers located on the perimeter of the task force as its early-warning system. This alternative was restricted by the fact that the cruisers and destroyers could only range out to a distance where they were still in visual contact with the carriers. Thus, in reality, the Japanese had a very primitive early-warning system for incoming American aircraft. In addition, the lack of radar also resulted in the Japanese directing the CAP manually, where they utilized four different air officers on four separate carriers to direct the CAP to where they were needed most. The manual system had the potential to create confusion in directing the CAP to the most effective area of combat.[21]

The fourth flaw in Japan's Midway operational plan going into battle was defensive in nature, and this flaw was related to the function and placement of its antiaircraft guns on the carriers. Of the four carriers, *Akagi* was affected by this flaw the most. The ship was not equipped with the more modern five-inch/.40-caliber guns but still had the older 4.7-inch/.45-caliber guns, which did not have the elevation or the rate of fire of the newer guns. The guns were placed amidships and low on the hull rather than around the four quarter sections of the carrier. The guns could not be aimed forward or toward the rear. The island on the port side blocked the ability of the port battery to aim the guns forward even more. If aircraft were to attack in the area of the port bow, the 4.7-inch guns could not effectively aim at them, leaving only the 25mm antiaircraft guns as the carrier's only defense. Thus, *Akagi* was very vulnerable to attack by U.S. dive-bombers. *Kaga* was equipped with the five-inch antiaircraft guns, but the carrier's fire-control system had the older Type 91 model as compared to the other Japanese carriers. The older model was slow in tracking incoming aircraft, and it relied on an aircraft flying straight and level. The older model was also produced at a time when aircraft were slower and concern for a ship's vulnerability came from planes flying level at high altitudes, not from aircraft flying at speeds greater than 200 miles per hour and diving in on a target. The other carriers had installed the newer Type 94 systems, but they were barely more effective than the older model. The Type 94 system had a narrow window in which it could fire at a dive-bomber that was closing in fast on a carrier. The newer system of antiaircraft guns would have less than one minute to locate their target and open fire. It was not that the Type 94 model (probably the best on any Axis warship at the time) was not effective against a torpedo bomber but that it just could not cope with the dive-bomber. The lighter Type 96 25mm automatic antiaircraft guns were mostly double-mounted, but a few guns on *Hiryu* had the newer triple-mounted model. The ammunition came in fifteen-round boxes, which led to the Japanese firing only one barrel at a time so that the other barrels could be loaded. This limitation reduced the firepower of the guns. The Type 96 25mm antiaircraft guns were similar to the Type 94 antiaircraft guns in two ways. First, both guns had a short range (8,000 meters), which meant that the 25mm weapons were only effective against a torpedo bomber, and second, the 25mm antiaircraft guns were virtually ineffective against the dive-bomber, not only because of its lighter firepower but because its target was moving swiftly in all three dimensions.[22]

A single director controlled the gun battery, which contained two to four weapon mounts. The Japanese carriers at Midway had the heavy (4.7–5 inch) antiaircraft guns grouped into batteries of three or four twin mounts apiece on both the starboard and port side of the carriers. The lighter guns (25mm) were clustered into five batteries, two of which were located on the port side of the carrier, and two batteries were placed on the starboard side of the ship with one battery positioned at the bow. The total number of aircraft that could be targeted by the antiaircraft guns on the Japanese carriers was not related to the number of gun mounts but rather to the number of fire-control directors that controlled the batteries. Based on these observations, the Japanese carriers at Midway would be able to defend themselves against a maximum of seven incoming aircraft. Thus, it would be the main responsibility of the CAP to stop the main influx of incoming planes that were attacking the carriers. The carriers' antiaircraft guns only had the ability to stop a few enemy planes that may have made it through the carriers' first line of defense.[23]

The relatively few warships that would surround the four carriers on their journey to Midway would offer little firepower for the defense of the carriers. The Japanese destroyers in 1942 were equipped with only a pair of twin 25mm mounts. Their five-inch guns were low-angled for excellent surface fighting but were totally ineffective as antiaircraft weapons. These guns were also not able to track a fast-moving plane and thus were useless in protecting the carriers against the dive-bomber. Only the heavy cruisers *Tone* and *Chikuma*, light cruiser *Nagara* and battleships *Haruna* and *Kirishima* could offer any assistance, but they would be too few in number to make any difference.

The fifth flaw in the Japanese operation plan for Midway was its naval policy, which insisted that the battleship, rather than the carrier, was the supreme weapon in naval warfare. The Japanese Navy at that time, in spite of all the evidence to the contrary (such as the role that airpower played in Japan's overwhelming successes in the early part of the war), refused to believe that airpower had surpassed the battleship as the most effective weapon in naval warfare. This fact explains why the Main Body and the Midway Invasion Force were all stationed from 300 to 500 miles to the west of the First Carrier Striking Force (comprised of only twenty ships). The Japanese high command still believed that it was the surface ships that needed to be protected rather than the carriers. Japan did not embrace the doctrine that airpower had replaced the battleship as the dominant weapon in naval warfare until 1944, by which time it was too late to influence the outcome of the war in the Pacific. Thus, the defense of the four carriers at Midway would not benefit from the formidable antiaircraft firepower of the ships in the rear, nor would they have the assistance of two of the experimental types of radar which were placed in the battleships in the Aleutian campaign. The placement of radar (although experimental) in the Japanese ships at Midway, instead of the battleships *Ise* and *Hyuga* in the Aleutians, would have improved the capability of the Japanese to defend their carriers against incoming enemy aircraft by detecting the enemy when its planes were further away from the Kido Butai and by directing its CAP to the incoming enemy aircraft.

This mistaken battleship-oriented naval policy also affected a tactical decision involving the Kido Butai in another way at Midway. The Japanese high command had two options at Midway: one was to assign to each carrier its own escort screen, and the other was to place the four carriers together with a common screen to protect all four of the carriers. In 1942, the wisest tactical decision for Japan would have been to give each carrier its own screen, since the Japanese carrier antiaircraft fire was inadequate in its ability to defend the carrier against the U.S. dive-bomber. In addition, the CAP could be launched and landed more effectively when the carriers had their individual escort screens. This option would allow carriers to be as far apart as ten or twenty miles, which would facilitate the landing and launching of its carrier aircraft on all four carriers, and would also create the possibility that one of the carriers might escape attack by incoming enemy planes.

This example is best exemplified by the carriers *Zuikaku* and *Shokaku* during the Battle of the Coral Sea, which had their own escorts and therefore permitted them to operate miles apart. The operational plan allowed carrier *Zuikaku* to escape detection by American aircraft by moving to and hiding under the overcast and rainy weather. However, at Midway, Admiral Yamamoto was forced to group all his carriers together with a common escort because he insisted on keeping all the other screening escorts to the rear of the Japanese carriers to protect his battleships. As a result, there was a paucity of screening ships available for the four carriers attacking Midway, and the carriers entered the eve of battle in a box formation approximately 1,300 yards apart and with a common escort screen for all four carriers.

The sixth flaw in the Japanese Midway operational plan was its failure to recognize that Midway was essentially an unsinkable fourth carrier for the United States. The Americans had seventy-six (though a number of these planes were obsolete) operational aircraft on Midway that would see action on the morning of June 4, 1942. These aircraft included twenty F2A-3 and four F4F-3 fighters, six TBF-1 torpedo bombers, four B-26 bombers, sixteen SBD-2 dive-bombers, eleven SB2U dive-bombers, and fifteen B-17s.[24] When the total of operational planes on Midway (76 aircraft) are added to the 221 operational planes on all three U.S. carriers (*Enterprise*, *Hornet* and *Yorktown*), the Japanese were facing 297 U.S. aircraft. On the other hand, the total number of operational aircraft on all four Japanese carriers was 227 planes, plus 21 non-operational Zeroes, which were being ferried to Midway for its future land-based fighter group, creating a total of 248 aircraft for Japan. This total represented a differential of forty-nine operational aircraft in favor of the United States.

The seventh flaw in the Japanese Midway operational plan was its decision to launch its aircraft against Midway from all four of its carriers.[25] The reason this tactical plan was adopted was because it took less time for the planes to be launched and recovered from four carriers than if the planes took off and landed from two carriers. However, this decision would also make the carriers more vulnerable to enemy attack because the carriers would not be able to launch or land their CAP while the Midway air strike was landing. Thus, the carriers' most important defensive weapon, their CAP, would not be able to refuel or rearm during this period of time, making the carriers more vulnerable to enemy attack. A more prudent decision would have been to launch the Midway air strike from only two carriers, allowing the remaining two carriers to be ready and armed with the proper ordnance if the American fleet were discovered. However, given the operational plan as it existed, Nagumo would now be faced with a dilemma: he could either immediately launch his remaining available aircraft or delay the launchings until all of the returning Midway flight had landed, were refueled and rearmed with proper ordnance and then made ready for takeoff from the flight deck. Nagumo would choose the latter decision.

Underpinning the flaw in this aspect of the Japanese Midway operational plan was the decision to attack Midway before confirming that a U.S. carrier fleet was not in the area. Once Japan decided to launch both the air strike on Midway and its U.S. carrier search mission simultaneously (0430), the roots of the dilemma (given the circumstances) were set in motion.

The best way this conundrum could have been avoided would have been for Yamamoto to insist on including six carriers in the Japanese Striking Force at Midway. If he had done this, the Japanese would have had a greater ability to deal with the situation by assigning two carriers to attack Midway and assigning four carriers to deal with the American carrier fleet if they were discovered. Thus, it was Japan, not America, who entered the conflict at Midway with significant impediments that would dampen its ability to decisively win the carrier battle. These hindrances included, foremost, its decision to attack Midway without having absolute certainty that the Americans were not in the area, its lack of naval intelligence (particularly the ability to break the American code), its suboptimal scouting plan, its lack of radar, its being numerically outnumbered by U.S. aircraft, and its weak defensive posture, especially against the dive-bomber.

The Americans still had to execute their more simplified but still difficult plan, namely to first locate the Japanese Striking Force with their PBYs from Midway, and secondly to launch their aircraft and locate the Japanese carriers before the Japanese could launch their planes against the U.S. fleet. It was hoped that U.S. aircraft would catch the Japanese carriers when they were most vulnerable, namely, during the refueling and rearming of their aircraft in preparation for a launch against the U.S. fleet.

Thus, on the first two days of June 1942, the Japanese carriers were forging through a storm and closer to Midway as the Americans waited northeast of Midway for them to arrive. At this time, the Yamamoto Force (Main Force), which was then 600 miles to the rear of the Nagumo Force, had noticed the rain diminish, but now fog became a serious problem, which threatened the refueling effort of the Yamamoto Force with its oil tankers. Yamamoto was not able to locate the tankers in the fog. Finally, the tankers broke radio silence and radioed their position to the battleship *Yamato*, which could have exposed the position of the Main Force to the enemy (the United States did not pick up the radio signal). The Japanese surmised that their fleet movements toward Midway may already have been known to the Americans because of a marked increase in communication traffic coming out of Hawaii, in which 40 percent of the radio traffic was marked urgent. Yamamoto also knew that the Midway patrols had extended out to 700 miles because of an accidental encounter between a Wotje Japanese flying boat and a U.S. flying boat 500 miles northeast of Wotje. In addition, U.S. submarines had been spotted 500 miles northeast of Wake Island, which indicated an American submarine picket line 600 miles southeast of Midway. Fueling operations for the Main Force, which began on June 1, were discontinued because of the intense fog and were resumed on the next day.[26]

On June 3, the mist which surrounded the Nagumo Force now became a dense fog. The fog was so impenetrable that communications by flag signals or by search lights were impossible. The fleet needed to alter course in order to carry out its mission to attack Midway. The only source of communication left to send this message was by radio transmission. This alternative, however, created the possibility that Kido Butai's position would be detected by the Americans. The Japanese First Striking Force, in its present plan, did not have the flexibility to alter its course set for Midway. Since its mission was to attack Midway, it created a dilemma for Nagumo in deciding whether or not to break radio silence. Once again the dual purpose of the mission reared its ugly head for the Japanese. Captain Oishi Tomatsu, senior member of the staff, suggested to Nagumo that although the first priority of its mission was to destroy the American fleet, unless the air attack on Midway was made as scheduled, the entire invasion would be upset and the invasion force would be opposed by a very strong enemy on an intact Midway.

Nagumo's inquiry into the whereabouts of the American fleet was met by specious reasoning of his advisors which suggested that, even if the carriers had left Pearl Harbor, they certainly would not be waiting at Midway to ambush his fleet but rather would be in the South Pacific. Nagumo accepted their reasoning and decided to carry out the operational plan as directed. Rear Admiral Kusaka Ryunosuke, Chief of Staff, offered the suggestion to Nagumo that low-powered, inter-fleet radio be employed for sending the order to make the corrective course change for Midway. Nagumo agreed and proceeded to order a message that was to be sent by low-power, inter-fleet radio to affect a change in course. Although the transmission was picked up by *Yamato* 600 miles to the west, it was not detected by the Americans.[27]

As the Nagumo Force sailed southeast, questions arise about what enemy communications were known to Nagumo. First, Fuchida and Okumiya, in the 1958 book *Midway*, document that Nagumo had received the transmission that Operation K was a failure. Parshall and Tully in their 2005 book *Shattered Sword* provide evidence that reveals how the line of communications between all naval forces worked as the Japanese were sailing toward Midway. The intelligence was first transmitted from its source in the Pacific to the First Communications Unit, which was stationed in Tokyo. The Tokyo unit would then transmit the same information to all appropriate ships at sea. The fact that Nagumo received this intelligence proved the system could work. However, it is not clear that all transmissions by the First Communications Unit were received by Nagumo or indeed by Yamamoto.

Second, the authors Parshall and Tully point out from *Akagi*'s air group report that Nagumo received the intelligence about U.S. scouting aircraft searching out as far as 700 miles from Midway. This intelligence pointed out that the invasion force to the south, which was two days ahead of the schedule of the date set by the operational plan to invade Midway, could be detected by the Americans before the battle began.

Third, that the *Akagi* air group report also revealed an increase in enemy signal traffic, many of them marked urgent, should have alerted the Japanese that the American carriers were on an urgent mission somewhere in the Pacific.[28]

Any other intelligence Nagumo had or did not have is probably academic. He did know Operation K was a failure, but he had no information that the Japanese submarine cordons placed between Hawaii and Midway were going to arrive late at their positions. As a result, he was in the dark as to the location of the American carriers. Therefore, it would have been prudent for him to alter his plans to attack Midway and prepare solely for a carrier engagement with the U.S. fleet.

Nagumo had already shown his lack of flexibility in the Pearl Harbor attack when he refused to follow up on the raid with an air attack on the U.S. fuel tanks which were left untouched. Certainly, he had the latitude to do so, as a discussion of such a possibility was held by his staff and him aboard the *Akagi* at the time of the planning. Nagumo's character traits appear to be rigid in nature, and he appeared unwilling to accept the responsibility of any change in the operational plan that would reflect upon him, even though it could potentially benefit the military mission. This impression is confirmed by Fuchida and Okumiya, who described Nagumo in 1941 as becoming passive and having lost the fighting spirit he had once had. He would no longer take the lead in the development of planned operations; instead he now tended to de facto approve the recommendations of his staff without any comments of his own. This tendency to accept the recommendations of his staff was also present in other Japanese naval leaders. This was the case when Captain Oishi and Chief of Staff Kusaka recommended to Nagumo that he break radio silence in order to make a corrective action in their course toward Midway. They based their suggestions on the basis that the Kido Butai had a commitment to a fixed schedule in attacking Midway, rather than remaining resolute in making the prime and only objective of the Midway operational plan the destruction of the U.S. fleet carriers. Nagumo could have consulted Yamamoto through the First Communication Unit to discuss the tactical situation that lay before him—namely, the cancellation of the Midway invasion. His failure to do so sealed the fate of the Japanese empire and its ability to decisively destroy the American fleet at Midway. However, the ultimate responsibility for the failure of the Japanese to cancel the invasion clearly falls at the feet of Admiral Yamamoto, as he had apparently more intelligence before him than Nagumo and was the commander of the whole Midway operation.[29]

Yamamoto did receive information regarding the failure of Operation K. This account is documented by Fuchida and Okumiya, and by Admiral Ugaki Matome, Chief of Staff of the Combined Fleet, in their books *Midway* and *Fading Victory*, respectively.[30] Ugaki also documents that Yamamoto received intelligence that American patrols extended out 700 miles from Midway and that there was increased U.S. radio traffic marked urgent out of Hawaii, as well as that U.S. submarines had set up a picket line 600 miles west of Midway. On June 3, Yamamoto received a communication from Rear Admiral Tanaka Raizo, Commander of the Midway Transport Force, that his ships had been discovered by an American patrol plane about 600 miles from Midway. With all of this information in hand, Yamamoto failed to cancel the air attack on Midway, which would allow the Nagumo Force freedom of movement and allow Nagumo to prepare for an enemy carrier engagement. He could have sent the directive by communicating the transmission to the First Communication Unit in Tokyo, which would then relay the message to Nagumo.

Much has been written about the reasons why Yamamoto reacted in this passive way, including Japanese arrogance and the Japanese trait of rigidity of purpose with little room for adjustment and flexibility as circumstances dictate. Yet these reasons do not explain Yamamoto's reactions in the Battle of the Coral Sea. When the Japanese received intelligence—as acknowledged by Ugaki in *Fading Victory*—that a U.S. enemy plane east of Rabaul reported in plain language the sighting of a large Japanese convoy escorted by two destroyers on a course of 200 degrees, Japanese leaders concluded that the Americans might believe that this was the invasion force heading for Tulagi or Port Moresby, even though that convoy was a day too early to be an invasion force.[31] Based on this intelligence, Admiral Yamamoto released the carriers *Zuikaku* and *Shokaku* from their mission to protect the invasion force in its landing at Port Moresby and gave them precise orders to destroy the U.S. carriers that might be in the area of the Coral Sea.[32]

This directive, which was totally appropriate, was based on a suspicion that the Americans might know about the invasion of Port Moresby. Even though Yamamoto knew that the Japanese Midway Invasion Force had been discovered, he failed to release Nagumo from his obligation to attack Midway. Regarding the issue of Japanese arrogance, Ugaki reports that in an April 29 meeting, Yamamoto warned those present about self-satisfaction resulting from their previously successful operations. Yamamoto also added that they should learn from the early war lessons and that new ideas were needed to supplement their present thinking.[33] Thus, he reacted in exactly the opposite way in his decision making prior to the Battle of Midway than he did prior to the Battle of the Coral Sea. One explanation might be that he was not so intimately involved with the operational plans for the Battle of the Coral Sea as he was with the operational plans for Midway. To this day, the decision making of Yamamoto and his staff prior to Midway is difficult to understand and defies all military logic.

Almost the entire operational Japanese Navy was heading for the Aleutians and Midway on June 3, refusing to believe that the American fleet was waiting for them in ambush northeast of Midway. Japan really never gave serious thought to the fact that their JN-25B naval code had been broken until July 30, 1942.

5

The Battle of Midway Begins

Wednesday, June 3, 1942 (U.S. Date): The Aleutian Campaign

The Japanese Northern Force, consisting of the Second Mobile Force (carrier group), the Adak/Attu Occupation Force and the Kiska Occupation Force, departed from Ominato, a naval base on the northern shore of Honshu between May 25 and May 27. On June 3 at 0213, the Second Mobile Force, under the command of Rear Admiral Kakuta Kakuji, reached its launching position to attack Dutch Harbor. The pilots in the planes on carriers *Ryujo* and *Junyo* had no idea of what kind of weather to expect in this area of the north Pacific. It was seven degrees below zero Centigrade. Most of the maps of the area that the Japanese had were thirty years old. Only one photograph of the area existed, and that was almost as old as the maps. The pilots were not even certain where Dutch Harbor was located. The fog which was present began to lift, and at 0238 the planes began taking off. Eleven torpedo bombers (one of which crashed into the sea on takeoff) and six fighters were launched from *Ryujo*, and twelve dive-bombers and six fighters took off from *Junyo*. The low cloud ceiling caused the aircraft to fly independently to Dutch Harbor, which was located 180 miles to the northeast. Just after the Japanese launched their aircraft, a PBY discovered the task force and dropped a number of bombs, which failed to make any contact with the ships.[1]

The Japanese planes from *Ryujo*, upon their arrival over Dutch Harbor, found fair weather, but they failed to discover any ships in the harbor. Aerial photographs taken by one of *Ryujo*'s planes revealed that Dutch Harbor was better fortified than the Japanese anticipated, with modern warehouses, barracks, wharves and fuel tanks. At 0407, the bombers attacked the radio station and the oil tanks located there, while the fighters strafed a flying boat moored in the water. In a period of twenty minutes, the aircraft inflicted substantial damage on Dutch Harbor's infrastructure and killed about 25 sailors and soldiers. All of *Ryujo*'s planes then flew safely back to their carrier except one Zero fighter which was hit by antiaircraft fire over the target. That aircraft made a landing on the southern shore of Akutan Island. Five weeks later, the U.S. Navy discovered the plane and learned that the pilot's neck had been broken on landing but found the Zero fighter aircraft intact. This fortunate discovery provided the United States with valuable information about the technology of the Zero aircraft's performance.[2]

Junyo's aircraft ran into an American PBY flying boat on its way to Dutch Harbor, and the fighters shot the plane down. The time lost in the incident allowed the fog to close in over Dutch Harbor, which prevented any aircraft from attacking their targets. As a result, the planes returned to the carrier *Junyo*. The pilots of *Junyo*'s aircraft observed returning to their carrier five U.S. destroyers in Makushin Bay on the northern side of Unalaska Island. Twenty-four planes were then directed to the target, but again fog prevented an effective attack. When all the aircraft were recovered, the task force retired on a southwesterly course and out of range of U.S. single-engine aircraft. At this time, Rear Admiral Robert Theobold, Commander of the U.S. North Pacific Force, was 500 miles south-southeast of Kakuta's carriers.

On June 3, Japanese operations against Dutch Harbor ended. As an intense fog engulfed the entire Japanese carrier fleet, it moved closer to the enemy shore and retired.[3] On the positive side, the Japanese air attack on Dutch Harbor did result in some damage to its infrastructure, but far more important was its negative effect of removing two small carriers away from Nagumo's carrier force nearing Midway.

The United States had built a 5,000-foot runway on Otter Point, which was on the northern end of Umnak within supporting distance of Dutch Harbor. The runway was so frozen that the U.S. aircraft would bounce thirty feet in the air upon landing. There were only two radar aircraft systems operational in all of Alaska. When Nimitz learned in early May that Japan would attack the Aleutians, he mobilized Task Force 8, under the command of Rear Admiral Robert Theobold, which consisted of five cruisers, fourteen destroyers and six submarines, to protect the area. However, not all the ships involved joined up with the task force until hours after Japan struck Dutch Harbor on June 3.[4]

The North Pacific Force (Task Force 8) was assigned to cover the area south of Kodiak (east of Dutch Harbor) and take advantage of any military opportunities that might arise. However, Theobold had much less intelligence on Japan's Aleutian operation than Fletcher and Spruance had regarding Midway. For instance, Theobold never had any initial information on where the Japanese Aleutian carrier force was to attack and did not know until May 28 where the Japanese invasion forces were going to land. On that date, Nimitz alerted Theobold that U.S. intelligence revealed that Japan would invade Kiska and most likely Attu. The United States had Dutch Harbor defended by 5,387 men; Kiska was occupied by 200 to 300 Marines and ten civilians who operated the weather station; and Attu had a wireless station with a U.S. garrison of unknown strength. Theobold, interpreting the intelligence presented to him differently than Nimitz did, concluded that an invasion of the small islands of Attu and Kiska was a Japanese ploy to draw his forces to the west, where the Japanese carriers could inflict heavy damage to his ships. He believed that the invasion of Dutch Harbor was the real Japanese objective. Thus, he positioned his fleet 400 miles due south of Kodiak and waited for the Japanese to invade Dutch Harbor. He expected the Japanese forces to approach Dutch Harbor somewhere between Cold Bay and Umnak. The Japanese originally did intend to invade Dutch Harbor but canceled the plan because they discovered they lacked the ships needed for the success of the mission.[5]

Theobold had few options as to where to locate Task Force 8 (composed of cruisers *Indianapolis, Louisville, Nashville, Saint Louis* and *Honolulu*; destroyers *Gridley, McCall, Gilmer, Humphreys, Case, Reid, Brooks, Sands, Kane, Dent, Talbot, King, Waters*;

and six S-class submarines, S-18, S-23, S-27, S-28, S-34 and S-35). If Theobold sailed west and attacked the Japanese Northern Force Main Body, he might have run into the two Japanese carriers.

Although he would not have any support from the U.S. Navy, he would have the assistance of the Army Air Corps 9, which had twenty-one P-40s and fourteen bombers stationed at Cold Bay and twelve P-40s at Otter Point in Umnak. These planes were radar equipped so that the fog would not be an insurmountable obstacle. The pilots, however, were inexperienced in flying over water and had little knowledge of the Aleutian terrain. Theobold, therefore, decided to station his fleet south of Kodiak and east of the Japanese invasion forces, which would preclude his task force from participating in any possible action against the Japanese forces operating in the western Aleutians.[6]

Discovery of the Japanese Transport Force

On the same day, Ensign James Lyle (VP-23) was over four hours into his flight, searching the area southwest of Midway, when he spotted two Japanese converted minesweepers (*Tama Maru* No. 3 and *Tama Maru* No. 5). At 0904, he radioed the information back to Midway. Twenty minutes later, Ensign Jack Reid (VP-44), who was flying further west than Lyle, discovered the Japanese Transport Group. He immediately transmitted his finding back to Midway with the words "Main Body." A few moments later, he reported that the distance of the force from Midway was 700 miles and had a bearing of 262 degrees. At 0950, he reported that the transport force consisted of eleven ships. It took Midway's Air Commander Captain Logan Ramsey, USN, until 1100 to realize that the Transport Group was not the Japanese Main Body, as initially reported by Ensign Reid at 0925. At this time, Task Forces 16 and 17 were steaming 320 miles northeast of Midway. Fletcher, who had taken over tactical command of both task forces the day before when the task forces united, received word of Reid's report, and he correctly interpreted the finding that the Japanese force discovered by Reid was not the Japanese carrier force that the United States was expecting to attack Midway.[7] The report that the Transport Group was heading in Midway's direction and was just 700 miles away was the first indication that Hypo had correctly interpreted Japanese intelligence that Midway was the prime target of the Japanese mission.

At 1300, with news of Reid's report, *Yorktown*, which was now operating alone north of Task Force 16 as a precautionary measure, launched ten SBDs to the north out to a radius of 175 miles but found no evidence of any Japanese ships. As a result, Task Force 17 decided to head south to join up with Task Force 16, which was now ten miles to the south. The two task forces steamed ten miles apart to within 200 miles of Midway so as to be in position to intercept the Japanese carrier force on the morning of June 4 (U.S. date). Task Force 17 remained ten miles north of Task Force 16 as the fleets headed toward their launch points.[8]

At 1158, on Midway, Captain Cyril Simard, Naval Commander of Midway Island, directed a B-17 to be supplied with extra tanks of gasoline and to fly out and track the Japanese Transport Group. Thirty minutes later, six B-17s under the command of

5. The Battle of Midway Begins 69

Ensign Jack Reid, VP-44, and his patrol squadron's crew. Back row, from left: R.J. Derouin, Francis Mussen, Ensign Hardeman (co-pilot); Ensign Jewell M. "Jack" Reid, and R.A. Swannow. Front row: J. F. Grammell, J. Groovers, and P.A. Fitzpatrick (photo 80-G-19974, courtesy of Naval History and Heritage Command).

Lieutenant Colonel Walter Sweeney, U.S. Army Air Corps (USAAC), all loaded with a half load of four 600-pound bombs, took off and flew out to bomb the Transport Group. At 1623, the six B-17s reached their target flying between 8,000 and 12,000 feet and dropped their bombs. The Japanese were completely surprised by the attack, but no direct bomb hits were inflicted on any of the ships of the Transport Group. After releasing their bombs, the aircrews of the B-17s turned home, believing that they had succeeded in their attack because of the near misses witnessed by them at such a high altitude. The lone B-17 sent out by Simard to scout the Transport Group never found the ships and as such returned to Midway. By 2145, all the B-17 crews had returned to Midway.[9]

While the B-17s were returning home from their mission, Lieutenant William Richards, VP-44's Executive Officer, was ordered to lead four PBYs (three PBYs from VP-24 and one from VP-51) to carry out a night torpedo attack on the Transport Group. At 2115, four Catalina flying boats armed with Mark 13 torpedoes took off from Eastern Island and headed southwest. The crews of the mission had just arrived at Midway that afternoon after flying from Pearl Harbor on their ten-hour trip to Midway. As the torpedo-armed PBYs headed for the Japanese Transport Force, the Kido Butai, which had completed its refueling requirements, detached its five oilers from the task force.

Akagi's signal lamps subsequently proceeded to blink out orders that informed the fleet that on the dawn of the next day, Midway would be attacked by its carrier's aircraft. At 1025, *Akagi* then signaled to all the ships in the fleet the anticipated movements that the Japanese carrier fleet would take after the air strike for Midway was launched. The Kido Butai then increased its speed to twenty-four knots in order to reach Midway by dawn of the next day.[10]

Thursday, June 4, 1942 (U.S. Date): The Battle for Midway Begins

On 0115, the radar system on the four PBY aircraft heading toward the Japanese Transport Force detected about ten ships on their port side less than ten miles away. The most experienced pilot in the group of PBYs was Lieutenant William Richards, USN, who attacked first when he targeted the last ship in the first column—the oiler *Akebono Maru*. The PBY descended to 100 feet and closed to within 800 feet of the oiler when he let go of his torpedo. The torpedo ran true and hit the bow of the *Akebono Maru*, killing eleven sailors and wounding thirteen. The second PBY to strike dropped down to a lower altitude and dropped his torpedo on the *Kizozumi Maru*, only to miss the ship. As the plane pulled away, the PBY's .50-caliber machine gun opened fire on the deck of the ship, wounding eight of the Kure's Special Naval Landing Forces (SNLF) unit. The other two PBYs were ineffective in their attempt to damage any of the ships, one aircraft missing with its torpedo, the other unable to find the Japanese fleet at all. All four PBYs then returned to Midway.[11]

Fletcher at this time was 202 miles northeast of Midway. U.S. intelligence placed the Japanese carrier fleet to the northwest of Midway where they would close to within 200 miles of Midway before they would launch their air attack on the atoll. U.S. naval forces were stationed on Japan's eastern flank, which provided a great opportunity for the American carriers' aircraft to attack the Kido Butai at its most vulnerable moment, that is, while the planes returning from Midway were being refueled and rearmed on their respective carriers.

Due to the remote possibility that a Japanese carrier force was in the northeast sector of Midway, at 0430 Fletcher directed *Yorktown* to launch ten SBD dive-bombers to search the northeastern area off Midway while six fighters were ordered aloft to provide the day's first CAP. The ten aircraft (presently 200 miles northeast of Midway) flew out to a radius of 100 miles, which encompassed a total distance of 300 miles from Midway—the distance within which the Japanese carriers would have to be if they were to launch a successful air attack on Midway.[12]

At 0300, the first wave of Japanese aircraft had been brought up to the flight decks of all four carriers. The planes had been armed and fueled in the hangar decks, which

Opposite top: **Petty Officer First Class Maruyama Taisuke.** *Bottom:* **Petty Officer First Class Maruyama Taisuke and family. Family identification unknown; he is seated, in the center (courtesy Maruyama Taisuke and the International Midway Memorial Foundation).**

5. The Battle of Midway Begins

was entirely enclosed from the outside weather.[13] Ventilation in this area was provided only by mechanical means.

Once on deck, the planes' engines were warmed up for the flight to Midway. Three types of aircraft were brought up to the flight decks—B5N2 torpedo bombers, Aichi D3A1 dive-bombers and the Mitsubishi A6M2 fighters. A total of 108 aircraft were waiting to take off from all four carriers: eighteen dive-bombers and nine fighters from *Akagi*, eighteen dive-bombers and nine fighters from *Kaga*, eighteen carrier attack aircraft and nine fighters from *Hiryu*, and eighteen carrier attack aircraft and nine fighters from *Soryu*. The scheduled time for the launching was 0430 when the Kido Butai would be 240 miles from Midway.[14]

Petty Flight Officer First Class Maruyama Taisuke was one of crew

members in the carrier attack aircraft from *Hiryu*. He was the observer/navigator/bomb release airman for the aircraft.

The pilot of the aircraft was Seaman First Class Nakao Harumi, and the radioman was Seaman First Class Yoshiichi Hamada. His plane was one of eighteen carrier attack planes from *Hiryu* that would be included in the first wave that would attack Midway. Lieutenant Tomonaga Joichi (who replaced Fuchida as leader of the First Wave Striking Force because Fuchida was recovering from his onboard appendectomy) was assigned to be the commander of the entire air attack group attacking Midway. Tomonaga was stationed on *Hiryu*, and he was waiting for the signal to begin his launch off *Hiryu*.[15]

Pilot Murakami Yoshiki sat in his Type 99 dive-bomber aboard *Kaga*. In the back seat was his observer, Airman First Class Kuroki (first name unavailable). Murakami's plane was one of the eighteen dive-bombers from *Kaga* that would be in the first wave that would attack Midway. His engines were warming up as he awaited the signal to launch his dive-bomber.[16]

At 0430, all four carriers increased speed, turned southeast into the wind and began launching the first wave of aircraft. The fighters took off first, followed by the dive-bombers on *Akagi* and *Kaga* and by the carrier attack aircraft on *Hiryu* and *Soryu*. It took fifteen minutes for all 108 aircraft to become airborne. By 0445, all the launched aircraft circling the carriers turned southeast toward Midway. Lieutenant Tomonaga led the thirty-six Type 97 attack bombers from *Hiryu* and *Soryu*; Lieutenant Ogawa Shoichi led the thirty-six Type 99 dive-bombers from *Akagi* and *Kaga*, and Lieutenant Suganami Masaji led the thirty-six Zero fighters (nine from each carrier) on the flight.

All three leaders were well qualified to carry out the mission.[17]

The Japanese Search for the American Carriers: Timeline

Japan 0430: launches aircraft to Midway; 0430: launches three of seven search aircraft;

Petty Officer Second Class Murakami Yoshi (courtesy Murakami Yoshi and the International Midway Memorial Foundation).

5. The Battle of Midway Begins   73

0500: launches four search aircraft; 0645: Japanese attack Midway; 0745: *Hornet* and *Enterprise* launch their aircraft; 0820: search plane discovers a U.S. carrier; 0830: Nagumo begins recovery of the aircraft returning from Midway; 0834: *Soryu* launches D4Y1 Yokosuka Type 13D4Y1 aircraft; 0840: *Yorktown* launches its aircraft; 0845: *Chikuma*'s Number 5 plane launched to replace *Tone*'s Number 4 plane; 0918: aircraft

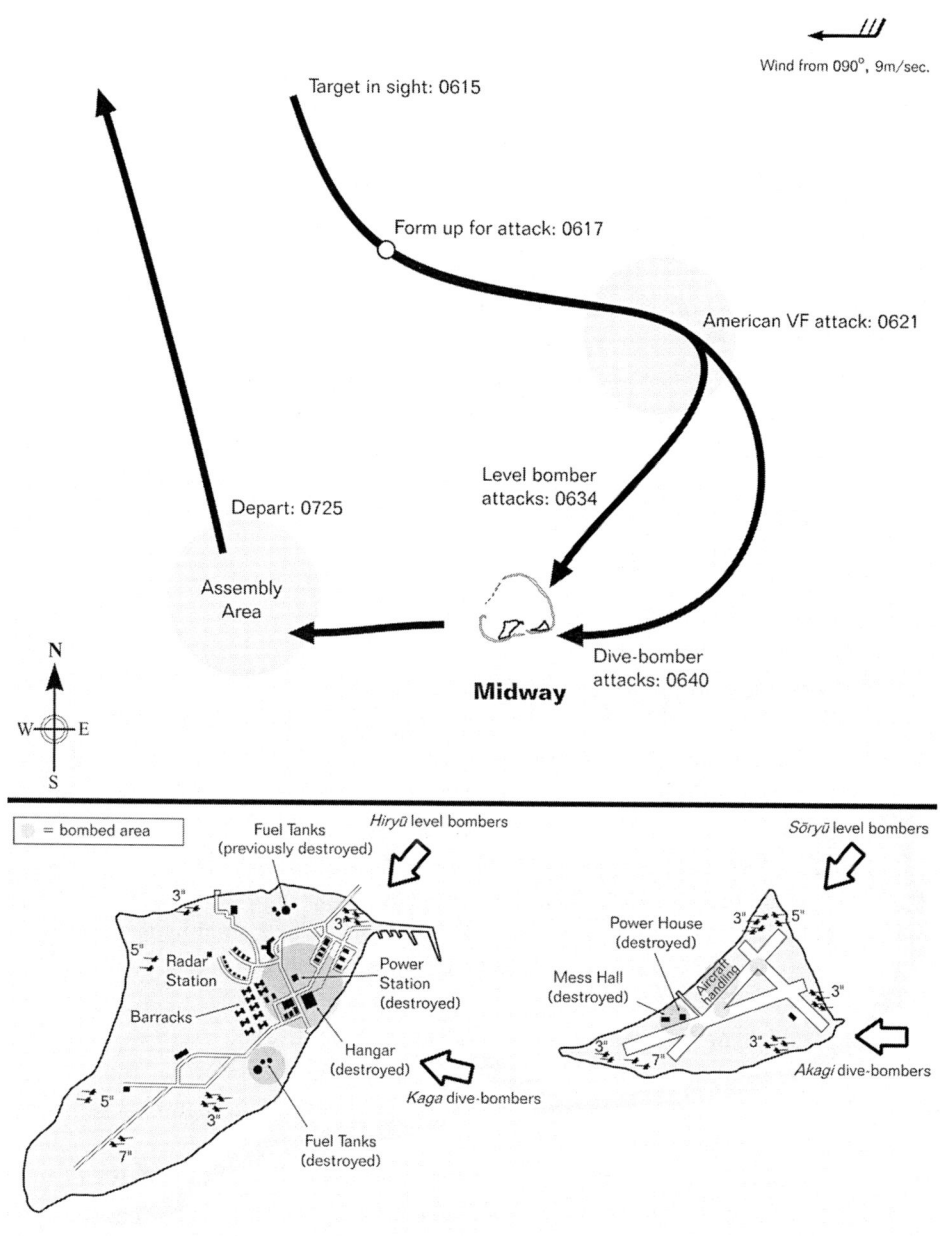

Japanese attack on Midway (courtesy of Jonathan Parshall).

returning from Midway recovered; 1022: *Akagi*, *Kaga* and *Soryu* are mortally damaged; 1110: *Chikuma*'s Number 5 search aircraft discovers *Yorktown* only; 1110: D4Y1 search aircraft discovers all three U.S. carriers but is unable to transmit the message; 1300: D4Y1 search aircraft drops tube on *Hiryu* the message about discovery of all three U.S. carriers; 1703: *Hiryu* is mortally damaged.

In early April of 1942, Japanese naval commanders created a flawed operational plan that was destined to doom Japan to defeat in the upcoming Battle of Midway. The plan was devised by Senior Operations Officer Captain Kuroshima Kameto, Chief of Staff of the Combined Naval Fleet, and approved by Rear Admiral Ugaki Matome and the Commander of the Combined Fleet Admiral Yamamoto Isoroku.[18] It was centered upon a dual mission: to destroy the American fleet and to attack and occupy Midway Atoll. There were many factors in the plan that contributed to Japan's defeat at Midway in June of 1942. The purpose of this work is to explore the serious consequences of Japan's indifference toward discovering the U.S. fleet at an early stage in the Battle of Midway and how that omission altered the outcome of the battle. One of the most significant flaws in the plan was to relegate only seven aircraft to the U.S. search area, which meant that, if the mission failed, it would be impossible for Japan to strike the U.S. carrier fleet first. Simply stated, this dearth of Japanese search aircraft led to the lack of early intelligence necessary for Japan to either strike first or counterattack all three U.S. carriers. Vice Admiral Nagumo Chuichi was unaware that the United States had three carriers in the area until approximately 1310 on June 4. By this time, Japan had lost three of its four carriers.

Preliminaries to the Battle of Midway began at 0430 on June 4, 1942 (U.S. date), when seven Japanese aircraft were designated to search the area east of the Kido Butai in a 180-degree arc.

Two torpedo bombers (Nakajima B5N2 Type 97), one each from *Akagi* and *Kaga*, would cover search lines number 1 (181 degrees) and number 2 (154 degrees); two of cruiser *Tone*'s search planes (E13A1 Type O reconnaissance aircraft) would cover search lines number 3 (123 degrees) and number 4 (100 degrees); cruiser *Chikuma* would send two of its E13A1s to cover search lines number 5 (77 degrees) and number 6 (54 degrees); and battleship *Haruna* would send search E8N2 Type 95 reconnaissance aircraft along search line number 7 (31 degrees). The plan stipulated that all the search aircraft would fly out 300 miles, turn port for sixty miles and then head back to their respective ships, except for *Haruna*'s plane, which would fly out only 150 miles before returning to its battleship.[19]

The search planes from *Akagi* and *Kaga*, and the aircraft from *Haruna*, were launched on time at 0430, exactly as the first wave of planes took off to attack Midway. However, the planes from *Tone* and *Chikuma* were delayed thirty minutes (0500) by engine and catapult trouble.

Chikuma's Number 1 plane, flying the number 5 search line during its outbound leg, should have passed over Task Force 17 (*Yorktown*). The fact that the pilot did not observe the task force meant that either he was flying above the clouds or he was off course. To the south was *Tone*'s Number 4 plane (pilot Petty Officer First Class Amari Hiroshi) flying along its assigned course. The delay in his departure actually led to his discovery of one of the American carriers. There is also speculation that other factors

5. The Battle of Midway Begins 75

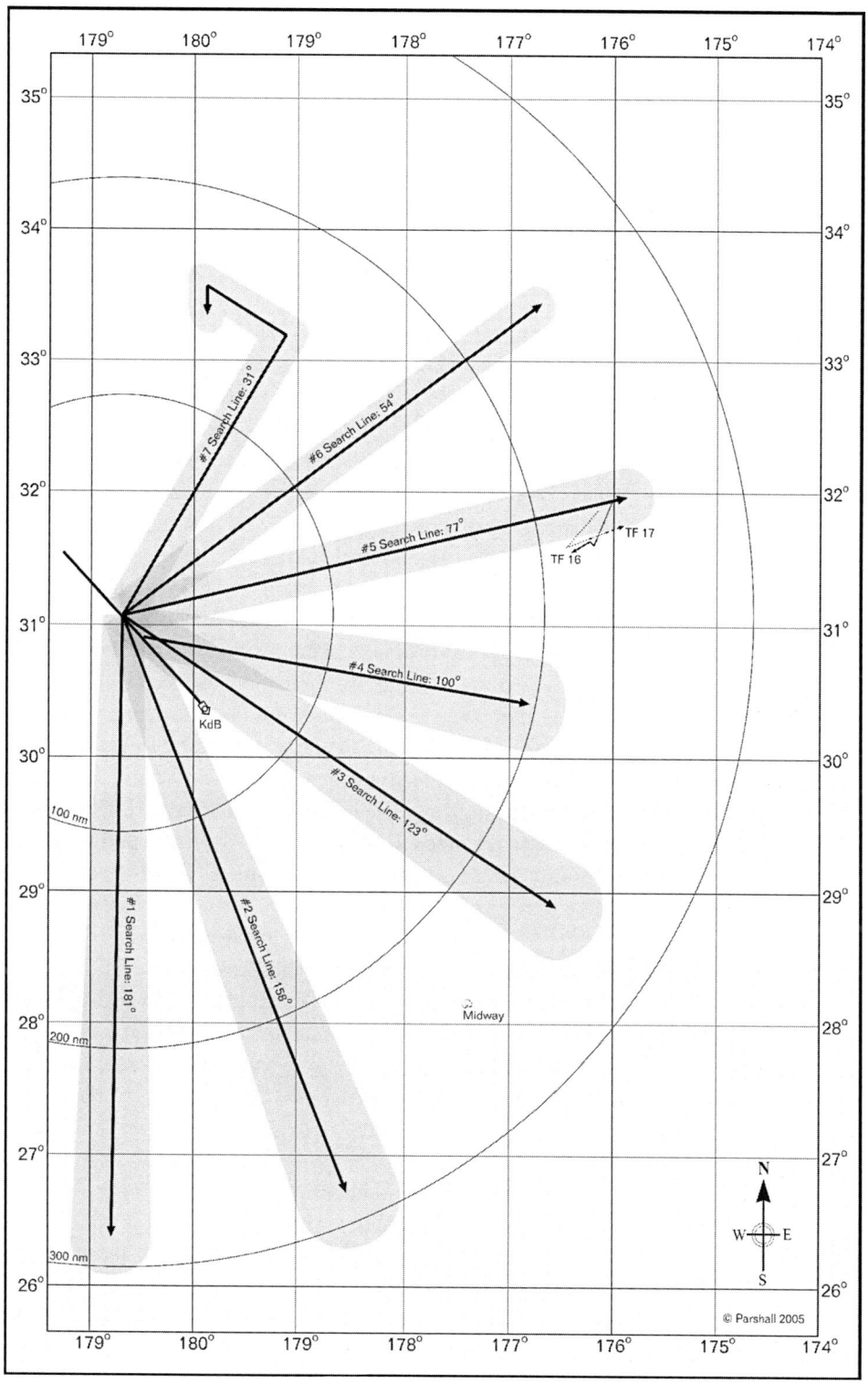

Japanese search pattern (courtesy of Jonathan Parshall).

may have played a role in his discovery—that he made his dogleg turn after flying just 220 miles or that he was off course. Unfortunately he died during the war, so we will never know precisely how he made his discovery.[20] Nevertheless, at 0740, on his return leg, Amari radioed back to Nagumo that he observed "an American naval force 240 miles from Midway, bearing 150 degrees, cruising at twenty knots." Thirty minutes later (0810), he identified the ships as "five cruisers and five destroyers." Finally, at 0820, Amari radioed to Nagumo that "the enemy force *appeared* to be accompanied by a carrier bringing up the rear." The carrier sighted by Amari has been presumed to be *Enterprise*, because his plane was detected on *Enterprise*'s radar (not by sight), and the scout plane was subsequently targeted by *Enterprise*'s CAP.[21]

Earlier, at 0650, *Enterprise* and *Hornet* had separated from each other with each carrier becoming the center of its own task force. *Enterprise* was surrounded by three cruisers and five destroyers, and *Hornet* was surrounded by three cruisers and four destroyers. Thus, at 0815, when *Enterprise*'s radar detected a plane about thirty miles to the southeast, it was positioned at the center of its task force and not bringing up the rear as reported by Amari. There is also no explanation for why he reported "five cruisers" as *Enterprise* had only three cruisers in its group. Even if he sighted two cruisers from *Hornet*'s group, Amari never reported sighting *Hornet*. Amari's report is difficult to reconcile with the facts, but one dictum is certain, that no Japanese attack aircraft found *Enterprise* or *Hornet* that day.

At about 0820, *Enterprise*'s command directed its CAP to fly to and intercept Amari's search plane. For over an hour the Japanese float plane effectively eluded the American CAP by hiding in the clouds. At 0845, *Chikuma* was ordered to send its Number 5 plane to replace Amari's search aircraft which was running low on fuel. Five minutes later, despite his fuel situation, Amari was ordered to stay where he was and to keep his radio on so that Nagumo could use the radio signal for direction finding for his attack aircraft. At 0855, Amari reported that he observed ten torpedo bombers heading toward the Kido Butai. These aircraft had been launched from *Yorktown* at 0840 and were actually twelve in number.

At 0930, Amari was ordered to continue to observe the American carrier fleet—most likely *Yorktown* and not *Enterprise*. It is speculated that Amari's aircraft must have flown toward *Yorktown* when his aircraft was pursued by *Enterprise*'s CAP. This conclusion is supported by the fact that at 1110, when *Chikuma*'s Number 5 plane (piloted by Petty Officer First Class Takezaki Masatake) flew out to the reported coordinates given to him by Amari, he came upon *Yorktown* only.

Soryu's D4Y1 experimental aircraft Yokosuka Type 13D4Y1 (later code-named Judy), launched at 0834 (piloted by Iida Masatada), also flew to the site reported by Amari. Arriving at that location at 1110, he found an empty sea. As Iida turned to make his flight back to *Soryu*, he noticed an American aircraft returning to its carrier, which he followed. By doing so, Iida discovered the presence of all three carriers, which at this time (1115) were now in roughly the same area. Radio difficulties prevented him from transmitting the information to Nagumo; however, it would not have made any difference because at that time, three Japanese carriers were already burning and were incapable of any operations.

At 1300, Yamaguchi Tamon learned of the existence of three U.S. carriers from a

5. The Battle of Midway Begins

captured U.S. pilot (Ensign Wesley Osmus, VT-3). Yamaguchi also learned that *Yorktown* had been operating independently of the other two carriers (as of 0840 when Ensign Osmus took off from *Yorktown*). This information was confirmed shortly thereafter by *Soryu*'s D4Y scout plane whose pilot, upon returning from his mission and finding *Soryu* on fire, flew over to *Hiryu* where he found its deck occupied with torpedo planes. Unable to land, he dropped the intelligence in a message tube.[22] Thus, it was not until shortly after 1300 that the Japanese knew with certainty that there were three U.S. carrier forces.

Historians have had lengthy discussions about the fact that on June 4 at 0820, Admiral Nagumo made a poor decision when he decided to recover all the planes returning from Midway rather than to immediately launch all of his available aircraft to attack the American fleet. What has not previously been taken into account is that Nagumo, at 0820, had only one unconfirmed report of the presence of a single American carrier. He was not aware that two other U.S. carriers were positioned in the area northeast of Midway. Had Nagumo immediately launched all of his available aircraft at 0830, his carrier fleet would have been less vulnerable to the destructive forces of the U.S. bombing attack that occurred at 1022, which was catastrophic because of the number of Japanese aircraft loaded with fuel and ammunition in the hangar decks below. Even if Nagumo's planes had been launched, he had only one unconfirmed report of one American carrier's position. Therefore, the best that Japan could have hoped for was the destruction of one of three U.S. carriers.

The dual-mission basis of the Japanese plan, in and of itself, played a significant role in Japan's defeat at Midway because it guaranteed that the Japanese carrier force would lose its flexibility of movement, necessitating that it remain relatively stationary during the time that it launched and recovered its aircraft for its attack against Midway. Unable to maneuver, this action left the Japanese carriers exposed to attack by U.S. carrier and land aircraft.

Another significant factor in America's victory was the United States' foreknowledge of Japan approaching Midway from the northwest and attacking the atoll in the early morning hours of June 4. This intelligence presented the United States with the opportunity to strike first and place a limit on the amount of time that Japan would have to discover the American fleet if Japan were to strike the U.S. fleet first. This was especially true since the Japanese had not given reasonable credence to the possibility that the United States would be waiting, ready to ambush the Kido Butai. If Japan had been seriously concerned about the U.S. fleet being present, it would not have attacked Midway without being absolutely certain that the Americans were not in the area. The Japanese attack on Midway also opened the door for the Americans to strike the Japanese carriers when they were most vulnerable—with all their aircraft aboard loaded with fuel and ammunition. Therefore, it was imperative that Japan be certain that the Americans were not in the area by providing a sound number of search aircraft to scout the waters northeast of Midway. Their failure to do so helped turn the tide of battle in favor of the United States because it allowed the United States to strike first. Interestingly, U.S. intelligence in the Battle of the Coral Sea (May 3–8) had the same foreknowledge of Japan's battle plan, but unlike the conflict at Midway, the Japanese task force had the flexibility to move its fleet at will. This tactical asset at the Coral Sea allowed

Japan to attack the United States at the same time that it was being attacked by the Unites States. Thus, the flexibility of movement factor is one illustration of why the outcomes of the two battles were different.

Two conclusions can be drawn from the foregoing: (1) At 0600, Japan had an opportunity to strike *Yorktown* first if *Chikuma*'s Number 1 search aircraft on its outward leg on the fifth search line had detected Task Force 17. Even in this best case scenario, Japan would have only been capable of launching sixty-four attack aircraft to attack *Yorktown*, since 108 planes had already been launched to attack Midway at 0430. The available Japanese aircraft would have had to be launched by 0630 because it was one and a half hours' flying time to *Yorktown* (Japanese aircraft would have arrived at 0800), and *Yorktown* did not launch its planes until 0840. At 0630, the Midway strike force was already engaged in its attack on the atoll, and these planes would have needed to be rearmed and refueled before they became operational. The foregoing presents the only possibility where Japan had the opportunity to strike *Yorktown* first. Again, even if this situation had actually occurred, only *Yorktown* would have been vulnerable because neither *Enterprise* nor *Hornet* were known to Nagumo until early afternoon. (2) At 0830, Nagumo had an opportunity to counterstrike the U.S. forces (*Yorktown*) with thirty torpedo planes and thirty-four dive-bombers aboard his four carriers. There has been much discussion in the literature as to Nagumo's decision at this time not to launch all his available aircraft before recovering his aircraft returning from Midway. The fact is that, as was the case in the morning, only the location of *Yorktown* was known at this time. The irony in the battle is that *Yorktown* was lost anyway on June 7, without either of the previously suggested events ever taking place. The root of Japan's defeat at Midway lay in its failure to recognize the need for more search aircraft to make completely sure that a U.S. carrier force was not waiting in ambush before launching its attack on Midway. Superimposed on this concept is the fact that U.S. intelligence enabled the American carrier force to lie in secret northeast of Midway, waiting to strike the Japanese carrier force first and at its most vulnerable time—with most of its aircraft in the hangar deck loaded with ordnance and fuel. The end result was the U.S. sinking all four Japanese carriers and the irreversible loss of Japanese naval supremacy in the Pacific.

Japan Prepares the Second Wave of Aircraft

Once the decks had been cleared, preparations were made to get the second wave ready for action. The second wave was composed of eighteen Type 99 dive-bombers, each positioned on *Hiryu* and *Soryu*. On *Akagi*, there were seventeen Type 97 carrier attack planes (torpedo bombers) and twenty-six carrier attack planes on *Kaga*. Thirty-six Zero fighters (nine on each carrier) brought the total number of planes in the second wave to 115 planes.

Lieutenant Commander Itaya Shigeru on *Akagi* would lead the fighter group, Lieutenant Commander Egusa Takashige on *Soryu* would head the dive-bomber squadron, and Lieutenant Commander Murata Shigeharu would be the leader of the torpedo bomber group. All three pilots were the elite of the naval air arm and were kept in reserve if the American carrier fleet was in the area. The second wave of aircraft waited patiently to see if the Japanese search planes launched between 0430 and 0500 found any evidence of the U.S. carrier fleet.

Fuchida and Okumiya, in *Midway*, report that around 1015, aircraft were being brought up from the hangar deck to the flight deck. At 1020, Nagumo gave the order to launch when ready, and *Akagi* began to launch its aircraft. At the same time, Fuchida and Okumiya admit that during the U.S. attack the "refueling and rearming operations were in full swing." It is important to appreciate that at this time, operations on a carrier permitted either the launching or the landing of planes or the spotting of planes from the hangar deck. Thus, Zero fighters could not be taking off from *Kaga* with a deck load of spotted aircraft. All of the CAP up to that time had been launched by *Kaga*. It is unlikely but possible that *Hiryu* and *Soryu* initially had spotted their dive-bombers on their respective flight decks but then brought them down to the hangar deck so that these two carriers could contribute to the carriers' CAP.[23]

At 0350 on Midway, the first of six F4F-3s under the command of Captain John Carey, USMC, took off to provide air cover for the B-17s and PBYs, which were to follow twenty-five minutes later. The B-17s' and PBYs' mission was to accumulate intelligence on the Japanese fleets approaching Midway. At 0415, eleven VP-23 PBY-5s took off from the Midway lagoon, and eleven PBY-5As took off from the airstrip on Eastern Island. VP-44 again covered the southwestern sector while VP-23 searched the northwestern sector.[24]

A few minutes later, fifteen B-17E bombers under the command of Lieutenant Colonel Sweeney took off, joined up over Kure Island (the last island in the Hawaiian chain) and headed west to attack, observe and photograph the Japanese Midway Transport Group (in addition, one B-17D was sent to act as a pathfinder and photograph plane). One of the B-17E bombers developed engine trouble in one of its engines and had to return to Hickam Air Force Base in Hawaii. At 0450, Captain John Carey's six F4F-3s were ordered to land, but only four of the fighters got the word so the other two fighters remained aloft. The thirty-eight other operational planes on Midway were warming up their planes, poised to take off.[25]

Americans Find the Japanese Carrier Force

At 0552, Lieutenant Howard Ady, USN, in his VP-23 PBY detected the Japanese Carrier Striking Force. He reported two carriers, three battleships, four heavy cruisers and six to eight destroyers (actually the Japanese striking force had only two battleships, two heavy cruisers and one light cruiser in its group). The reason why Ady reported only two carriers was that battleship *Kirishima* and light cruiser *Nagara* had laid down a smoke screen which hid the other two carriers. The initial report sent by Ady was erroneous in that it placed the Japanese carrier force 175 miles away from the U.S. carrier force lurking to the northeast. In actuality, the Japanese striking force was at least 200 miles southwest of the American carriers. At 0607, with receipt of this intelligence, Fletcher ordered Admiral Raymond Spruance to head southwest toward the enemy at twenty-five knots. Consulting with his staff, Spruance decided to launch his

The plane of Captain John F. Carey (USMC), June 24, 1942 (photo 80-G-11636, courtesy Naval History and Heritage Command).

aircraft from carriers *Enterprise* and *Hornet* at 0700. Assuming that the Japanese maintained their present course and speed, Task Force 16 would close the distance between themselves and the Japanese to 155 miles. Meanwhile, Fletcher held his northeasterly course in order to recover the scout planes he had sent aloft to search the sector that was northeast of the American carriers.

Fletcher scouted this area because only two carriers were reported by Ady, and naval intelligence had already felt very confident that the Japanese would strike Midway with at least four carriers.[26]

At 0544, Lieutenant William Chase, USN, in his VP-23 PBY, sent out a report in plain language that he observed over fifty planes about 100 miles northwest by north of Midway, heading toward the atoll. When Captain Simard received the information, he diverted the B-17Es to the reported location of the Japanese carriers. Soon after Chase's report, Midway's radar detected many planes eighty-nine miles from Midway. The air-raid alarm was sounded, and at 0600, all the operational aircraft on Midway began to launch from Eastern Island's airstrip. First to take off were VMF-221's seventeen Brewster F2A-3 (one F2A-3 returned due to engine trouble) and six F4F-3 Marine fighters (the two tardy F4F-3s from that day's CAP joined the group of four F4F-3s over

5. The Battle of Midway Begins

Midway). The F2A-3 aircraft was under the overall command of Major Floyd Parks, USMC, and the six F4F-3s were under the leadership of Captain John Carey, USMC. The first, fourth and fifth divisions of VMF-221 were vectored out from Midway to intercept the oncoming Japanese planes while the second and third division of VMF-221 were orbiting ten miles away in case other Japanese aircraft might approach Midway from another direction.[27]

After the fighters took off, six TBF-1 Avengers (VT-8 detachment), but not then flying from *Hornet*, under the command of Lieutenant Langdon Fieberling, USN, took off. The planes climbed to 2,000 feet and while heading northwest at a speed of 160 miles per hour toward the Kido Butai were briefly attacked by three Japanese fighters accompanying the inbound Japanese first wave against Midway. Next, four U.S. Army B-26 Marauder medium bombers from the Sixty-Ninth Bombardment Squadron flew off Eastern Island's airstrip and followed the TBFs to the northwest. This group of planes was under the command of Captain William F. Collins, Jr., USA.[28]

Soon after the TBFs and B-26s took off, VMSB 241 sent sixteen Douglas SBD-2 dive-bombers under the command of Major Lofton Henderson, USMC, into the air. These planes were followed by twelve Voight SB2U-3 dive-bombers, which were under the leadership of Captain Benjamin Norris, USMC. Each plane carried a 500-pound bomb. However, one of the Voight dive-bombers turned back (leaving eleven SB2U-3s to make the mission) when the left side of its engine cowling (a removable metal covering over the engine) had blown off. The two squadrons of aircraft united twenty miles

VMSB-241. All present are USMCR: Front row (seated, L–R): Lt. Albert W. Tweedy; Lt. Bruce Prosser; Maj. Lofton R. Henderson, USMC (CO); Capt. Leo R. Smith, USMC (XO); Lt. Elmer G. Glidden, Jr. Middle row (kneeling): Lt. Thomas J. Gratzek; Lt. Robert W. Vaupell; Lt. Daniel Iverson, Jr.; Lt. Jesse Rollow, Jr.; Lt. Harold G. Schlendering; Tech. Sgt. Clyde H. Stamps, USMC. Rear row (standing): Lt. Maurice A. Ward; Lt. Richard L. Blain; Lt. Sumner H. Whitten; Lt. Thomas F. Moore, Jr.; Lt. M. DeLalio; Lt. Bruce Ek; Lt. Leon M. Williamson; T Richard Fleming; Lt. Robert J. Bear; Lt. Howard C. Frazer, USMC; and Lt. Bruno P. Hagedorn (courtesy of Naval History and Heritage Command).

east of Midway before departing northwest to head for the Japanese carriers. As they left for the carriers, they observed the incoming first wave of Japanese aircraft heading for Midway.[29]

The Midway airstrip on Eastern Island was now clear of all operational aircraft. The time was 0615, and the first wave of the Japanese striking force now caught sight of the atoll. The Japanese aircraft began to form their final approach to the islands. In the lead were the carrier attack planes, followed at a higher altitude by the carrier dive-bombers and then by the Japanese fighters who were trailing the formation. This disposition of aircraft initially favored the U.S. Marine fighter aircraft.

The first wave of incoming Japanese planes

Lieutenant Jesse Rollow, Jr., USMC, VMSB-241 (courtesy Jesse Rollow, Jr., and the International Midway Memorial Foundation).

were expecting good fortune as they observed a beautiful sunrise similar to the one that presented itself on the morning of the Pearl Harbor attack. The rising sun was felt to be a good omen for the events that would follow. After flying for almost two hours, the first wave arrived at 0615, where they could see the outline of Midway Atoll. They elected to fly to the east in order to approach the atoll from the northeast. Suddenly at 0621, and thirty miles out from Midway, the formation was attacked from above by seven F2A-3 and three F4F-3 Marine fighters. The Marine fighters immediately attacked two of *Hiryu*'s carrier land-attack planes in the first chutai (air group division—six or nine aircraft), whose pilots were Flight Petty Officer Second Class Miyauchi Masaji and Flight Petty Officer Second Class Ohisa Haki. The former plane immediately broke into flames and caught fire as the aircraft headed toward the sea. The latter aircraft also caught fire but was able to stay in formation until its chutai began its bombing run on Midway when the pilot finally lost control of the plane and also headed into the sea. Three additional carrier attack planes were damaged, including a hit on the commander's plane, Lieutenant Tomonaga.[30]

The basic building block of the Japanese air formation was the placement of three planes in an inverted V arrangement, which they called a shotai. A group of two (six planes) or three shotai (nine planes) was called a chutai. In its attack on Midway, Japan flew the carrier attack planes Kate (torpedo bombers/kankos) in a six-plane chutai.

A third plane piloted by Lieutenant Kikuchi Rokuro, leader of *Hiryu*'s second chutai, caught on fire when bullets

Top: Lieutenant (Major) Daniel Iverson, USMC, VMSB-241, and wife Margaret Hough Fisher Iverson (courtesy the family of Daniel Iverson, Jr. and the International Midway Memorial Foundation). *Bottom:* Lieutenant Daniel Iverson's aircraft, flown with VMSB-241, rescued from the depths of Lake Michigan in 1994. The plane, along with many others, saw its wartime career end when it was ditched during carrier landing training exercises. It has since been restored, and is on display at the National Naval Aviation Museum, in Pensacola (U.S. Navy photo, courtesy International Midway Memorial Foundation).

from enemy guns severed his oil line. He tried to return to the *Hiryu* but was forced to crash-land his plane into the waters off Kure Island. The three-man crew climbed into their raft but were never rescued.[31]

The Marine fighters were soon joined by the remaining thirteen aircraft that had been ten miles away. After the initial ten Marine fighters made their first pass, Japanese Zero fighters pounced on the scene and in less than ten minutes shot down thirteen F2A-3s and two F4F-3s and irreversibly damaged seven other fighters. The Japanese counterattack was very effective, resulting in the destruction or damage of twenty-two of the twenty-three Marine aircraft. After the Zero counterattack, only two marine fighters remained operational to defend the airspace over Midway.[32]

During their approach to Midway, the thirty-six Japanese dive-bombers never broke formation as they were not attacked by U.S. fighters. Unimpeded, the dive-bombers began to fly into their formation for a bombing run against Midway. The eighteen dive-bombers (kanbaku) from *Akagi* were assigned to attack Eastern Island along with the eighteen carrier attack planes (kankos) from *Soryu*. The eighteen dive-bombers from *Kaga* and the remaining fifteen carrier attack planes from *Hiryu* would direct their attention to Sand Island. The carrier attack aircraft would approach Midway from the northeast, while the dive-bombers would attack the atoll out of the east.[33]

On Midway, the eight seventy-seven-foot Elco motor torpedo boats stationed at Sand Island got underway just as the Japanese aircraft were approaching Midway. The two other torpedo boats (PT-29 and PT-30) were patrolling the waters off Kure Island. The PBYs returning from their torpedo run against the Japanese Midway Transport Group picked up on their radio that an air-raid warning was in progress over Midway. The pilots then directed their aircraft southeast toward the island of Lisianski to avoid the attack.

A fourth plane piloted by Petty Officer First Class Sakamoto Noriyoshi of the second shotai received a direct hit and plummeted into the lagoon near Sand Island. A fifth plane piloted by Warrant Officer Nonaka Satoru was also shot down over Midway, resulting in the loss of five of *Hiryu*'s carrier attack planes in its assault on Midway. Three Japanese carrier land-attack planes were also lost from *Soryu*. Those planes were piloted by Petty Officer Third Class Kayahara Yoshihiro of the first chutai, Petty Officer First Class Mori Juzo of the second chutai and Petty Officer First Class Ochi Masatake of the third chutai, respectively. Thus, in the first wave, *Hiryu* and *Soryu* lost eight of its carrier's land-attack aircraft.[34]

VMSB-241, which had rendezvoused about twenty nautical miles east of Midway, could witness the Japanese aircraft as they approached the atoll and observe the islands' antiaircraft fire.[35]

The antiaircraft firepower over Midway added to the numbers of Japanese carrier land-attack planes (kankos) lost over Midway. The Japanese aircraft were surprised by the intensity and accuracy of the American antiaircraft fire, but their pilots were still able to maintain their course on the mission's flight pattern. On Eastern Island, the Japanese land-attack planes from *Soryu* and the dive-bombers from *Akagi* eliminated the power plant; severed the gasoline line serving the aircraft on the ground, which resulted in the future fueling of the planes by hand; damaged the sick bay; and demolished the command post. On Sand Island, the dive-bombers from *Kaga* and the land-attack planes from *Hiryu* destroyed the water lines; set three oil storage tanks on fire, which created a thick blanket of smoke that could be seen miles from the atoll; destroyed the laundry facility and the dispensary; demolished the navy mess hall, galley, brig and contactor's buildings; destroyed the torpedo and bombsight facilities; and burned the seaplane hangar to the ground.

However, Midway still had formable defenses with its antiaircraft guns intact and its airstrip on Eastern Island still operational. Although Midway's fighter support had been eliminated and the operational integrity of Midway's thirty-seven aircraft that had taken off before the attack was unknown, the atoll still presented a formable defense against a Japanese invasion by its transport group. Thus, at 0715, Lieutenant Tomonaga radioed Nagumo that a second attack on Midway was necessary as they headed back to the Kido Butai.

The first wave of Japanese planes, which had arrived over Midway at 0630 to make their bombing and strafing runs, now flew to the north of the atoll at 0645 where all of the remaining planes would rendezvous to head back to the Kido Butai. There, Tomonaga radioed Nagumo that the attack was finished and that the first wave was heading back to the carriers. At 0700, the surviving Japanese aircraft left the Midway area to return to the Kido Butai. The loss of aircraft by the Japanese in its attack on Midway was significant. *Hiryu* was the hardest hit with the loss of five carrier attack aircraft (kankos) and another four kanko aircraft considered unfit for further duty due to significant damage to the aircraft. Thus, of the seventeen carrier attack planes that made the attack on Midway (one carrier attack plane [a torpedo bomber] aborted its mission), only eight carrier attack aircraft remained operational, and one carrier attack plane needed repairs.

Two of *Hiryu*'s nine returning fighters were deemed unfit for further action. *Soryu* lost four carrier attack aircraft as a result of its attack on Midway; however, four of the remaining fourteen carrier attack planes that made it back to *Soryu* were judged non-operational, leaving ten carrier attack aircraft for future operations. *Soryu*'s nine fighters returned intact and operational.

Akagi lost one fighter over Midway and all eighteen of its dive-bombers returned safely, but one dive-bomber was considered unfit for future military action. *Kaga* lost two fighters: one fighter was shot down over Midway, and the other fighter was able to land safely on board *Kaga* but was too damaged to remain operational. In addition, *Kaga* lost one dive-bomber to antiaircraft fire over Sand Island. In total, eleven Japanese aircraft were lost in the attack on Midway, and in addition, another fourteen planes were too heavily damaged by enemy fire to remain operational.

Thus, the first wave lost 23 percent out of its total striking force (25 out of 108 planes) in its attack on Midway. The loss of 23 percent of its striking force points out another serious inherent flaw in Japan's decision to attack Midway; that is, rather than adopting a naval plan that would place the primary naval focus on the possibility that the U.S. carrier fleet might be lurking to the northeast waiting to ambush the Kido Butai, Yamamoto elected to include an attack on Midway as part of his operational plan.[36]

At 0630, as Midway was being attacked, *Yorktown*'s ten SBDs radioed back to Fletcher that there was no evidence of an enemy task force to the northeast of Midway, and shortly thereafter, the SBDs returned to the carrier. Having landed the SBDs and the CAP fighters, the carrier turned to the southwest at a speed of twenty-five knots to catch up with Task Force 16 to the south. Pre-war doctrine envisioned that U.S. carriers would operate together as a single large striking force.

In reality, *Enterprise* and *Hornet* would tactically operate independently of each other, but in close contact. Thus, all the carriers' aircraft would take their own navigational courses to the Japanese carriers. This was most fortunate for the Americans, as Commander Stanhope Ring, who was the senior commander, would have been in charge of this massive strike; instead, Ring was in charge of only *Hornet*'s strike force, as each carrier sent its strike force out independently of the other. Had this not been the case, both *Enterprise* and *Hornet*'s aircraft would have gotten lost, and the outcome of the battle would have been inextricably altered in favor of the Japanese.

When *Hornet*'s four squadron commanders of Scouting Eight, Bombing Eight, Torpedo Eight and Fighting Eight and Commander Stanhope Ring (Commander, *Hornet* Air Group) met to discuss the navigational course they should take to the Japanese carriers, there was disagreement in the group. So Ring declared that he would plot the course. The leader of *Hornet*'s torpedo squadron's group (VT-8), Lieutenant Commander John Waldron, did not agree with the course to be taken, but Ring was adamant. Waldron for the moment accepted the decision of his commander. Ultimately, it was Ring who with his squadron flew in the wrong direction and thus failed to discover the Kido Butai. This episode points out that although the United States had a significant advantage—through intelligence—as to where the Kido Butai would be at the time that its carriers were most vulnerable to American air attacks, it still would require the proper execution of America's tactical plan to achieve success.[37]

At 0650, Task Force 16 separated, with each carrier being the center of its escorting ships. Heavy cruisers *Northampton*, *Pensacola* and *Vincennes* with destroyers *Balch*, *Benham*, *Aylin*, *Monaghan* and *Phelps* sailed with *Enterprise* (a total of nine ships). Heavy cruisers *Minneapolis*, *New Orleans* and light cruiser *Atlanta*, with destroyers *Maury*, *Ellet*, *Worden* and *Conyngham*, sailed with *Hornet* (a total of eight ships). The winds were light that day, only about five miles an hour and out of the southeast. At 0656, both carriers turned southeast into the wind as they increased their speed to twenty-eight knots.[38]

At 0700, *Hornet*, having launched its CAP, sent aloft its ten-plane escort of F4F fighters (VF-8), whose section leader was under the command of Lieutenant Commander Samuel Pat Mitchell, whose fighters bided their time over *Hornet*, waiting for the remainder of the carrier's strike force to take off. Finally, *Hornet*'s thirty-four SBDs were ready to take off.

The first fifteen aircraft to take off were SBD scouting bombers (VS-8), led by Lieutenant Commander Walter Rodee. The next two planes were piloted by Commander Ring and his wingman Ensign Clayton Fisher from Bombing Eight, each car-

Opposite top: **Ensign George Gay, USN (left) and Lieutenant Elbert Scott McCuskey, USN, June 4, 1942 (photo NH-90482, courtesy of Naval History and Heritage Command).** *Bottom:* **On the USS *Enterprise* (CV-6), SBD-3 warming up, June 4, 1942 (courtesy Naval History and Heritage Command).**

5. The Battle of Midway Begins

rying a 500-pound bomb. Next were the seventeen planes of Bombing Eight (VB-8), armed with 1,000-pound bombs and led by Lieutenant Commander Robert Johnson. At 0746, the fifteen TBD-1s (VT-8) left the carrier and were the last aircraft to leave the *Hornet*. Their leader was Lieutenant Commander John Waldron. The planes climbed to 19,000 feet and departed from the area at 0754 at the rear of the strike formation.[39]

At 0706, *Enterprise*, having flown her CAP off the carrier, spotted the first sixteen scouting bombers (VS-6) from the thirty-seven SBDs on the flight deck. One of the scouting bombers developed engine trouble and was unable to make the mission. The fifteen dive-bombers (VS-6) were led by Lieutenant Wilmer Gallaher. Lieutenant Commander Clarence Wade McClusky, Air Group Commander, and his two wingmen of Bombing Six took off next. The first six of the SBDs carried only a 500-pound bomb. The remaining twelve SBDs carried two 100-pound bombs, as well as a 500-pound bomb. Eighteen dive-bombers of Bombing Six were spotted, but mechanical troubles kept three aircraft from making the mission. Thus, fifteen SBDs lifted off from *Enterprise*, with each plane carrying a 1,000-pound bomb. Bombing Six was under the leadership of Lieutenant Richard Best. The SBDs climbed to 20,000 feet and waited for their fighter escort and the torpedo bombers to be launched. Ten F4F fighters led by Lieutenant Richard Gray were next spotted and launched. The last aircraft to be launched were the torpedo bombers, which could not be spotted until the last SBD took off because the TBD required the entire deck to take off with a 1,000-pound bomb load. Finally, the fourteen TBD-1 planes lifted off *Enterprise* under the command of Lieutenant Commander Eugene Lindsey and headed out on their mission. At 0745, with the SBDs circling overhead and wasting gasoline, Rear Admiral Raymond Spruance, Commander of Task Force 16, became concerned over the time that was being taken in launching and the effect it had on the SBDs' fuel reserves, so he ordered the SBDs to depart from the area. Finally, the first F4F fighter began taking off from *Enterprise*, and it took until 0800 for Task Force 16 to complete launching all of its available aircraft against the Kido Butai, thus setting in motion a series of events that would inextricably alter the outcome of the Battle of Midway.[40]

Midway's Aircraft Find the Kido Butai

At 0705, the four B-26 bombers were spotted by *Akagi*'s bridge-top lookout closing in on the Japanese carrier fleet. Arriving at the same time, the six TBF torpedo bombers from Midway began their run against two of the Japanese carriers in the area. The TBFs were the first group of Midway-based aircraft to attack the Japanese carriers. The VT-8 detachment dropped down to within 150 feet of the ocean. The Japanese had thirty fighters in the air, and a number of them immediately attacked the VT-8 detachment. Five of the six TBFs were consequently shot down.

The remaining TBF's crew consisted of pilot Ensign Albert Earnest, radioman Aviation Radioman Third Class Harry Ferrier and gunner Seaman First Class Jay Manning. The plane had sustained seventy-odd bullet and cannon shell hits, and Manning was killed and Earnest and Ferrier were wounded. Earnest discovered he could steer the plane with his trim tabs, and somehow he was able to fly the plane back to Midway.[41]

5. The Battle of Midway Begins

TBF Earnest's plane, June 24, 1942 (Ensign Albert K. Earnest, USN, photo 80-G-17063, courtesy Naval History and Heritage Command).

The four B-26 bombers did not observe the Japanese carriers until five minutes later. The bombers then began their run in on the Japanese carriers while trying to avoid the antiaircraft fire from the screening ships. Six Zero fighters arrived, and the B-26s lowered their altitude to within 200 feet of the sea. The Japanese fighters were able to shoot down two of the four B-26 bombers.

Captain Collins, leader of the group and pilot of the first plane, was able to release his Mark 13 torpedo at *Akagi* but missed by a wide margin. First Lieutenant James Muri, pilot of the fourth plane, also released his torpedo on *Akagi*, but his torpedo went wide of its target. The surviving two B-26 aircraft subsequently found their way back to Midway.[42]

Having received the message from Tomonaga at 0700 that a second strike was necessary on Midway, and with none of the Japanese search planes reporting sighting of the American fleet, Nagumo ordered the carrier attack planes (kankos) of the second wave on *Akagi* and *Kaga* that had been armed with torpedoes to be replaced with bombs for a land attack. These planes had initially been armed with torpedoes so that they would be combat ready for an attack on the American fleet if one were sighted. *Hiryu* and *Soryu* had only dive-bombers in its second wave, which were located in the hangar deck. These planes would not be armed until they were spotted on the flight deck, unlike the carrier attack planes which were armed in the hangar deck.

During this time, the Japanese continued to increase their fighter CAP because of the incoming attack by the ten planes from Midway. This action prevented them from

B-26, June 4, 1942. Lieutenant James Muri, USAAC, second from left in front; rest of crew unidentified (photo USAF-22850-AC, courtesy of Naval History and Heritage Command).

raising any offensive aircraft from the hangar deck to the flight deck, if any of the U.S. fleet were discovered. It is speculated by Parshall and Tully in their book *Shattered Sword* that, had *Chikuma*'s Number 1 plane spotted *Yorktown*, 200 miles away from the Kido Butai, it would have been at 0630 at the earliest. It was Japanese naval policy to keep all its operational aircraft in the hangar deck until spotting the aircraft. It is also true that the functional capability of the Japanese carrier was that its flight deck could only be used for landing or launching or spotting aircraft at any given time. It is estimated that it takes at least forty-five minutes to spot aircraft from the hangar deck to the flight deck; therefore the earliest the planes could have been launched from the carriers to attack *Yorktown* would have been 0715. This would have given the planes barely enough time to reach *Yorktown* before *Yorktown* launched its own aircraft at 0838. The basis for this reasoning is that it would take at least an hour and a half for the Japanese aircraft to reach *Yorktown* which was 200 miles away. Taking into account that the Japanese carriers were under attack by the ten planes from Midway at 0710 and that more CAP aircraft were needed to protect the carriers, it would have been difficult for the Kido Butai to launch its air attack against *Yorktown* at that time. Even though it is remotely possible that the Japanese could have launched their aircraft before the first air attack returned from Midway, the best case scenario for the Japanese would have been that they would have found *Yorktown* and sunk the carrier. However, it is important to point out that at that time, the Japanese did not know the whereabouts of *Enterprise* and *Hornet*, which were thirty miles south of Task Force 17. In addition, Task Force 16 had already launched its aircraft at 0700, which was too late for the Japanese to attack the U.S. carriers with all their planes on deck. The foregoing appears to be academic since U.S. sources have reported that the location of *Yorktown* was just outside the search arc of *Chikuma*'s Number 1 search plane—a point that will be further discussed later.

The preceding describes one of the most critical flaws inherent in the Japanese Midway operational plan, namely that the fixation on attacking Midway first was pivotal in the destruction of the four Japanese carriers at Midway. It deprived the Japanese of the opportunity to strike the U.S. fleet first, which was the only scenario in which Japan could achieve total victory at Midway. The decision by the Japanese to attack Midway afforded the United States an incredible advantage because, through the brilliance of U.S. intelligence, Fletcher and Spruance now knew the exact course and location of the Japanese carriers as they approached Midway.

This advantage afforded the U.S. task force the opportunity to attack the Kido Butai first and at a time when the carriers were most vulnerable—with all its carrier aircraft on board. If the Japanese had not been wedded to attacking Midway first and had concentrated on destroying the U.S. fleet, they would have had flexibility of movement (as they did at Coral Sea), and the United States would not have known for certain the location of the Japanese fleet.

By 0715, none of the U.S. carriers had been sighted by any of the Japanese scout planes, and so the transition of changing the carrier attack aircraft (kanko) from torpedoes to bombs continued.

Tone's Number 4 aircraft was launched a half hour late (following its course along the 100-degree bearing), and its pilot either decided not to follow its assigned course out to the 300-mile destination or he was off course when his plane made a left turn at 220 miles out on his dogleg back to the fleet.

Evidence obtained from U.S. Navy records place Task Force 16 and Task Force 17 in the search area of *Tone*'s Number 4 aircraft, whereas Japanese sources place the U.S. task forces to the north, which was the area covered by *Chikuma*'s Number 1 search plane. The foregoing explanations given for the *Tone* Number 4 plane help explain why this aircraft and not *Mikuma*'s Number 1 aircraft discovered an American fleet at 0728.

At 0720, Petty Officer First Class Amari Hiroshi, pilot of the *Tone* Number 4 Aichi E13A float plane, immediately radioed back to the Nagumo fleet that he had sighted ten ships, distance 240 miles from Midway, heading southeast at twenty knots. Nagumo received the message sometime before 0745. In the narrative summary of the operation in the official report, Nagumo states he received the message at 0500 (0800 Midway time). In the same document, however, in the detailed action log portion of the narrative, there are entries at 0745 and 0747, which establish that Nagumo gave orders acknowledging Amari's report. At 0745, Nagumo gave orders to reverse the initial order to rearm the Japanese carrier attack aircraft (kankos) on board *Akagi* and *Kaga* with bombs and now rearm them with torpedoes. These orders are consistent with the fact that Nagumo received the Amari message before 0745. In addition, the conclusion that Nagumo received Amari's message at 0745 is supported by American intelligence in Hawaii that at 0747 Nagumo sent in the clear that *Tone*'s Number 4 plane was directed to determine the types of ships seen and remain in contact.[43]

At 0758, the *Tone* search plane reported back to Nagumo that the ten-ship fleet seen had changed course to 080 degrees, but the float plane did not radio back the types of ships seen. The officers on the deck of *Akagi* were totally frustrated and at 0800 sent out another message for the scout crew to immediately report back the types of ships being observed.

At 0800, as Nagumo was in contact with *Tone*'s search plane, *Hiryu* and *Soryu* were attacked by the fourteen B-17E bombers from Midway. *Kaga* was still landing the last four aircraft of its CAP, after which the carrier sent seven fighters airborne to supplement the CAP. The B-17Es were attacked randomly by the Zeroes, but the high-altitude combat (20,000 feet) was not ideal for the fighters and so they inflicted little damage to the B-17E bombers. However, all fourteen of the B-17Es were unaware that they had missed their targets, as it was erroneously reported upon their return to Midway that the B-17Es had set three carriers on fire.

After the attack by the six TBFs and four B-26s at 0705, all four carriers were engaged in sending off and landing their CAP during the lulls that followed the American attacks during that morning. Clearly, Nagumo realized that the CAP was his best defense against U.S. air attacks, and not the carriers' antiaircraft guns.

At 0811, just as the sixteen SBD-2s from Midway arrived and were closing in on *Hiryu*, *Tone*'s Number 4 plane radioed Nagumo that the ten ships it was observing were five cruisers and five destroyers. Nagumo and his staff were relieved that there were no American carriers present. Ten minutes later at 0821, the float scout plane signaled that a ship in the rear of the ten-vessel formation appeared to be a carrier. The message astonished Nagumo and his staff, but some present on the bridge still clung to the words "appears to be" as a justification that it still was not certain that a U.S. carrier was present. However, the size of the American fleet present went against this conclusion, and Nagumo proceeded to make his subsequent decisions on the basis that at least one U.S. carrier was in the corridor northeast of Midway. At 0830, *Tone*'s search plane reported back that two additional enemy ships had been observed and appeared to be cruisers. The American fleet seen by the *Tone* search aircraft was most likely *Enterprise*'s portion of Task Force 16, which contained *Enterprise* and eight other ships (three cruisers and five destroyers). *Enterprise* had separated from *Hornet* and its seven-ship screen at 0650 and was off in the distance. However, it took forty-five minutes (at 0813) for *Enterprise* and heavy cruiser *Northampton* to sight the *Tone* Number 4 scout plane. Nine minutes later (at 0822), *Enterprise* directed two of its fighter CAP to bring down the Japanese float plane.

However, the plane hid in the cloud cover and avoided the fighters. Running low on fuel, at 0830, the plane radioed back to Nagumo that he was heading back to the carriers, but he was ordered to continue his observation of the U.S. fleet.[44]

At 0800, the Japanese carriers sighted the sixteen SBD-2 dive-bombers approaching from the southeast. The SBD-2s left Midway after the B-26s took off, but their

5. The Battle of Midway Begins

slower speed and their more northerly navigational course caused the aircraft to arrive an hour later than the B-26s.

Most of Major Henderson's pilots were inexperienced because the recently delivered SBD-2 planes did not arrive on Midway until May 26, leaving the pilots little time to practice dive-bombing techniques with the aircraft. At 0811, Henderson led his squadron of sixteen aircraft into a shallow dive as it began its attack on *Soryu* and *Hiryu*. The planes were immediately attacked by nine Japanese Zeroes, and eight of the SBD-2s plummeted into the ocean. One of the sixteen SBD-2 radio/gunners was able to shoot down a *Hiryu*'s Zero, piloted by Warrant Officer Kodama Yoshimi. Among the aircraft lost in that attack was that of Major Henderson, the leader of VMSB-241, who bravely led his men in the attack on Carrier Division Two. The airfields on Midway and Guadalcanal would subsequently be named after him as well as the destroyer *Henderson*. The eight remaining SBD-2s now focused their attention on carrier *Hiryu*. Multiple attempts were made at hitting the carrier, but only one near miss was obtained. The surviving eight SBDs then returned to Midway.

Nautilus at periscope depth had remained in the vicinity of the Kido Butai since 0710. Forty-five minutes later, its commander, Lieutenant Commander William H. Brockman, Jr., observed four Japanese ships in the distance. The boat dove down to ninety feet and closed the distance between itself and the Japanese vessels, identified as one battleship, one light cruiser of the Jintsu class and two cruisers of the Yubari class. The battleship Brockman sighted was *Kirishima*, and the light cruiser was *Nagara*. The two other cruisers misidentified by Brockman as Yubari-class cruisers were actually Kagero-class destroyers. Brockman decided to attack the battleship, but as he prepared to make his run, the submarine was detected by an antisubmarine float plane, which dropped a bomb near the submarine. Brockman immediately dove down to ninety feet to escape being hit. At 0824, *Nautilus* again came up to periscope depth, but light cruiser *Nagara* and the destroyer *Arashi* both came over to the area to drop depth charges in order to keep *Nautilus* at bay.[45] *Nautilus* would be the only U.S. submarine of the twelve Midway Patrol Group that was to play an unwitting role in altering the outcome of the Battle of Midway, which will be described in the pages that follow.

At about 0815, Tomonaga and his Midway attack force were due to return from the atoll. After the four-hour mission, the aircraft would be low on fuel, and some planes would be damaged and would need to land immediately on the carriers. Nagumo and his staff were now faced with a tactical decision which they had only fifteen minutes to resolve because Tomonaga's planes were low on fuel. Should Nagumo immediately land the returning force from Midway or first send off all the available operational aircraft on board the four carriers to search and destroy the one carrier (*Yorktown*) that Amari had discovered on his scouting mission? However, Japanese scout aircraft had been known to make mistakes in the reporting of the location of their discoveries. Indeed, this is exactly what happened in Amari's initial report in which he placed the location of the ten U.S. ships sixty miles north-northeast of where they were actually located.[46]

To add to the confusion was the question of why the search pattern of *Chikuma*'s Number 1 scout plane did not discover the American force (*Yorktown*). Previous explanations given were that either the plane was flying above the clouds or it was off course.

A more likely explanation is that the Japanese report, placing the U.S. task forces inside the search arc of *Chikuma*'s Number 1 search plane, was in error. This conclusion is drawn because American sources place the U.S. forces sixty miles to the southeast and outside the search arc of the flight path taken by *Chikuma*'s Number 1 scout plane.

Therefore, this evidence refutes the assertion that *Chikuma*'s Number 1 search plane missed sighting the U.S. forces at 0630, and therefore any speculation that the American fleet was sighted by *Chikuma*'s Number 1 scout plane is purely academic. Thus, it is highly improbable, and more likely impossible, that Nagumo would have ever had an opportunity to launch his aircraft in an attack on U.S. forces (*Yorktown*) at an earlier time (0630).[47]

The only logical explanations for the discovery of a U.S. carrier force are that either Amari, the pilot of *Tone*'s Number 4 plane, was in error or the coordinates of U.S. forces given by American sources are wrong. The former possibility appears to be closer to the truth. Nagumo questioned the validity of the location of U.S. forces as given by Amari, as many of the Japanese search planes in the past exercised great freedom in the reporting of the location of enemy ships. Nagumo continued to ponder his decision as Tomonaga's planes were circling above the carriers waiting to land.[48]

At 0820, the Amari scout plane had reported that a U.S. carrier appeared to be present. Nagumo and his staff were astonished to hear this news, but some of his staff held out hope that this was report was not true because Amari used the words "appears to be." At 0830, Amari then reported that two additional cruisers were seen. An 0830 time was reported by Fuchida and Okumiya in *Midway*, while Parshall and Tully state in *Shattered Sword* that the time was 0845. The size of the force observed by *Tone*'s scout plane Number 4 (thirteen ships) indicated to Nagumo that there must be a U.S. carrier in the group. Nagumo also knew that the Americans knew his exact location for at least one and a half hours (since the first attack by the TBFs and B-26 aircraft from Midway at 0700). Thus, an initial strike by a U.S. carrier force was most likely underway.

A discussion by Nagumo and his staff aboard *Akagi* occurred to decide whether or not to launch all operational aircraft available against the U.S. carrier force or first to land Tomonaga's air group hovering overhead and then rearm and refuel all the aircraft before launching an attack against the U.S. carrier force (one U.S. carrier suspected). On the one hand, Nagumo could have ordered all available aircraft to be launched against the one U.S. carrier, but he was not certain that the American force even contained a carrier and he might misdirect his aircraft to attack a U.S. naval task force that did not include a carrier as was done in the Battle of the Coral Sea.

However, with an hour having elapsed since the Americans attacked his position, prudence should have dictated that waiting an additional two hours (two and half hours total since the American attack occurred) to rearm and refuel his planes and subsequently launch his aircraft at 1030 would present a real opportunity for the United States to strike the Kido Butai first.

This dilemma was created by a grave error in the Japanese Midway plan that included an attack on Midway as part of its mission. The flaw resulted in loss of *flexibility of movement* for the Japanese fleet, which is essential if victory is to be achieved in a naval battle. It also permitted American intelligence to learn exactly where the Kido

5. The Battle of Midway Begins

Butai would be en route to Midway because of its fixed position in an attack on the island naval base. This information presented an opportunity to the United States not only to strike the Japanese task force first, but to do so when it was most vulnerable, that is, with all of its aircraft on board being rearmed and refueled.

In spite of the fact that Lieutenant Commander Ono Kenjiro, Staff Intelligence Officer, had calculated that the American carrier force was just 200 miles away from the Kido Butai and thus already within striking distance, Nagumo decided to land Tomonaga's returning air group first before launching an all-out attack against the American forces.[49] Even the urgings of Rear Admiral Yamaguchi Tamon, Commander of Carrier Division Two, could not persuade Nagumo to launch all available aircraft immediately, although it placed at risk Tomanaga's air group, who were short on fuel. Yamaguchi felt that to do otherwise would be too risky and dangerous, but Nagumo did not take his advice and instead gave the order to land Tomanaga's air group.

If Nagumo waited, he would have eighteen carrier attack planes from *Akagi*, about twenty-seven carrier attack planes from *Kaga*, eighteen dive-bombers from *Hiryu* and sixteen dive-bombers from *Soryu* (a total of seventy-nine carrier aircraft). If he had launched immediately, he would have twelve carrier attack aircraft from *Akagi*; eighteen carrier attack aircraft from *Kaga*, eighteen dive-bombers from *Hiryu* and sixteen dive-bombers from *Soryu*, for a total of sixty-four carrier aircraft (a difference of fifteen aircraft). The Japanese also had forty-seven Zero fighters (thirty-five of these fighters operational) on all four carriers. The latter would have been a formidable force to send against the Americans. Utilizing a dozen of the Zero fighters for escorting the bombers would still leave thirty-five fighters to serve in the CAP as defense for the carriers. Although there were other options open to the Japanese at this moment, the bottom line is that Nagumo did not send any aircraft to attack the American carrier task force.

One must remember that even if the Japanese did launch their available aircraft, the best they could hope for would be the destruction of *Yorktown*, as *Enterprise* and *Hornet* were not yet discovered by the Japanese. When they failed to launch their aircraft at 0815, the odds for total destruction of their carrier fleet by the United States was greatly increased because all their aircraft fueled and rearmed would be on board if the United States attacked.

At 0827, the third wave of U.S. aircraft arrived from Midway—the eleven Marine SB2U-3s. The pilots, deciding that *Akagi* and *Hiryu* were too far away, headed for the battleship *Haruna*. *Haruna* made swift and evasive turns to avoid being hit by the bombs released by the dive-bombers. Although there were five or six near misses, *Haruna* escaped the attack unscathed. Zero fighters then dove in on the SB2U-3s, shooting two of them down and driving the remaining planes off to the southwest.[50]

At 0830, *Soryu* launched a new Yokosuka Type 13 reconnaissance aircraft (later code-named Judy) to fly to the site indicated by *Tone*'s Number 4 scout plane. The aircraft had a maximum speed of 343 miles per hour and a range of 850 nautical miles. At the controls was pilot Petty Officer First Class Lida Masatada, and in the rear seat was Support Operations Officer (SPO) Kondo Isamu. The plane headed northeast toward the designated area.

At 0820, two U.S. fighters from *Enterprise*'s CAP vectored out toward the Japanese scout plane from heavy cruiser *Tone* in the hope of ambushing the aircraft. The fighters, however, were unable to attack the elusive float plane whose pilot hid the aircraft under cloud cover. The *Tone* scout plane, which had been thirty miles away from *Enterprise*, must have then flown farther to the northeast to avoid the U.S. fighters. As a result, Amari was now able to detect two of the heavy cruisers in Task Force 17 but was unable to sight *Yorktown*. At 0850, Amari radioed Nagumo that he was returning to the Kido Butai. Nagumo emphatically replied that the pilot should not only stay where he was but that he should also keep his radio transmitter on so that the plane's radio frequency could be used as a direction-finding device for the Japanese aircraft to find the American fleet. Amari then reported that ten torpedo planes (actually it was the fifteen U.S. TBD-1 torpedo planes from *Hornet*) were heading toward the Japanese carriers.[51]

At 0855, Nagumo contacted Yamamoto to inform him that an enemy carrier, five cruisers and five destroyers were discovered at 0800, 240 miles northeast from Midway, and that the Kido Butai was now steaming toward the enemy task force. Nagumo failed to mention to Yamamoto the other events that had involved the Kido Butai between 0700 and 0900. Yamamoto for his part had already intercepted the messages between *Tone*'s Number 4 plane and the Kido Butai and appeared unconcerned about the presence of a U.S. task force.

At 0900, *Nautilus*, which continued to harass the Kido Butai, was tailing the Japanese fleet, waiting for an opportunity to attack one of the Japanese ships. Light cruiser *Nagara* spotted the submarine and closed in at high speed to drop depth charges on *Nautilus*. Destroyer *Arashi*, seeing the cruiser chase *Nautilus*, joined the chase and remained behind to keep the submarine submerged by dropping continuous depth charges on the submarine. This action allowed the Kido Butai to get out of range and out of harm's way.[52]

At 0850, *Kaga* completed its landings of Tomonaga's planes; *Akagi* was finished at 0859 and both *Soryu* and *Hiryu* completed their landings at 0910. Perhaps *Soryu* and *Hiryu* took longer to land the returning Midway planes because those carriers were lowering the aircraft that had been brought up to the flight deck from the hangar deck by Yamaguchi anticipating an earlier Japanese attack on U.S. forces at 0820. At 0917, with all aircraft aboard, Nagumo ordered a change in the course of the Kido Butai to the northeast to close the distance to the enemy.[53]

At 0800, Task Force 17 continued to steam south and was now only ten miles north of Task Force 16. Fletcher delayed the launching of his aircraft out of concern that not all of the four Japanese carriers (only two Japanese carriers were known to Fletcher to have been discovered thus far) had been found, in which case he would be in position to direct his planes to the remaining Japanese carriers in the new location. At 0838, Fletcher finally decided to send aloft part of his contingency of available aircraft to the initially reported Japanese location—northwest of Midway—because he had become aware that the Japanese had found a U.S. task force. At 0836, he gave the order to launch a normal departure by ordering the slowest planes to take off first, followed by the faster aircraft.

Of the aircraft on board *Yorktown* (CV-5), only VS-5 scouting dive-bombers originated on the carrier. Returning from the Battle of the Coral Sea, *Yorktown* sustained losses to its squadrons of bombing dive-bombers, torpedo planes and fighters. Those aircraft had been replaced with aircraft from *Saratoga* (CV-3), which was under repair in the state of Washington because of a submarine torpedo attack in January 1942. Thus, the torpedo planes (VT-3), bombing dive-bombers (VB-3) and fighters (V-3) on board *Yorktown* had all been transferred from *Saratoga* to *Yorktown*.

The seventeen SBDs from Bombing Three (VB-3) under the command of Lieutenant Commander Maxwell Leslie, each loaded with a 1,000-pound bomb, were followed by the twelve TBD-1s from Torpedo Three (VT-3) under the command of Lieutenant Commander Lance Massey and then by six F4Fs from Fighting Three (VF-3) under the command of Lieutenant Commander John *Jimmy* Thach, who would escort the group out to the target.

Thach had originally been on *Saratoga* when the carrier was torpedoed in January 1942 and on *Lexington* when that carrier was sunk in the Battle of the Coral Sea in May 1942. The entire group in unison, under the command of Lieutenant Commander Oscar Pederson, flew toward the Kido Butai at a heading of 230 degrees. The fighters would fly 5,000–6,000 feet above the torpedo bombers and below the high-flying dive-bombers, which were at 20,000 feet. *Yorktown* had launched its planes in an orderly manner and in less time, as compared to Task Force 16. *Yorktown* was the only one of the three U.S. carriers at Midway for which all three squadrons of aircraft (torpedo planes, dive-bombers and fighters) would arrive over the Kido Butai at the same time and had the best opportunity to effect a coordinated attack on the enemy. The last plane left the carrier deck at 0905. There had been an adjustment made to their navigational course in flying to the enemy carrier's position to 230 degrees because the reported location of the Kido Butai was now several hours old. The pilots planned to fly to the calculated location, and then, if the enemy was not found, they would turn to the northwest to head back along a reciprocal bearing of the enemy's reported course before returning back to *Yorktown*. This course of action gave the Americans the best chance of finding the Japanese carriers.[54]

Fletcher kept in reserve seventeen SBDs from Scouting Five (VS-5) under the command of Lieutenant Wallace Short and six F4Fs from Fighting Three (VF-3) under the command of Lieutenant Richard Crommelin for a second strike if the other carriers were found.

Hornet's Aircraft's Ill-Fated Flight

At 0820, Lieutenant Commander John Waldron, leader of VT-8's squadron of fifteen TBD-1s, was heading toward the enemy, but he became convinced that they were flying in the wrong direction. He immediately contacted Air Group Commander, Commander Ring, but the two could not come to an agreement. Thus, Waldron told Ring that he was changing his course to the southwest and heading to the enemy in that direction. Lieutenant James Gray of VF-6, having climbed halfway to the assigned 20,000-foot altitude and not having a perfect view of the situation, observed a torpedo squadron below him which disappeared into cloud cover and then came out of it.

Assuming it was Lindsey's VT-6, he changed his course to actually cover Waldron's VT-8 torpedo bombers. This confusion occurred because each of the air groups from

Hornet and *Enterprise* flew to the target independently and under the charge of each air group's commander.

Since the air groups from these carriers were in the same vicinity, it was easy for Gray to confuse *Hornet*'s torpedo bombers with those of *Enterprise*.[55]

How the narrative unfolded is important because the actions of *Hornet*'s planes that day resulted in only *Hornet*'s fifteen torpedo bombers finding the Kido Butai as the two squadrons of SBD dive-bombers and one squadron of F4F fighters got lost and never found the enemy carriers (depriving the United States of forty-four planes and three-quarters of *Hornet*'s aircraft). The original plan was for thirty-four dive-bombers to fly at 20,000 feet and the torpedo planes at 1,500 feet. The ten fighters could cover either the torpedo planes or the dive-bombes but not both squadrons.

The TBD-1s were slow and would approach the Japanese carriers at 100 feet and on a fixed course, which made the aircraft very vulnerable to Japanese fighters. Waldron obviously supported the plan whereby the torpedo bombers would be covered by the fighters, as did Lieutenant Commander Samuel *Pat* Mitchell, Commander of *Hornet*'s fighter group. The Captain of *Hornet*, Marc Mitscher, who disagreed with Waldron and Mitchell, took the position that the fighters should try to cover both the dive-bombers and the torpedo bombers. He felt that the best chance the F4F Wildcat had against a Zero fighter was to attack from above, so that all the fighters should fly above the dive-bombers and torpedo planes with the expectation of protecting both the dive-bombers and the torpedo planes. Mitscher decided not to split the fighter group as was done in the Battle of the Coral Sea where neither group benefitted and the dive-bombers fared worse than the torpedo planes. In reality, with the fighters as assigned by Mitscher, they would actually only cover the dive-bombers, leaving the torpedo bombers, at least initially, to fly to the target without fighter protection. Mitchell and Waldron were obviously displeased with the decision, but Mitscher's decision stood.[56]

At 0607 that morning, Mitscher received news that Fletcher had ordered Spruance to attack the Japanese carriers, but Spruance decided not to execute that order until 0700 so as to close the range between the enemy task force and his own carriers. Thirty minutes later, the four squadron leaders met with Mitscher, Ring and Commander Apollo Soucek, Air Officer of *Hornet*, on the carrier's bridge for a final briefing. Disagreement ensued as each pilot was asked to resolve the navigational problem using the available data. The results varied among the pilots, so no consensus was arrived at. As a result, Ring decided that his navigational course would be chosen, which proved to be inaccurate.[57]

At the meeting, Waldron and Mitchell again tried to convince Mitscher to send some of the fighters with the torpedo planes. When Mitscher rebuffed that suggestion, Waldron pleaded with Mitscher to send at least one fighter or at worse loan a Wildcat fighter to his squadron which could then be flown by a pilot of his torpedo group. The answer from Mitscher was still in the negative, and at that point Mitscher ordered Waldron out of the bridge and to his torpedo bombers, which were warming up on the flight deck.[58]

At 0700, *Hornet* launched its aircraft in a deferred departure; that is, each of *Hornet*'s planes, after taking off, would circle the carrier until all planes were launched, and then the aircraft would head toward their target in one formation, 150 miles away. The

SBD-3 warming up on the *Yorktown* (CV-5), June 4, 1942, (photo NH-100740, courtesy Naval History and Heritage Command).

purpose of this decision was to facilitate a coordinated attack on the enemy's carriers. This deferred departure also carried with it the consequences of devouring a significant amount of gasoline in the Wildcat fighters' 144-gallon capacity-fuel tank and in the fuel tanks of the SBD dive-bombers, which had to climb to an altitude of 20,000 feet. At 0800, all the planes were in formation and headed out to the enemy carriers.

The initial navigational course they flew was nearly due west at 265 degrees. However, this course was inconsistent with the battle map report submitted by Mitscher with his after-action report on June 11, which placed the dive-bombers and fighters flying in a southwesterly direction at 239 degrees. Mitscher's report also stated that this navigational course actually took them south of the Kido Butai because Nagumo had changed his course to the north. But other available evidence does not support Mitscher's account on that day, reporting that Ring (SBDs) and Mitchell (F4Fs) actually flew west at 265 degrees, which took their air groups 80–100 miles north of the Kido Butai. Thirty-five minutes into the flight, Waldron and his fifteen torpedo bombers, ignoring Ring's command to stay with the group, broke away from the dive-bombers and fighters and headed southwest. The navigational course plotted by Waldron was south of the original course decided upon by Ring in the meeting on *Hornet*'s bridge, which originally was to be at 239 degrees southwest.[59]

It remains a mystery why Ring did not follow the southwest navigation course he himself prescribed on *Hornet*'s bridge. One explanation is that the westerly course at 265 degrees was ordered by Mitscher. In an account written by Ring, he asserts that the interception course flown by him on that day was predetermined, but he does not state by whom (however, only a higher authority than Ring could dictate a change in navigational course, and that person would be Mitscher). The reason for Mitscher's changing the navigation course may lie in the fact that the Japanese carriers were assumed to be operating independently of one another. Nimitz had suggested in his original orders to his task force commanders that "one or more [Japanese] carriers may take up close positions" for an attack on Midway while "additional carrier groups may be operating against U.S. surface forces." Mitscher must have been aware that Fletcher had sent a communication to Spruance at 0648 (one that Mitscher must have picked up) that only two out of four Japanese carriers anticipated by U.S. intelligence to be present at Midway had been located.[60] Thus, Mitscher may have directed *Hornet*'s air resources to that end (finding and destroying the missing two Japanese carriers, even though he had no idea of where those carriers might be). If this scenario is true, then it remains a mystery why Mitscher and Ring did not share the reason for the change in the navigational course with the other squadron commanders.

The preceding information documents that Waldron did (strictly speaking) disobey orders by changing his course from due west to southwest, but he did so with honorable intentions.

Waldron was following the navigational course set forth by Ring at the meeting on the bridge of *Hornet*. Thus, at 0755, when Waldron called Ring over the radio and broke radio silence to inform him that he was going in the wrong direction, it was Ring, the Commander, *Hornet* Group (CHAG), who insisted on not conforming to the navigational course he previously set forth. At 0830, Waldron decided to change his navigational course and lead his TBD-1 squadron to the southwest. Waldron, who was one-eighth Sioux, claimed that his Indian heritage gave him a sixth sense about the future. Having made this statement, he deserves the credit for having turned his squadron to the southwest, and in addition, Waldron modified his course to 234 degrees rather than the 239 degrees originally planned by Ring. This corrected course would take Waldron's squadron directly to the Japanese carriers.

At 0900, James Gray's ten fighters (VF-6) continued to cover Torpedo Eight (VT-8) until he lost the group under cloud cover. Gray felt the cloud cover would protect the torpedo bombers from Japanese fighters. At 0910, Gray saw the wakes of the Japanese fleet. Gray tried in vain to contact Lieutenant Commander Wade McClusky, and thinking VT-8 was VT-6, Gray assumed McClusky's SBDs were close by. Given the circumstances, Gray decided to stay around for McClusky to arrive.

Ring, *Hornet*'s thirty-four SBDs and the ten F4F fighters continued on their flight due west. However, by this time, the fuel gauges in the fighters began to indicate that they were close to the point of no return. At 0900, the fighters' fuel gauges read below the half-empty mark.

Ensign J. E. McInerny, one of the VF-8s' pilots, having tried unsuccessfully by head signals to get his leader Lieutenant Commander Pat Mitchell to order a return of the fighters to *Hornet*, broke formation, and shortly thereafter, eight of the fighters followed him. Mitchell for the moment stayed on course, but once he realized that his squadron had abandoned him, he also turned around and sped after the departed fighters to gain the leadership position of the squadron. At 0900, all ten fighters headed back to *Hornet*, leaving the thirty-four SBDs to fly on their own without fighter protection.[61]

5. The Battle of Midway Begins

Ring and the dive-bombers following him were probably unaware that the fighters had left them as no radio silence was broken when the fighters departed. The thirty-four planes continued west until 0920 when a few of their radiomen picked up Waldron's radio messages requesting to speak to Stanhope Ring, but Ring did not reply. Waldron's words to the men of his squadron, warning them of incoming Japanese fighters, and his statement that two of his torpedo planes were headed into the water were picked up by the radiomen of *Hornet*'s dive-bombers as they flew west. Now Ring knew that Waldron's torpedo squadron had found the enemy carriers and that Waldron's planes were now under heavy attack by Japanese fighters. If Ring heard the radio communication, he did not reply. Moments later, Waldron again tried to reach Ring on the radio, but again there was no answer from Ring.[62]

Hornet's dive-bombers, having now flown over 200 miles, were close to running out of fuel. Lieutenant Commander Robert Johnson, Commander of Bombing Eight's dive-bombers, felt the time had come to make a run at reaching Eastern Island's airstrip on Midway, and if on the way they ran into the Kido Butai, they would attack its carriers. He signaled his wingman, who then followed Johnson to the south. Sixteen dive-bombers of Bombing Eight then proceeded to peel off and fly south with Johnson, except for Ring's wingman, Ensign Clayton Fisher, who stayed with him. The remaining fifteen planes of Lieutenant Commander Walter Rodee's Scouting Eight stayed with Ring and Clayton and continued to fly west.

At 1000, when Johnson realized they could not find the enemy carriers, he turned the squadron's course to the northeast. Shortly thereafter, the seventeen dive-bombers ran into an American PBY whose pilot signaled them the course to Midway. However, Lieutenant Alfred Tucker of VS-8, who detected the YE homing signal from *Hornet*, decided with two other pilots not to fly to Midway, and instead the three aircraft (SBDs) headed toward *Hornet*.[63] *Hornet* used a dedicated YE transmitter that sent out a single different Morse code letter to each thirty-degree quadrant of the compass. The aircraft received the signal on their ZB receiver. Three of the aircraft led by Tucker turned to the northeast to look for *Hornet*. The remaining fourteen planes under the command of Johnson headed for Eastern Island. Two of these planes ran out of fuel before reaching Midway, and a third had to ditch in the lagoon off the Midway Islands. The eleven surviving planes were refueled and rearmed on Eastern Island. The SBDs of VS-8 then took off and found their way back to *Hornet*. Tucker's group of three SBDs, which flew directly to *Hornet*, landed safely on deck. Thus, only three SBDs from VS-8 were lost on the ill-fated flight.[64]

The ten F4F fighters were now running precariously low on fuel. Mitchell could not detect *Hornet*'s YE signal but Lieutenant Stan Ruehlow in his squadron could, so Mitchell relinquished the lead to Ruehlow. The fighters headed east toward *Hornet*, but by unwittingly dropping down to 8,000 feet to conserve fuel, the planes missed the carrier because at that altitude the ZB receivers were unreliable. Now out of fuel, the F4Fs ditched into the sea. The men who survived remained in their rafts in the water for four days and were subjected to shark attacks before eight of the ten pilots were rescued by some of the eleven PBYs assigned to the search. Two pilots, Ensign Markland Kelly and Ensign C. R. Hill, were never found.[65]

Ring and his group of sixteen SBDs (VS-8) maintained their course and continued to fly west. Loaded with only 500-pound bombs, they were able to use less fuel and fly further. But after flying over 225 miles over a one-and-a-half-hour period of time, the pilots began to worry about running out of fuel. At this point, Rodee, Commander of Scouting Eight, decided to turn around and head back to *Hornet*. All of the other pilots followed his lead except Ring, who was left alone. As a result, Ring decided to fly back to *Hornet* alone. No one has ever explained this extraordinary action by Ring. He actually picked up the YE-ZB homing system, not from *Hornet* but from *Enterprise*. His course was true, and he eventually found *Hornet* and was the first one to land on the carrier at 1118. Ring did not report to the bridge but went straight to his stateroom. Mitscher only learned what had happened after Walter Rodee landed and reported to him on the flight of this flawed mission.[66]

Analysis

So why then did Ring fly due west on a 265-degree course rather than the 239-degree course he agreed to on the *Hornet*'s bridge? One possible explanation was that Mitscher instructed Ring to change the navigational course of his mission (already described). American intelligence had indicated that there would be at least four Japanese carriers, and only two enemy carriers had thus far been sighted. If Mitscher were responsible for the change in the navigational direction, he would not have sent all of his available aircraft to search and destroy the other two Japanese carriers (without any confirmation of their location). The second possibility was that Ring, who was known to be an incompetent navigator, did not have his calculated course rechecked by Mitscher before the flight took place. It is unlikely that Mitscher would have left such a crucial decision regarding the navigational course of this mission in the hands of Ring. The fact that the direction of the navigational course was challenged by two of *Hornet*'s squadron commanders was reason enough for him to double-check Ring's course. The evidence appears to indicate that both Mitscher and Ring were complicit in the decision to change the navigational course of the mission.

The Body of Evidence

Mitscher submitted an action report one week after June 4, 1942. He stated that the course that his four squadrons (VT-8, VB-8, VS-8 and VF-8) flew that day was 239 degrees to the southwest and that the enemy was 155 miles away from *Hornet*. This course was diagrammed on a map Mitscher submitted with his action report on June 11. Mitscher contended that Ring missed the Kido Butai because Nagumo changed course to the north and Ring flew south of the Japanese task force. The following evidence refutes this report. After *Hornet* had completed launching all of its aircraft at 0754, Waldron flew with Ring for about forty-five minutes on his flight to the Kido Butai. At 0830, Waldron disobeyed Ring's radio command to stay with the formation.

After telling Ring he was going in the wrong direction, Waldron changed his course to fly in a southwest direction. It took Waldron's squadron about forty minutes to discover the Kido Butai.

If Ring's navigation course was 239 degrees instead of the actual navigation course of 265 degrees, Waldron would not have reached the Kido Butai in about forty minutes, and Waldron, flying in a southwest direction, would have missed the Japanese task force entirely as he would have been flying well to the south of where the Kido Butai was actually located.

Mitscher should have double-checked Ring's calculations, because if he did not, Mitscher would share in the blame for the disastrous effects of Ring's change in the navigational course of the mission, namely, the effective loss of the airpower of a U.S. carrier at Midway and failing to provide VT-8 with fighter support.

The foregoing conclusions may explain why Mitscher did not insist on an action report, not only from Ring, but from any of his other squadron commanders. It may also explain why Mitscher did not hold Ring responsible, either for incompetence (if, indeed, Ring was incompetent) or for following Mitscher's orders.

Another episode involves *Hornet*'s role in assisting *Enterprise* in the search for and destruction of *Hiryu*. At 1403, sixteen Dauntless dive-bombers had taken off from *Hornet*. Two of the SBDs from the sixteen planes that took off had to return to the carrier because of engine failure. The delay in the landing of these two planes prevented any other planes from taking off due to the time factor. Among the stranded planes were those of Stanhope Ring, the Air Group Commander, and Walter Rodee, the Air Squadron Commander. This occurrence raises the question of whether Mitscher purposely kept these two pilots in the rear because of their drastic mishandling of the morning mission.

Evidence indicates that Ring, who was noted for his allegiance to "doing it by the book," never submitted an after-action report to Mitscher. To date, after seventy-five years, this report has not been found, nor have any after-action reports ever been found from squadron commanders Rodee, Johnson or Mitchell (Waldron died in action), even though they were mandatory under navy regulations. The absence of these after-action reports by the squadron commanders could not have gone unnoticed by Admiral Ernest King, Commander in Chief, Nimitz, or Spruance, and they apparently were not insisted upon by any of them.

The lack of after-action reports by the squadron commanders and Mitscher's erroneous map diagram all point to a cover-up of the episode by the U.S. Navy. King, Nimitz and Spruance must have decided that the incident should not reach the awareness of the public after the great victory by the United States at Midway. It is obvious that an inquiry into the details of the flight should have occurred and insubordination charges brought against those individuals responsible. Supportive evidence that Mitscher's after-action report was considered to be inaccurate can be obtained from Spruance's own written words: "Where discrepancies exist between *Enterprise* and *Hornet* reports, the *Enterprise* report should be taken to be more accurate." Without any action reports filed by the squadron commanders (most unusual) after the battle, Mitscher's Midway report demonstrating that the *Hornet*'s planes flew on a course of 240 degrees southwest was the only evidence that gave testimony to the morning's events. As a result, his map was considered accurate with no evidence to the contrary to refute that premise. This falsehood continued to be accepted until recently when Craig Symonds, in his book

The Battle of Midway, presented evidence to the contrary from Japanese sources. Mitscher claimed, or at least signed, the report that asserted that Stanhope Ring and his air group had flown a course of 240 degrees and had missed the Kido Butai because Nagumo turned north instead of heading toward Midway. The key fact here is that Nagumo did not turn to the north until 0917 (a critical fact unknown at that time to Mitscher when he signed the report), so that if Ring was truly flying on a 240-degree course, he would have intercepted the Kido Butai before it turned north.

Certainly, Waldron discovered the Japanese carrier fleet at 0918, before it turned north. Bowen Weisheit, author of *The Last Flight of C. Markland Kelly*, in his interviews with surviving fighter pilots of Mitchell's squadron, learned that their navigation course was 265 degrees due west. In addition, Rodee wrote the navigation course down in his flight log book, since he never was asked to submit an official after-action report. To add to the evidence was the fact that the radar operator stated that he tracked *Hornet's* air group out as far as he could on a course heading of 265 degrees. However, Clayton Fisher, Ring's wingman, testified that the air group flew on a southwest heading of 240 degrees, but most of the testimony points to the fact that Ring did fly due west at 265 degrees. This scenario is best explained by the conclusion that Mitscher was responsible for *Hornet's* air group flying due west at 265 degrees because he was trying to locate and destroy the other two Japanese carriers. It is likely that Mitscher checked Ring's calculations, so Ring appears to have been following the course set forth by Mitscher. One other suggestion was that *Hornet's* magnetic compass was off by fifteen or twenty degrees that day, but *Hornet's* pilots reported that 265 degrees was the actual direction they were flying on their *flight to nowhere*.

It is reasonable to assume that the U.S. Navy was not interested in a scandal of this nature being reported in the press after the Battle of Midway. A truthful report of the flight would have necessitated that formal charges be brought against Waldron, McInerny, Mitchell, Johnson and Rodee, and possibly others. Therefore, instead of court-martial hearings—the logical outcome of this insubordination—these individuals were recommended for medals. Certainly, one would assume that Admirals King, Nimitz and Spruance were knowledgeable about the *flight to nowhere* and its repercussions and were in total agreement to the terms of this proposed cover-up. The incident was most likely concealed because of the embarrassment it would have caused the Navy at the time of a great victory, as well as keeping up morale on the home front.

The foregoing discussion is consistent with the fact that, after the Midway battle, Ring and Mitscher were ordered by Nimitz (who was most likely directed to do so by King) to command Patrol Wing Two, a shore-based assignment, removing Mitscher as a carrier commander and Ring as a squadron air commander and grounding them on a land-based assignment of much less importance. Mitscher remained there until December 1942. In April 1943, he was placed in charge of air assets in the Solomon Islands. In January 1944, he received command of the Fast Carrier Task Force (Task Force 58), which was associated with Spruance's Fifth Fleet, where he distinguished himself with success in this role and was rewarded with a promotion to vice admiral. Ring's virtues of loyalty and punctuality eventually enabled him to be placed in command of a new escort carrier *Siboney* in May 1945. After the war, his officer skills culminated in his promotion to the rank of vice admiral.

Analysis

The foregoing episode points out that in spite of U.S. intelligence outlining Japan's tactical plan to seize and occupy Midway, the Americans still needed to take advantage of the information by properly executing their countermoves against the Japanese offensive.

Effectively, all of *Hornet*'s SBDs and F4F fighters were taken out of the equation for the U.S. counteroffensive against the Kido Butai. Even the third component of *Hornet*'s offensive aircraft—the torpedo bomber—would soon make its attack on the Japanese carriers without fighter support. Thus, in essence, the Japanese at this time tactically held an edge over the Americans in carriers by a 2:1 margin. So, in spite of the fact that the U.S. aircraft launched their aircraft first, a 2:1 Japanese advantage in carriers now gave the Americans a theoretical chance of destroying only one Japanese carrier, with the loss of one American carrier. It would now take an extraordinary set of circumstances for the United States to decisively destroy the Japanese carrier fleet.

While it is true, as reported by Parshall and Tully in their book *Shattered Sword* published in 2005, that the United States did not face overwhelming numerical odds at Midway, at this moment in time in the battle, Japan effectively had a tactical advantage of 2:1 over the United States in the number of carriers. *Hornet*'s SBDs and fighters had been effectively taken out of the battle, and the fifty-two aircraft from the unsinkable fourth carrier of Midway had been ineffective in their attacks on the Japanese carriers.

Some of the reasons for the failure of Midway's aircraft were that most of the aircraft were either obsolete or slow, and the one aircraft that the Japanese carrier was most vulnerable to, the dive-bomber, was present on Midway in name only, as the pilots had not yet learned how to dive-bomb. Good fortune played a major role for the Americans at Midway, and thus the description of a *miracle* at Midway is appropriate.

Waldron realized that the course to the Japanese fleet plotted by his superiors earlier that morning had to be modified. Having flown due west at 265 degrees with Ring for twenty minutes, he changed his squadron's course to 234 degrees to the southwest. Torpedo Eight was flying in two sections, with Waldron leading one section of eight aircraft and Lieutenant James Owens leading the other section of seven planes. What is interesting is that each of the planes did not take a bombardier, and thus, only the pilot and the gunner/radioman were present in the three-man aircraft. The possible reasons for the exclusion of the bombardier may have been that only two crewmen were necessary, or that the bombardier's absence would lighten the load of the TBD and thus conserve fuel. After flying for thirty minutes, and unsure of the exact location of the Kido Butai, Waldron directed his squadron to spread out in an effort to find the Japanese carriers. Shortly after the order, Waldron saw the smoke of many ships on the horizon on his starboard side. The time was 0916.[67]

Based on the earlier report from Petty Officer Amari, who was scouting an American fleet, Nagumo already knew that U.S. torpedo planes were heading for the Japanese task force. The last of Tomonaga's aircraft landed at 0917, and Nagumo's fleet was now heading northeast.

Nagumo added six fighters to the eighteen already in the air, and twenty-four Zeroes headed out to meet the fifteen incoming TBD-1 Devastator torpedo bombers.

Waldron left his radio on as the squadron entered battle, and his messages were picked up by Ring's group over eighty miles away, but they were not heard by Gray or any of the men flying high above VT-8's torpedo bombers. The reason given by Gray twenty-one years later was that *Hornet* and *Enterprise* used two different radio frequencies.[68]

The torpedo bombers decreased their speed to 110 knots as the planes drew closer together. The Japanese carriers turned west so as to present a smaller target to the incoming torpedo planes. At 0930, when the TBDs were eight miles out from the carriers, the Devastators were attacked by the Japanese fighters. The torpedo bombers could tolerate the Zero's machine guns but not their 20mm cannon fire. Twelve of the torpedo bombers were shot down, and the remaining three TBDs headed toward *Soryu*. Within minutes, only Ensign George Gay, who was last in the formation, was airborne. His plane had been hit so badly that the controls of his torpedo release mechanism were defective, and he was not sure if he had actually released his torpedo. Within a few moments, his plane was again attacked by the Japanese CAP, and his plane was now headed into the water. Gay was able to climb out of the aircraft with his raft, but he was not able to save Robert Huntington, his gunner/radioman, who appeared to be dead and was inextricably caught in his seat harness. Gay floated in the water with his seat cushion over his head as the Japanese fighters, having shot down the last TBD, left the area. The time was now about 0932.[69]

At 0706, *Enterprise* began to launch its aircraft. Fifteen SBDs of Scouting Six took to the air, followed by the leader of the group, Lieutenant Commander Wade McClusky, and his two VS-6 wingmen. The first six planes carried a single 500-pound bomb, and the last twelve planes carried a 500-pound bomb plus two 100-pound bombs. Fifteen SBDs from Bombing Six then took off, each carrying a 1,000-pound bomb, and climbed to 20,000 feet to wait for the arrival of the carrier's ten fighters and fourteen torpedo bombers. An unexpected delay in launching the remainder of the planes was due to the repair of a TBD engine, and this led Spruance to give the order for all of the SBDs to depart from the area and head to their target without the torpedo bombers and fighters. The SBDs flew to the southwest at a heading of 231 degrees. At about 0800, the last TBD lifted off from *Enterprise* and headed to the Kido Butai on a heading of 240 degrees. The entire *Enterprise* contingency of aircraft on the mission consisted of ten F4Fs, thirty-three SBDs and fourteen TBDs, for a total of fifty-seven aircraft.[70]

On the way to their target, the fourteen torpedo bombers (VT-6), under the command of Lieutenant Commander Eugene Lindsey, broke up into two sections, each with seven planes. Similar to VT-8, the TBD-1s were manned by only a pilot and a gunner/radioman. The planes were flying to the Kido Butai without fighter support (VF-6) as James Gray mistakenly covered VT-8 earlier that morning. Lindsey, like Waldron, flew directly to the target and, like Waldron, the contingent of SBDs from *Enterprise* were not with the TBDs, as they had departed earlier and were on a different course to the target. At 0930, Lindsey became aware of smoke in the distance off his starboard wing and soon saw the wakes of numerous ships to the north by northwest. Lindsey would have missed the Kido Butai had it not been for Waldron's squadron, for in the VT-8 attack, the Japanese carriers were forced to take evasive action and lay down a smoke screen to hide and protect the Kido Butai. It was precisely the smoke

5. The Battle of Midway Begins

screen that drew Lindsey's attention to the Japanese task force. Thus, Waldron's group was responsible for Lindsey's planes finding the Japanese carriers.[71]

Lindsey, VT-6's skipper, observed only three Japanese carriers scattered in the distance. He tried unsuccessfully to contact McClusky, and running low on fuel, he decided to attack the Japanese carriers alone. *Kaga* was the closest carrier, and Lindsey, turning his squadron due north, divided his group in two so that the target could be attacked from both sides. At 0938, about thirty Zeroes were overhead of the Japanese carriers, five of which were in the process of landing. A warning shot by heavy cruiser *Tone* alerted the Zeroes to the new attack by *Enterprise*'s torpedo bombers, approaching *Kaga* from the south. *Akagi* then reinforced the CAP by launching six Zeroes. The U.S. torpedo planes, flying at only 100 knots, seemed to close in on *Kaga* at a very slow pace.

Lieutenant Arthur Ely, leading the second section, dropped his planes down to sea level, flying just above the waves in order to gain speed. Lindsey, meanwhile, was having trouble reaching *Kaga*'s port bow.[72]

James Gray, flying at 22,000 feet on the far side of the Kido Butai, was now running low on fuel, having been in the air for almost an hour. Both Lindsey and Ely tried to reach Gray for help but received no answer. This time all aircraft involved from *Enterprise* were using *Enterprise*'s radio frequency. Gray later justified his decision to apparently not answer either Lindsey or Ely by stating that his fighter squadron was low on fuel and therefore was not capable of engaging in any dogfight which would quickly use up his squadron's remaining fuel, meaning that all his fighters would wind up in the water. At 0952, Gray decided to radio Spruance to report the presence of two Japanese carriers, two battleships, and six destroyers. This was the first message that Spruance had received since Task Force 16 launched its planes. At 1000, Gray decided to leave the area and head back to *Enterprise*. He also felt that his squadron represented one-third of *Enterprise*'s fighter strength and that his planes would be needed to defend the carrier against a Japanese air attack. Before he left, he tried once again to reach McClusky, but to no avail.[73]

About twenty miles to the west, VT-6 was engaged in a deadly struggle with the Japanese CAP. Ely again tried to reach Gray but failed. His section was under heavy attack by Japanese Zeroes. Five of the seven TBDs from the second section were shot down, including Ely's TBD.

The two remaining aircraft were able to head back to *Enterprise*. Lindsey's first section was now facing *Kaga*'s stern, as the carrier had turned around. Nearing *Kaga*, Lindsey's section was pounded upon by Zero fighters, resulting in Lindsey again calling Gray several times for assistance, but again there was no reply. The aircraft of the first section of VT-6 fought back as best they could. However, only three planes survived the onslaught and were able to head back to *Enterprise*. In the attack, five or six torpedoes were launched by VT-6, but the unreliability of the American torpedo and skillful handling of the Japanese carriers by their commanders assured that no hits occurred. At 1015, the attack was over. Of a total of five TBDs that survived the attack, four planes returned, one of which was discarded overboard the next day due to numerous bullet holes, and the fifth plane was ditched into the sea on its way back to *Enterprise*. It took seventeen days for Machinist Albert Winchell and Gunner/Radioman Third Class Douglas Cossett to be rescued by a PBY, which discovered their raft on the open sea.[74]

All the aircraft from *Yorktown*, including the TBDs, followed a course that took them directly to the Kido Butai in just over one hour. *Hornet*'s TBDs took one and a half hours, and *Enterprise*'s TBDs required one hour and forty minutes to reach the Japanese carriers. The crews of VT-3 torpedo bombers were the first to spot the Kido Butai, again as a result of the black smoke laid down by the Japanese screening ships. The leader of the torpedo squadron, Massey brought his group down from 2,500 feet to 150 feet above the water. A few moments later, Lieutenant Commander Maxwell Leslie, leader of VB-3 dive-bombers, spotted the Japanese carriers and asked Massey if he was ready to begin a coordinated attack. Massey replied in the affirmative. Suddenly Massey's squadron was attacked by Japanese Zeroes so that he had to immediately make his run on the Japanese carriers, thus ending any thought of a coordinated attack.

At this time, the Zeroes in the air had fought off two U.S. torpedo attacks, one from the northeast and one from the south, in the course of an hour and were low on ammunition as they approached the third squadron of U.S. torpedo planes, which was also flying in from the northeast.

James Thach had only six F4Fs with him, and so he was not able to effectively implement the Thach weave, which required the F4F fighters to operate in groups of four. Thus, Thach made up one group of four and directed Warrant Officer Tom Cheek to protect the rear of the torpedo bombers as Thach's group would maintain his present altitude—5,500 feet above them. Every Zero from all four carriers was now in the sky, a total of forty-two fighters. The numbers of Japanese Zeroes permitted the Japanese fighters to attack both the U.S. fighters and the torpedo bombers. *Yorktown*'s six F4F fighters were overwhelmed, and one of the U.S. fighters in Thach's group was immediately shot down. In the ensuing dogfight between the Zeroes and the remaining five U.S. fighters, Thach and his men were unable to protect VT-5's torpedo bombers because the five remaining U.S. fighters were too engaged with the great number of Zeroes attacking them.[75]

After departing from *Enterprise* at 0745, Lieutenant Commander Wade McClusky, commander of *Enterprise*'s air group of thirty-three SBD dive-bombers, flew on a southwesterly course.

McClusky was flying with Lieutenant Wilmer Gallaher's Scouting Six's seventeen dive-bombers, with two of those aircraft acting as wingmen for McClusky. One aircraft from Scouting Six developed mechanical difficulties and had to return to *Enterprise*; the remaining thirty-two SBDs continued on their mission. At 0920, McClusky's group arrived over the area where he believed the Kido Butai should be located, but the sea was devoid of any ships.

Seventy miles to the north, Waldron was directing his torpedo group to attack the Kido Butai over the radio, but his transmissions were not heard by any of the radiomen of McClusky's dive-bombers. A number of the aircrafts' fuel gauges were already past the halfway mark, due to their prolonged circling over *Enterprise* while the SBDs waited for the others to take off and due to the consumption of fuel utilized in their long climb to 20,000 feet. Had Spruance not ordered McClusky's group to depart independently at 0745, McClusky's search for the Kido Butai would have ended before he sighted the Kido Butai for lack of fuel. Now, McClusky was willing to risk the loss of some of his aircraft due to the shortage of fuel in order to continue the search for the Japanese carriers. He veered the group to a course that was due west for thirty-five miles and, finding no sign of the Kido Butai, turned his group of planes to the northwest, conducting a modified box search. In the process, two of the dive-bombers in Bombing Six's group ran out of fuel and headed toward the sea. One crew of the downed planes was later rescued, but the other aircraft was never found.[76]

At 0955, McClusky noticed a lone ship (*Arashi*) heading northeast at high speed (thirty-five knots), its wake leaving a telltale sign for McClusky to follow. Deducing that the ship was heading back to its task force, McClusky turned the squadron north by northeast where, ten minutes later, he came upon the Kido Butai.

Machinist Tom F. Cheek, USN, VF-3 (courtesy Tom Cheek and the International Midway Memorial Foundation).

When Lieutenant Richard Best's (leader of Bombing Six) wingman ran out of oxygen, Best brought the fifteen SBD dive-bombers down to an altitude of 15,000 where the men could breathe more easily. This action placed Best's squadron below Scouting Six and 1,250 feet behind them.[77]

Nautilus, one of the ten submarines that was directed by Nimitz to survey the waters north and west of Midway, had been making every attempt to attack the Kido Butai but was repulsed by a Japanese cruiser and destroyer. The submarine was over 350 feet long and displaced 2,700 tons.

Nautilus had two large six-inch guns, one located aft and the other on the foredeck. The ship held thirty-six torpedoes which could be released from any of its ten torpedo tubes. One must remember that the Mark 14 torpedo still had a flawed detonation mechanism. *Nautilus* was to play a critical role in the Battle of Midway by virtue of its persistent tactics against an aggressive defensive posture posed by the Japanese Navy. The Japanese destroyer *Arashi* kept the submarine at bay beneath the waves by repeatedly dropping depth charges on the vessel. This action prevented *Nautilus* from firing any torpedoes. While *Arashi* was dropping depth charges on the submarine, the Kido

Butai was actually moving closer to *Nautilus*. When *Arashi* moved away from the area, Lieutenant Commander William Brackman brought the submarine up to periscope depth and realized that now he was right in the middle of the entire Japanese task force. Brockman's periscope was detected by battleship *Kirishima*, which fired on the submarine as *Arashi* came speedily back to the area occupied by *Nautilus*. Brockman fired two torpedoes at *Kirishima*, but the first tube did not fire and the fate of the second torpedo was unknown. He then brought the submarine down to 150 feet.

Brockman continued to stay at this depth for forty minutes to avoid being detected by Commander Watanabe Yasumasa, Commander of the Japanese destroyer *Arashi*. At 0917, and while *Nautilus* was again under attack by *Arashi*, Nagumo changed course and headed north.

Kirishima and all the other big ships in the task force moved away, leaving only *Arashi* behind to deal with *Nautilus*. The submarine used this opportunity to fire a torpedo at *Arashi*, but its skipper easily avoided the torpedo. Brockman, then still submerged, silently changed course and left the area. *Arashi* had dogged *Nautilus* for two hours (0800–1000) and had dropped at least twenty-eight depth charges. Watanabe decided the Kido Butai was now far away to the northeast from *Nautilus* and that the U.S. submarine could do no harm. As a result, he ceased his attacks on the submarine and headed back to the task force at a full speed of thirty-five knots. This action resulted in a wide V-shaped wake that could be seen for miles.[78]

At 1002, at the same time that *Nautilus* was free of *Arashi*, Massey's torpedo bombers were undergoing an attack by over thirty Zeroes in their sector. Thach's fighter support and the fact that Massey lowered his altitude permitted VT-5 to almost get past the first pass by the Zeroes, and only the tail end TBD of the squadron was lost in the attack. The TBD burst into flames and headed toward the sea. Its pilot, Ensign Wesley Osmus, was able to bail out, but his gunner/radioman, Aviation Radioman Third Class Benjamin Dodson, Jr., was unable to extricate himself from the plane.

Osmus, who failed to secure his raft from the crippled aircraft, was found by the crew of *Arashi* swimming alone in the water. The destroyer then picked him up and headed back to rejoin the Kido Butai.[79]

After the first wave of Zero fighters made their pass, Massey continued to press on toward *Hiryu*, which was now closest to his formation. The Japanese CAP had now been increased by fresh Zeroes from *Soryu*, bringing their numbers now in the air to forty. When VT-3 was about two miles from *Hiryu*, the Japanese fighters began a vicious attack on Massey's squadron. Of the twelve original torpedo bombers, only five TBDs got through the Japanese gauntlet to continue their attack on *Hiryu*. The seven planes lost along the way included the TBD belonging to Massey. The remaining five aircraft continued on toward *Hiryu*, but only two TBDs survived the attack on that ship. Of a total of twelve original torpedo planes, only two were able to head back to *Yorktown*. One TBD, whose pilot was Radio Electrician William Esders, his radioman/gunner Aviation Radioman Second Class Robert Brazier, ran out of fuel before reaching the carrier and headed into the sea. Esders was able to get the severely wounded Brazier into the raft, but the radioman/gunner died shortly thereafter. Esders was picked up the next day by destroyer *Hammann*.

Another TBD, whose crew consisted of pilot Machinist Harry Corl with radioman/

gunner Aviation Radioman Third Class Lloyd Childers, was somehow able to survive the Zeroes' attack and headed back to *Yorktown*. However, Childers's plane also ran out of gas, and the aircraft ditched into the sea before reaching its carrier.[80]

Analysis

Of the forty-one torpedo bombers from the three American carriers *Enterprise* (fourteen TBDs), *Hornet* (fifteen TBDs) and *Yorktown* (twelve TBDs), only four torpedo planes, all from *Enterprise*, made it safely back to their carrier. Three torpedo bombers (one TBD from *Enterprise* and two TBDs from *Yorktown*) ran out of fuel attempting to reach their carriers; fortunately, most of their crews were rescued. In summary, none of the *Hornet*'s and *Yorktown*'s torpedo bombers returned safely to their carriers. Of the four torpedo bombers from *Enterprise*, one was so badly damaged by bullet holes that it was deemed expendable and was discarded overboard. The loss of thirty-eight of the forty-one torpedo bombers from all three U.S. carriers was not rewarded with even one direct hit on any Japanese carrier. At 1015, all the aircraft hurled at the Kido Butai from Midway and all the torpedo bombers from all three American carriers had not inflicted any damage to the Japanese Navy at Midway. This is not to say that the U.S. torpedo bombers did not play a significant role in the outcome of the Battle of Midway.

Radio Electrician Wilhelm G. Esders, USN, VT-3 (courtesy Wilhelm G. Esders and the International Midway Memorial Foundation).

What the foregoing demonstrates is that, as important as U.S. intelligence was for creating an opportunity for the Americans to obtain a decisive victory against the Japanese Navy at Midway, it still required execution of a plan and good fortune to bring this objective to fruition. In spite of repeated air attacks from Midway and from three U.S. carrier torpedo squadrons, not one hit was inflicted on any of the ships in the Kido Butai. Fate would now have to intervene for the Americans to achieve a decisive victory at Midway.

Fate is an interesting phenomenon in that it is a series of seemingly unrelated events that are linked together to produce an end result. One could conclude that fate at Midway produced a miracle, because the sequence of events in the battle led to an extraordinary result; that is, the carrier planes from *Enterprise* and *Yorktown* independently arrived on the scene of the battle at the same time, creating an uncoordinated

coordinated attack, which led to the subsequent destruction of three Japanese carriers. Parshall and Tully, in their book *Shattered Sword*, devote a number of pages to declaring that Midway was not a miracle against overwhelming Japanese odds, and to an extent that is a true statement. As was previously discussed, what is not true is that a miracle did not occur at Midway. At 1015, the Japanese Navy was able to resist every air attack the United States could throw against it. It tactically outnumbered the Americans at this time by a 2:1 margin as a result of the loss of two-thirds of *Hornet*'s aircraft and because of the failure of many of the planes that originated from Midway. It is also true that only half of *Yorktown*'s dive-bombers and fighters and all of its torpedo bombers had attacked the Kido Butai.

Enterprise's SBDs, under McClusky, were low on gas and had not yet located the Japanese carriers. At this moment, a culmination of seemingly unrelated events came together to produce an astonishing result. The first unrelated event revolves around Admiral Spruance, who gave the order at 0745 to no longer restrain *Enterprise*'s SBDs from leaving the area by ordering the planes to proceed toward the target. Up to this time, he had kept the SBDs from departing until the torpedo bombers and fighters were airborne so that all the squadrons of aircraft could leave together. If Spruance had not made that decision, McClusky's dive-bombers would have been forced to end their search for the Kido Butai when they found the sea empty at the designated navigational coordinates because their low fuel reserves would have been exhausted from waiting around for the remainder of *Enterprise*'s aircraft. The second unrelated event was the persistence of *Nautilus* actions in trying to attack the ships of the Kido Butai. *Nautilus*'s aggressiveness led to *Arashi* being assigned to stay behind with the submarine as the Kido Butai moved away to the north. As a result, McClusky was able to spot the destroyer's wake and follow it back to the Kido Butai. In the absence of this occurrence, *Yorktown*'s seventeen SBDs, six fighters and twelve torpedo bombers would have been the only aircraft available for the attack on the Japanese carrier force. The third unrelated event was the fact that, although *Enterprise*'s dive-bombers took off a little over one hour earlier (0745) than *Yorktown*'s dive-bombers (0900), all of the SBDs from both carriers arrived at the target within minutes of each other. This astonishing occurrence allowed an uncoordinated coordinated attack to play out against the Japanese carriers by both U.S. carrier groups of dive-bombers and *Yorktown*'s torpedo bombers. While VT-3 torpedo bombers were not actually synchronized in their attack with its dive-bombers, the net result was the same, as their assault on *Hiryu* kept Japan's CAP down at sea level and allowed the SBDs of both *Enterprise* and *Yorktown* to dive down on the Kido Butai unmolested. Thus, it was a miracle (fate) that played a pivotal role in America's victory at Midway, justifying the titles of Walter Lord's *Incredible Victory* and Gordon Prange's *Miracle at Midway*. The turning point of the battle was about to unfold.

6

The Turning Point

At 1010, due to the recurrent attacks by torpedo bombers during the previous forty-five minutes, the well-integrated Japanese carrier box formation no longer existed. Each carrier had to move independently in order to avoid the American torpedo attacks. *Kaga* was now the southernmost carrier and the first one seen by McClusky's group of dive-bombers. Two miles north and about seven miles to starboard was *Akagi*, fourteen miles to the north was *Hiryu*, and twenty miles away and almost unseen was *Soryu*.[1]

Yorktown's dive-bombers arrived at the same time as *Enterprise* by coincidence: McClusky's (CV-6) group coming from the south and Leslie's (CV-5) group from the east were on their way to their targets. Leslie's group attacked *Soryu*, which was nearest to him, and McClusky's planes attacked *Kaga* and *Akagi*, which were nearest to his aircraft. It was U.S. naval doctrine that each squadron of dive-bombers would attack a different capital ship. Ordinarily, the lead squadron (VS-6) of SBDs, under the command of Gallaher, would strike the carrier that was most distant (*Akagi*), while Best's rear squadron (VB-6) would attack the carrier that was nearest (*Kaga*). This would leave Best's squadron of SBDs carrying the heavier 1,000-pound bomb ordnance to attack the nearest carrier *Kaga*. Lieutenant Richard Best, who commanded the rear squadron (VB-6), assumed the doctrine would be followed by Gallaher. McClusky saw the two carriers not as north and south of each other but rather as east and west. McClusky could not give hand signals to Best who was 5,000 feet below him, so he went on the radio and told Gallaher to attack *Kaga* and Best to attack *Akagi*. Best never heard the order and proceeded to attack *Kaga*, which was the nearest carrier to his plane. Unknown to Best was the fact that the Gallaher squadron was a mile above him and preparing to dive down on *Kaga* as ordered by McClusky.

The sixteen SBDs of Gallaher and the McClusky aircraft came diving down past Best just as he was preparing to push over. A massive collision of all planes involved was avoided by a matter of a short distance. Best was able to reverse his attempt to begin his dive on *Kaga*, but ten aircraft of his group (VB-6) joined in on the attack on *Kaga*. As a result, a total of twenty-seven SBDs attacked *Kaga*. Only Best and his wingmen, Lieutenant (jg) Bud Kroger and Ensign Fred Weber, would attack *Akagi*.[2]

At 1010, the Japanese had thirty-five Zeroes in the air: fourteen were flying patrol close to all four carriers, and the other twenty-one were either chasing VT-6 torpedo bombers to the southeast or lingering in that area. At 1015, *Soryu* and *Hiryu* launched three fighters each, bringing the total CAP in the air to forty-one. Most of the CAP

113

stationed away from the carriers were now pursuing the twelve torpedo bombers from *Yorktown*. There were reasons why it happened that the Japanese concentrated their CAP in the vicinity of VT-3 and left the skies at higher altitudes unguarded. One reason, as explained in a previous chapter, was that the CAP was under the supervision of four independent air officers on each carrier, who rarely communicated with each other, with the result that the Zeroes were randomly directed to a particular vector site as they saw fit. Another reason was that the lack of radar, which the Americans had on board all three carriers (*Enterprise* and *Yorktown* had the latest CXAM radar, while *Hornet* had SC radar, an earlier form of radar), was extremely costly to the Japanese in the Battle of Midway. Its absence denied the Japanese the ability to be forewarned of the presence and the direction of incoming enemy aircraft while the aircraft were miles from their target. Not having radar blindsided the Japanese to the incoming dive-bombers from *Enterprise* and *Yorktown*. Thus, they were not able to direct any of their CAP to the SBDs' sectors of arrival before the U.S. planes reached their destination. The Japanese CAP was fixated on VT-3 because the Japanese feared the torpedo bomber more than the dive-bomber. In addition, the slow speed of the U.S. torpedo bomber resulted in all the dive-bombers from *Yorktown* and *Enterprise* completing their attacks before VT-3 had finished its torpedo run against *Hiryu*. In addition, the Japanese used only one radio frequency and had faulty radios in their aircraft, which limited communication to and among their planes, thus impairing the CAP in its defense of the Japanese carriers. As a result, all the SBDs from both U.S. carriers arrived over the Kido Butai unmolested as they prepared for their dive on the Japanese carriers.[3]

Analysis

The most critical flaw in the Japanese Midway operation was that of including an attack on Midway Atoll in the plan rather than having one mission which was to seek out and destroy the anticipated American carrier response. The inclusion of the invasion on Midway Island in the plan resulted in a serious tactical disadvantage to the Japanese, whereby its carrier aircraft, which were being fully armed and fueled, would be detained in their hangar decks for change of ordnance because their mission was changed from a land target to a sea target. This action alone accounted for the Japanese carriers being placed in a vulnerable position to a U.S. air attack. Fuel lines were not drained or filled with CO_2, and huge amounts of munitions were not placed safely below in the magazines, which would have significantly limited any damage done to the Japanese carriers should they be hit by U.S. dive-bombers. The carrier attack planes on *Soryu* and *Hiryu* were armed with their ordnance in the hangar deck, while the dive-bombers were usually not armed with their bombs until they reached the flight deck. These circumstances alone, more than anything else, ensured the total destruction of the Japanese carrier fleet at Midway. Even *Shokaku* (a carrier similar in size to *Akagi* and *Kaga*) at the Battle of the Coral Sea, in spite of sustaining two direct hits by 1,000-pound bombs from twenty-four SBDs from *Yorktown* and one direct hit from fifteen SBDs from *Lexington*, was never in danger of sinking, in part because its fuel lines had been secured, and its munitions supply had been properly placed in the magazine area.[4] In addition, most of

Shokaku's planes were aloft attacking the American carriers and not on board with their fuel tanks full of gasoline. Thus, *Shokaku*'s fires were quickly extinguished, and no major explosions occurred.

One subject that deserves attention is the fact that all of the Japanese torpedo bombers and dive-bombers were below (in the hangar deck) on all four carriers at the time that VT-3, VB-6, VS-6 and VB-3 (three of the four squadrons on *Yorktown* came from *Saratoga* [CV-3]) arrived at 1010.

This statement is contrary to what Fuchida and Okumiya reported in *Midway*, in which Fuchida states that all of the Japanese strike forces on all four carriers were in the process of bringing up their planes from the hangar to the flight deck. He also states that *Akagi*'s aircraft were warming up their engines on the flight deck in preparation to launch its planes. Five minutes were all that was required to have all of its aircraft airborne. The issue is not why Fuchida wrote this statement but the fact that all aircraft of the strike force were actually below in the hangar deck at the time of the U.S. attack. Proof of this assertion is made from four pieces of evidence. The linchpin of this proof arises from the fact that a Japanese carrier at that time could only land or launch one aircraft at a time, so that no other aircraft could be spotted on the flight deck. The first confirmatory evidence comes from the Japanese war history series (Senshi Sosho) which specifically states that during the U.S. attack on the Kido Butai, all four carriers had their carrier attack aircraft (torpedo bombers) below in the hangar decks and that only fighters were situated on the flight deck.[5] Second was the testimonial of Lieutenant Richard Best, Commander of VB-6, to this author that he saw, prior to his attack, only Zero fighters on the deck of the *Akagi*. Lieutenant Commander Maxwell Leslie, commander of VB-3, observed no planes on the deck of *Soryu*.

Lieutenant Richard H. Best, USN, VB-6 (courtesy Richard H. Best and the International Midway Memorial Foundation).

Third are the reports from the Japanese side, which include Petty Officer First Class Maruyama Taisuke's statement to this author that his carrier attack planes on *Hiryu* were ready for an attack on the U.S. carrier force but were not launched (implying that the attack aircraft were in the hangar deck). He was in the flight ready room of *Hiryu*, and not in his plane on the flight deck, when he learned that *Akagi* was finished, indicating that his aircraft had not yet been brought up to the flight deck. In addition, Warrant Officer Morinaga Takayoshi, pilot of a torpedo bomber from *Kaga*'s squadron of attack planes, stated that only two or three aircraft were on the flight deck of *Kaga* near its stern when the attack occurred. Lastly, keeping in mind that no Japanese aircraft could be spotted while planes were landing or being sent aloft, at 1013, *Hiryu* sent up three Zeroes, and at 1015, *Hiryu* also sent up a shotai of three planes to complement its CAP. Thus, no other aircraft could have been spotted at his time. While it is true that the Japanese had ample time to refuel and rearm all available planes in the contemplated strike force by 0920, the incessant U.S. air torpedo attacks on the Kido Butai caused its CAP to be very active in the defense of the four carriers and as such prevented Nagumo from spotting his aircraft from the hangar deck to the flight deck. This was particularly true because it would take about forty-five minutes for each carrier to spot all the carrier attack aircraft from the hangar deck to the flight deck, and that occurrence would have prevented the ability of each carrier to reinforce the CAP and land aircraft from the CAP that were running out of fuel and ammunition. These conclusions are based on the fact that the Japanese carrier at that time could neither land nor launch aircraft at the same time, which prevented the spotting of aircraft during this time. During the U.S. air attacks from its carrier task forces, the first priority for Japan was the defense of the carriers and not the destruction of the U.S. fleet.

The time was 1019 and *Hiryu* flashed a message to *Kaga* that enemy dive-bombers (VS-6) were overhead *Kaga*. At 1022, *Kaga*'s five-inch guns began to fire aggressively at the incoming dive-bombers which were approaching the carrier at a steep angle. The sixth U.S. SBD in line on the way down was hit and sent spiraling into the sea. *Kaga* had just turned into the wind to launch some of its Zeroes to augment the CAP. The carrier turned hard to starboard in an attempt to avoid the dive-bombers' bombs. However, the pilots of these SBDs were experienced compared to the SBD pilots that flew from Midway and attacked the Kido Butai earlier that morning. The first three dive-bombers' bombs missed the carrier, but the fourth SBD, under the command of Lieutenant Gallaher, dropped his 500-pound bomb on the flight deck near the elevator. The bomb descended to the upper hangar deck where it detonated, causing fire in the berthing compartments. The next two aircraft missed *Kaga*, but the seventh plane released its bomb on the forward elevator where the bomb hit the fighter storage spaces. The force from the explosion knocked out the bridge's window so that control of the carrier had to be mandated to emergency steering from the engine room. A third bomb landed directly on the bridge, making it impossible to control the direction of the ship from above, as many high-ranking officers were killed and a fire began to blaze in the bridge. A fourth bomb landed directly amidships and slightly to port.

The carrier was now going around in a clockwise circle, and it was impossible to tell how many other SBDs had additional hits on the carrier. The initial bomb hits destroyed both the carrier's port and starboard fire mains and the emergency generator which supplied power for *Kaga*'s firefighting equipment and its CO_2 fire suppression system. After the attack, the carrier was virtually devoid of any ability to fight its out-of-control fires.

The major reason for the ultimate demise of *Kaga* was that the hangar deck was littered with various types of ordnance (twenty torpedoes, twenty-eight 800-kilogram bombs and forty 250-kilogram bombs), and bomb carts were just lying around near the hangar bulkheads. In addition, the carrier attack planes were filled with aviation gasoline and armed with torpedoes.

This explosive environment was just waiting to ignite. The ordnance could not be moved to the flight deck to be thrown overboard because the elevators were either destroyed or unusable, and due to the sheer weight of the torpedoes (1,800 pounds), none of this ordnance could be moved.

Kaga's fuel system was unsecured at the time of the U.S. attack, and a number of fuel lines had been ruptured by the bombing attack causing fuel to leak onto the hangar deck's floor. The aircraft on board the hangar deck itself contained over 10,000 gallons of aviation fuel. *Kaga* was exceedingly vulnerable for this explosive situation to ignite.[6]

At 1025, *Soryu* was the next carrier to be hit by U.S. bombs. Lieutenant Commander Leslie of VB-3 began his dive at 14,500 feet and began to strafe the carrier with his .50-caliber machine guns because he, along with three other pilots, had already jettisoned their bombs. This mishap occurred because the pilots in these three aircraft inadvertently dropped their bombs on the way to their target due to a faulty electrical bomb release mechanism. This mishap left only thirteen SBDs from *Yorktown* to attack *Soryu*.[7]

Soryu's hangars had three fireproof bays, but three *Yorktown* pilots from VB-3, beginning with Lieutenant (jg) Paul Holmberg, dropped their 1,000-pound bombs into each one of the fireproof bays. Holmberg's bomb detonated on the starboard side of the upper hangar, where five-inch ammunition lay ready for gun mounts Number 1 and Number 3. Lieutenant Harold Bottomley got the second hit, which descended into the lower hangar deck where *Soryu*'s dive-bombers were located. The subsequent explosions left the carrier without its boilers, and therefore power to operate the ship was lost. A third bomb landed on the Number 4 arresting wire and descended to the upper hangar deck where Type 97 attack aircraft (kankos) were being rearmed after the Midway strike. The bomb created massive fires in the rear of the upper hangar deck. Now the carrier was on fire along the whole length of the ship in both the upper and lower hangar decks.

There was no way for the crew to fight the blaze because the means to combat the fires had been destroyed by the bombs. *Soryu*'s fate was now sealed as fires from bow to stern would lead ultimately to its demise with over 419 Japanese crew members dying in the process.[8]

At 1026, Best rolled over and began his dive on *Akagi*, and at 1,500 feet he released his 1,000-pound bomb at a point near the bridge of the carrier. His bomb destroyed the fireproof curtain between the hangar and the midships elevator, the 4.7-inch ready ammunition lockers on the port side, and, most importantly, the eighteen torpedo bombers fueled and rearmed waiting to be spotted on the flight deck. Initially, the fire was localized, but due to the fact that the hangar deck was full of aircraft fully fueled and armed with ordnance, and the fact that it was not possible to flood the rear magazines due to damage of valves controlling the water system, the fires and explosions got out of control. In addition, Captain Aoki Taijiro, skipper of *Akagi*, was unable to properly operate the CO_2 system which appeared to malfunction due to damage by Best's bomb. Explosions would shortly follow, which would result in fires extending the length of the carrier and its ultimate demise.[9]

At 1040, Best's wingman, Lieutenant (jg) Edwin Kroeger, followed Best down to *Akagi* and dropped his bomb on the port edge of the flight deck forward of the midships elevator. The bomb exploded in the sea near the side of the carrier. The other wingman,

Ensign Fred Weber, followed Kroeger down and released his bomb, which landed on or near the port side of the stern of *Akagi*.

In *A Glorious Day in Our History*, Robert Cressman et al. reported that Weber's 1,000-pound bomb landed among *Akagi*'s Type 97 carrier attack aircraft (torpedo bombers) and destroyed the water mains and jammed the carrier's rudder. On the other hand, Parshall and Tully reported in *Shattered Sword* that Weber's bomb was a near miss, just off the port side of *Akagi*'s stern. They believe the more reasonable explanation of the carrier's rudder jamming was due to huge shock waves sent through the carrier's hull structure, fixing the rudder in a thirty-degree attitude, oriented to the starboard position. It was difficult for them to believe that a bomb that hit the flight deck near the stern would affect the rudder, which was located in the bowels of the ship. The interpretation by Parshall and Tully seems to be a more plausible explanation as to why Captain Aoki's order at 1042 to change the navigational course of *Akagi* could not be carried out.

The fourth carrier, *Hiryu*, escaped the wrath of the U.S. dive-bombers and avoided the torpedo runs made by VT-3 against the carrier. At 1035, VT-3 was just finishing its torpedo attack against *Hiryu* as the U.S. dive-bombers, having released their ordnance, were trying to leave the area and head back to their respective carriers—*Enterprise* and *Yorktown*.

At 1037, *Kaga* sustained a huge explosion from the combination of massive amounts of leaking aviation fuel from the damaged main fuel lines and the heat and spark of the spreading fires, which ignited the aviation gasoline. This was followed by six more massive explosions, and immediately all the lights on the ship went out. Commander Amagai Takahisa, the Air Officer of *Kaga*, was now in charge of fire control, because all the senior officers above him had been killed. He was an aviator and had little to no experience fighting fires on board a ship or taking charge of serious inflammatory situations. His lack of experience did little to assist the firefighters in their attempt to control the fires.[10]

At 1043, *Akagi*'s fires, which had been confined to the hangar deck, had now spread to the flight deck. Two Zero fighters, which were unable to get off the flight deck, caught fire and sent plumes of black smoke into the command station. Nagumo's staff encouraged the admiral to leave the carrier, but he refused, in spite of the fact that *Akagi* was motionless in the water, its radios were not functioning and he was no longer capable of commanding the carrier. Finally, under the influence of Rear Admiral Kusaka Ryunosuke, First Air Fleet air command, Nagumo submitted. With all avenues of escape from the bridge blocked by fires, Nagumo and other members of his staff went out of the windows at the front of the bridge on a rope that was secured to the frame of the windows. The group landed first in an area on the front of the island, fourteen feet below them, and then they had to descend another six feet to get to the flight deck itself. The last officer off the bridge, Commander Fuchida Mitsuo, *Akagi* Air Group Commander, was on his way down the line when an explosion knocked him to the flight deck, where he sustained two broken legs and fractures of his ankles and arches. The heat from the fire singed his clothes, and at that point, two sailors picked him up and carried him to the anchor deck on the front of the carrier where Nagumo and others were located. In addition to Nagumo, this group included Kusaka; Fuchida; Lieutenant Commander

6. The Turning Point 119

Nishibayashi, Staff Flag Secretary; and Commander Genda Minoru, Staff Air Officer of the First Fleet, whose hand was burned. The four men were all then transferred to cruiser *Nagara*.[11]

At 1045, *Soryu*'s fires and explosions grew so severe and extensive that Captain Yanagimoto Ryusaku gave the order to abandon ship. Men began jumping into the water, as others were thrown into the water by the explosions on the carrier.[12]

At 1045, Rear Admiral Abe Hiroaki, Commander of Cruiser Division Eight, received a message from heavy cruiser *Chikuma* that Scout Plane 5 had observed five more American cruisers and destroyers about 130 miles from Midway. At 1047, Abe informed Yamamoto of the intelligence as well as the fact that *Akagi*, *Kaga* and *Soryu* were all burning. Included in the message was information that the Kido Butai was retiring to the north and that *Hiryu* was preparing to attack the enemy carriers. Abe proceeded to immediately send an order for Admiral Yamaguchi to attack the enemy carriers.[13]

While Yamamoto's Main Body was engulfed in a dense fog about 600 miles to the west, he received news of the U.S. air attack on the Kido Butai. Yamamoto was stunned by the communication that *Akagi*, *Kaga* and *Soryu* were all ablaze as he returned the message to the chief signalman.

At 1050, when Admiral Yamaguchi received the directive from Admiral Abe, he was already in the process of launching a counteroffensive against the U.S. carrier fleet. The eighteen-dive-bomber group would make up the mainstay of the 1054 strike force and would be under the command of Lieutenant Kobayashi Michio. The Type 99 dive-bombers would be escorted by six Zero fighters. Two-thirds of the dive-bombers were equipped with 250-kilogram semi-armor-piercing bombs, while one-third of the aircraft were carrying 242-kilogram high-explosive land bombs fused for immediate contact detonation. At 1054, *Hiryu* turned into the wind and began launching its aircraft. Four minutes later all the planes were airborne. Yamaguchi then sent a communication to the remaining force that *Hiryu* had just initiated its counteroffensive against U.S. carrier forces.[14]

Analysis

The foregoing narrative is further proof that Fuchida's assertion, in *Midway*, that the Kido Butai had its strike force on the decks of all four carriers, ready to take off, was not true.

If the *Hiryu* strike force had been spotted on its flight deck, it would have begun launching those planes at the latest at 1035, after *Yorktown*'s torpedo bombers had completed their torpedo run against *Hiryu* and the U.S. dive-bombers had left the area. Instead, the dive-bombers did not take off until 1054, almost thirty minutes after the U.S. attack began. This time frame allowed thirty-five minutes for *Hiryu* to bring the eighteen dive-bombers up from the hangar deck to the flight deck, which is what actually took place. Only four minutes were needed to launch the dive-bombers into the air. Notably, the carrier attack planes from the first wave of the Midway strike force were still below in the hangar deck being rearmed and refueled. *Hiryu*'s torpedo bombers were not sent aloft at this time because they were not ready, and it would take about one to two hours before the planes would be refueled and rearmed and ready for combat.

At 1110, Yamaguchi received a message from *Chikuma*'s Number 5 scout plane (which had relieved *Tone*'s scout plane Number 4) that the enemy fleet was only ninety miles away from the Kido Butai. Because the scout plane's pilot had actually discovered Task Force 17 (*Yorktown*) and not Task Force 16 (*Enterprise*), the Japanese were not aware at this time that the Americans had two task forces in the area.

While *Chikuma*'s Number 5 plane was making its report at 1110, *Soryu*'s new reconnaissance bomber Yokosuka D4Y1 (whose maximum speed was 343 miles per hour with a range of 850 nautical miles) was reporting the disposition and location of Task Force 16. However, the new bomber's radio was not working, and it was not until early afternoon that Yamaguchi and Nagumo learned that the Americans had two separate task forces and as many as three carriers.

Yamaguchi steered *Hiryu* on a thirty-degree course toward U.S. carrier forces escorted by only two destroyers as protection against a U.S. submarine attack, because the other destroyers were tied up attending to the burning carriers. The men were still servicing the carrier attack planes which had attacked Midway by rearming the aircraft with torpedoes. Only seven of the carrier attack planes (torpedo bombers) that had attacked Midway were operational, so two (one of the planes was Tomonaga's aircraft) of the returning torpedo bombers were repaired and added to the strike force. A third torpedo plane was added when a torpedo plane from *Akagi* landed on *Hiryu*'s deck because *Akagi* was on fire. Therefore, a total of ten torpedo planes were being made ready to take off *Hiryu* within a one- to two-hour period.[15]

At 1130, Nagumo felt that the remaining ships of the Kido Butai should engage the U.S. carrier forces in a daylight surface action with the significant gun and torpedo arsenal of its surface forces. He reasoned that the enemy force was only ninety miles away, and by closing the distance this option would be possible. First, though, he had to organize the surface ships that had been scattered except for the six destroyers that had been assigned to assist the burning carriers *Akagi*, *Kaga* and *Soryu*.

At 1158, the Kido Butai's surface force was organized and proceeded to the northeast at a speed of twenty-four knots to close the distance to the U.S. carrier fleet. At noon, Nagumo received a message from Vice Admiral Kondo, Commander of the Invasion Force Main Body, who was about 220 miles away, that his force was proceeding to join the Kido Butai at a speed of twenty-eight knots. *Hiryu* at that time was trailing the Nagumo's surface fleet as it headed to the northeast of Midway. At 1110, after flying for a little over an hour, *Chikuma*'s Number 5 search plane, which had relieved *Tone*'s Number 4 search plane, reported that the U.S. fleet, a mere ninety miles away, was withdrawing to the east. As a result, Nagumo gave up on the idea of a daylight surface battle and contemplated a night action. Nagumo was on-board *Nagara*, fearful of U.S. air attacks on *Hiryu*, the Mobile Fleet ordered *Hiryu* to turn around with the Kido Butai and proceed due west. It was at this time that Yamaguchi told Nagumo that he was planning a dusk strike against the U.S. carriers.[16]

As Kondo's Midway Invasion Force was heading to Midway, both Nagumo and Yamaguchi knew that the fleet had no aircraft to supplement *Hiryu*'s depleted airpower. In addition, not only were light carriers *Junyo* and *Ryujo* not included in the Midway operational plan, but no contingency was made that the carriers could provide additional airpower if the operation plan at Midway did not go well. The Aleutian carriers were now located 1,856 miles to the north, and it would take at least several days for the carriers to arrive at Midway.

Analysis

It is clear that Yamaguchi had been conforming to Nagumo's orders as he had before the U.S. attack on *Akagi*, *Kaga* and *Soryu*. Yamaguchi never made the case to Nagumo (or to himself) that after the dive-bombers were launched at 1054 or at the very least at 1250, when ten torpedo planes and six fighters were sent aloft from *Hiryu*, he should retire to the west at high speed.

If he had taken this action, *Hiryu* would have been respectively 235 miles or 150 miles further west and out of range of U.S. planes in the former case and at the outer limits of the SBDs' fuel capability in the latter case. Nagumo, for his part, permitted Yamaguchi to decide the fate of the *Hiryu* and gave no serious thought of trying to preserve the remaining Japanese carrier so as to fight on another day. Even though *Hiryu* had only thirty-seven aircraft on board at 0930—ten fighters, eighteen dive-bombers (kanbaku) and nine carrier attack planes—and twenty-seven CAP fighters (sixty-four aircraft), which now represented only 25 percent of the Kido Butai's original force, Nagumo and Yamaguchi failed to see the wisdom of trying to save *Hiryu* rather than placing the carrier in a vulnerable position where the carrier could be destroyed by U.S. aircraft. Instead, the remaining Japanese carrier *Hiryu* had continued to close the distance to the enemy along with the Japanese surface force, in lieu of retiring to the northwest where its planes still had the capability to reach U.S. forces. This decision would place *Hiryu* in harm's way, as it was now clearly within range (less than ninety miles away) from U.S. dive-bombers.[17]

On the other hand, the Americans had lost twelve fighters, thirty-eight torpedo bombers and twenty-one dive-bombers, a casualty rate of almost 40 percent of the original complement of planes that were launched. *Yorktown*'s seventeen SBDs of Scouting Five were the only effective reserve force present until the returning planes could be recovered and reorganized. These SBDs were spotted on *Yorktown*'s flight deck along with twelve fighters and were waiting for orders to take off. Since the intelligence reports that Fletcher had received (both by Lieutenant Ady at 0535 and at 1115 by one of Gray's fighter pilots) were that only two Japanese carriers had been observed, Fletcher decided that two other Japanese carriers could be lurking northeast of Task Force 17. Accordingly, at 1150 he sent the seventeen SBDs and twelve fighters to search the area northeast of *Yorktown* out to a radius of 200 miles. Even with the current small air force of *Yorktown*'s seventeen dive-bombers and twelve fighters, once the Americans reorganized the returning aircraft, they would have an effective fighting force of more than sixty dive-bombers, compared to the eighteen Japanese dive-bombers heading toward the U.S. carrier fleet. In addition, the United States had all of its carriers intact and thus three flight decks on which to land, compared to only one flight deck for the Japanese.[18]

Akagi, *Kaga* and *Soryu*'s fires continued to rage. At 1135, *Akagi*'s hangar deck was rocked by a very intense explosion. Even so, *Akagi* still had the best (though slim) chance to contain its fires because the carrier suffered only one direct hit which, at least initially, led only to a contained fire. Then the fire began to spread, and although the firefighting crews on *Akagi* fought the spreading flames for nine hours, the fires ultimately won out. *Soryu*, which had sustained three direct hits, was doomed to burn, and *Kaga*, which had been hit four times, was able to move but at a slow rate of only two knots. As its fires burned out of control, *Kaga* continued to be tracked by *Nautilus*.

The major flaw in the Japanese Midway operational plan reared its ugly head once more, that of assigning two missions to the Kido Butai: Midway and destroying the U.S. carrier force. It was this flaw that led to the situation in which the Japanese aircraft were below in the hangar decks being loaded with fuel and ordnance, leaving the Japanese carriers extremely vulnerable to U.S. air attack. It was the presence of aviation fuel and the ordnance on the planes that led to the explosions and fires which were resistant to control by water. Firefighting foam was equally ineffective. Once ignited by the bombs, the fires would burn until all the aviation fuel was consumed, and with that reality the three carriers were doomed to sink to the bottom of the ocean.[19]

At 1032, Kobayashi received a signal from *Chikuma*'s Number 5 plane which would guide the eighteen dive-bombers to the enemy carrier *Yorktown*. Ten minutes later, Kobayashi also received a message from *Hiryu* giving the location of *Yorktown*. Shortly thereafter, having received the signals, Kobayashi lost his fighter cover as the escorting Zeroes dove down on what were initially perceived to be U.S. torpedo planes but in reality were a section of *Enterprise*'s Scouting Six dive-bombers, under the command of Lieutenant Charles Ware, returning to *Enterprise* after successfully bombing *Kaga*. The Zeroes were unable to shoot down any of the American dive-bombers but in the process damaged two Japanese fighters, causing the planes to return to *Hiryu*. One fighter never made it back to the carrier and crash-landed into the sea near *Hiryu*. The other aircraft continued to fly on to *Hiryu*. The remaining four Zeroes then attempted to catch up to the Japanese dive-bombers which were now ahead of them, but were unable to do so. The Japanese dive-bombers were about to begin their attack on *Yorktown*.[20]

Four of *Enterprise*'s dive-bombers never made it back to their carrier as they had run out of fuel, and all four aircraft crashed-landed into the sea. One of the four downed aircraft, piloted by Ensign Frank W. O'Flaherty, had ditched into the sea, and he and his backseat gunner, Aviation Machinist Mate First Class Bruno Gaido, made it into a life raft. Unfortunately, they were picked up out of the water and taken prisoner by the crew from destroyer *Makigumo*. During their interrogation, even though O'Flaherty and Gaido informed the Japanese of details about Midway, they gave little or no intelligence regarding the American carriers. After the interrogation, the Japanese tied weights to their ankles and threw the two Americans overboard to their deaths.[21]

It was now noon and over an hour since Kobayashi took off, and Yamaguchi had not heard from his group leader. Actually, Kobayashi did send two messages to Yamaguchi, but he did not receive them. Ten minutes later, Yamaguchi did receive a signal from a pilot in one of the other dive-bombers in the group—that it was about to attack an enemy carrier. It was obvious to Yamaguchi that since the dive-bomber group came upon *Yorktown* in just over seventy minutes, the two enemy forces could not be that far apart, confirming *Chikuma*'s Number 5 observation that the enemy was only ninety miles away.[22]

At 1152, *Yorktown*'s radar discovered a number of unidentified aircraft approaching the carrier from forty-six miles out. Machinist Tom Cheek (VF-3), returning from his attack on the Kido Butai, had failed to catch the tail-hook wire and crash-landed into the barrier. When Lieutenant Commander Max Leslie's squadron (VB-3) returned from bombing *Soryu*, they were unable to land on *Yorktown* because of Tom Cheek's crash and were ordered to join *Yorktown*'s CAP in their effort to intercept the Japanese dive-bombers. The twenty F4F fighters, which were already in the sky to protect the carrier, had been vectored out to destroy incoming Japanese planes. The carrier's radar played a crucial role in preventing the Japanese dive-bombers from catching *Yorktown* in the vulnerable process of recovering aircraft as well as permitting the carrier to have time to remove aviation gasoline from the fuel lines, secure the watertight doors and dispose of an 800-gallon auxiliary gas tank by discarding it overboard. The Japanese dive-bombers were flying in a formation of two nine-plane chutai. At 1200, Kobayashi spotted the American carrier and reported back to *Hiryu* that he was attacking. U.S. fighters descended upon the incoming Japanese dive-bombers from above and destroyed nine dive-bombers, with two other dive-bombers being forced to release their bombs so that their planes could fly faster. The escorting Zeroes finally joined the melee, and three of the Japanese fighters were lost in the struggle, with the loss of only one American fighter. The remaining seven dive-bombers continued to make their run against *Yorktown*. The carrier was protected by a ring of cruisers and destroyers which provided heavy antiaircraft fire. The first Japanese chutai of three planes approached *Yorktown* from astern. The first dive-bomber was promptly shot down by 1.1-inch machine guns located aft of the carrier's island, just as the dive-bomber released his bomb. The bomb hit the carrier near its midships elevator, creating a twelve-foot hole in the deck. The second kanbaku followed with the same results; this aircraft was shot down by flak as his high-explosive bomb landed close astern resulting in loss of life on the port side of the superstructure deck, aft, and the port quarter of the flight deck. The third dive-bomber, the last plane from the first chutai, also approached *Yorktown* from astern and dropped his bomb alongside the carrier's stern. The plane escaped damage as the aircraft flew away just above the waves.[23]

The four planes from the second chutai now made their run on *Yorktown*'s starboard side. The carrier was still operating at a speed of thirty knots. The first plane missed the carrier with its bomb. The second plane, piloted by Warrant Officer Nakazawa Shimematsu, leader of the second chutai, released his 250-kilogram semi-armor bomb, which struck *Yorktown* directly amidships. Huge amounts of thick black smoke began to rise skyward from the carrier deck, and the carrier's speed slowed down significantly. The third plane, piloted by Warrant Officer Nakagawa Shizo, came in from the starboard bow and landed his 250-kilogram bomb on top of *Yorktown*'s forward elevator. Fires, erupting from the bomb hit, threatened the ship's magazine and forward aviation fuel depot.

However, the carrier's fire crew had already drained its fuel lines and replaced the fuel with inert CO_2 gas so that the threat to the area was minimized. The fourth and last plane dove down on the carrier, but his bomb only achieved a near miss. The attack by the seven dive-bombers from *Hiryu* resulted in three direct hits and two near misses.

At 1211, Kobayashi signaled *Hiryu* that fires were breaking out on the U.S. carrier. Suddenly, his transmission ceased and he was never heard from again. Only five of the original eighteen Japanese dive-bombers made it back to *Hiryu*; its air arm was now only a shell of its former self.

Yet, in spite of the loss of most of the aircraft from *Hiryu* and the presence of two undamaged U.S. carriers (*Enterprise* and *Hornet*), Yamaguchi failed to appreciate the tactical disadvantage the Kido Butai faced and as a result did not recommend to Nagumo that the *Hiryu* pull back to safer waters and out of range of a U.S. air attack. Yamaguchi became resigned to the fact that Nagumo wanted a surface attack against the Americans and that his carrier was just a pawn in the chess match and thus expendable. *Hiryu* continued to close the distance to the enemy with *Nagara* leading the surface force and heading directly into harm's way.[24]

Yorktown's damage-control crews were fighting the fires below the flight deck. Others were in the process of trying to place some of its boilers online, while other crew members covered the holes in the flight deck with steel and wooden beams. The carrier's radar was damaged and not working. At 1324, with repairs underway, Admiral Fletcher transferred his flag to the heavy cruiser *Astoria* by whaleboat.

At 1210, the Kido Butai had only *Chikuma*'s Number 4 plane available for scouting as *Chukuma*'s Number 1 plane was disabled and neither *Tone*'s Number 1 aircraft nor *Tone*'s Number 4 (Amari's plane) were ready to take off. Yamaguchi was still waiting for Tomonaga's ten torpedo planes and six fighters to be made available for action. He anticipated that the planes would be ready to go within the hour. This would set the time at 1330, almost two and one-half hours after the dive-bombers took off. The delay could not be accounted for by the CAP landings and takeoffs, as those aircraft operations ceased at 1134, and the CAP remained in the sky, allowing the attack aircraft to be launched when they were ready. The torpedo bombers, if ready, could have been brought up from the hangar deck to the flight deck within about forty-five minutes after the dive-bombers had been sent aloft. The explanations given for the delay by Parshall and Tully in their book *Shattered Sword* was that *Hiryu*'s hangar crews were either tired or Yamaguchi was hoping to locate and confirm a second target. Another possibility is that the crews were taking time to try to repair Tomonaga's left-wing fuel tank, at which they were unsuccessful. The hangar crews did repair one of the five damaged kankos that returned from Midway and made it operational. This feat increased the number of kankos available for service from eight to nine. The kanko from *Akagi*, which attempted to cover the search route at 1015, turned back (reasons unknown), only to find *Akagi* in flames, so he landed on *Hiryu*. This plane increased the number of Type 97 carrier attack aircraft for the 1330 mission to ten torpedo bombers. The 1330 departure time once again demonstrates that *Hiryu* did not have all its aircraft spotted at 1030, as described by Fuchida and Okumiya in *Midway*.[25]

At 1215, Nagumo was back in command and in communication with his battleships and escorting cruisers and destroyers from his new flagship cruiser *Nagara*. As he attempted to close the distance between the enemy and his own forces, Nagumo stayed in communication with Yamaguchi and *Hiryu*. His hope was for a day surface encounter with U.S. forces. He looked forward to the arrival of Kondo's Second Fleet, which included the small carrier *Zuiho*, but it was not due until the morning. Spruance was clearly not interested in having a daylight or a night surface action so he turned his forces to the north. At 1240, *Chikuma*'s Number 5 scout plane signaled to Nagumo that he had spotted one U.S. carrier, 130 miles from his launch point, which was speeding north at thirty knots. Realizing that the range between the two carrier forces was widening, Nagumo attempted to stay northwest of the U.S. fleet and wait until he learned of the results of *Hiryu*'s air attacks and received further information from his search aircraft before taking any further action. At 1245, he ordered the fleet to turn due north at a speed of twenty knots.[26]

At 1220, Yamamoto had released his tankers and headed south toward Nagumo's force. He ordered Kondo to send part of his forces to bombard Midway. At 1310, Yamamoto, finally postponed the invasion on Midway and Kiska.

Ten minutes earlier, Yamaguchi learned that *Arashi* had picked up out of the water Ensign Wesley Osmus, a torpedo bomber pilot whose plane was shot down by the Japanese CAP when Torpedo Three was on its initial approach to *Hiryu*. In the interrogation on *Arashi* that followed, it was learned that the Americans had not one but three aircraft carriers in the area—*Enterprise*, *Hornet* and *Yorktown*. Osmus then revealed that *Yorktown* was operating independently of the other two carriers. He also informed the Japanese of when *Yorktown* left Pearl Harbor and that all three American carriers were waiting to ambush the Kido Butai. All of this information was passed on to Nagumo and Yamamoto. After the Japanese learned of the new intelligence, the Commander of *Arashi*, Watanabe Yasumasa, ordered the execution of Osmus. When the Japanese took Osmus to the ship's stern to be thrown overboard, he grabbed the railing, and the Japanese took a fire axe to his head to force him to release his grip. His body then plummeted into the sea.[27]

Hiryu, which was steaming east and south of *Nagara* (Nagumo new flagship), continued to stay within eyesight of *Nagara*'s signal lamp, and the carrier was passively following *Nagara*, which was in the lead to the northwest of *Hiryu*. Thus, the last Japanese carrier was positioned as a backup to the battleships and cruisers rather than acting independently on its own with cruisers and destroyers on the periphery providing antiaircraft fire. More importantly, *Hiryu* should have withdrawn miles to the west earlier and out of harm's way of U.S. aircraft.

Nagumo was being kept apprised of *Yorktown* by *Chikuma*'s Number 5 scout plane. He then ordered a five-plane search line to be explored by the shorter-range Nakajima E8N2 Type 95 reconnaissance bi-winged airplane. Each plane was to search out to 150 miles, turn left for thirty miles and then return to the Kido Butai. Two of the five aircraft would be launched from heavy cruiser *Tone* and one each from heavy cruiser *Chikuma* and battleships *Haruna* and *Kirishima*.[28]

At 1315, as the ten torpedo bombers were warming up their engines, the five remaining dive-bombers and one Zero were returning from their attack on *Yorktown*. At the time of the takeoff, it was discovered that the repair crews were not able to seal Tomonaga's left fuel tank, as it was still leaking. It really did not make any difference, for when a Type 97 aircraft was carrying a heavy torpedo, the fifty-six-gallon outboard tank could not be fueled anyway because of the additional weight that the aviation gasoline added to the aircraft. Thus, only the eight-seven-gallon inboard tanks were fueled. With the flight deck spotted with the torpedo bombers, one of the returning dive-bombers flew over the carrier and released a message that gave the enemy position as ninety miles away at a bearing of eighty degrees. The communication also stated that the task force was composed of five heavy cruisers and that the one carrier was left burning. The intelligence was given to Lieutenant Hashimoto Toshio (Tomonaga's radioman/observer). Not knowing that he would not be flying with Tomonaga, Hashimoto did not pass the latest information on the location of *Yorktown* to Tomonaga, as they started out on their mission.[29]

At 1330, the ten torpedo bombers and six fighters were launched, and Tomonaga divided the command into two five-plane chutai, with himself in command of the first chutai and Lieutenant Hashimoto of the second chute. By this time, *Soryu*'s Yokosuka D4Y1 carrier bomber had returned from its reconnaissance mission and was the first plane to land after the torpedo bombers and escort fighters were launched. Previously finding the *Hiryu*'s deck spotted with aircraft at 1310, Iida had dropped a message tube onto *Hiryu*'s deck. With the flight deck now cleared, he proceeded to land his plane. Since the radio messages from the scout plane regarding the location and composition of the American task forces was not received earlier by Kido Butai due to radio problems, Yamaguchi learned for the first time that the American force contained three carriers—*Enterprise*, *Hornet* and *Yorktown* at 1310. This intelligence was consistent with the information learned by the Japanese from Osmus. Following the landing of *Soryu*'s reconnaissance plane, the *Hiryu*'s five dive-bombers and one fighter landed.[30]

Enterprise and *Hornet*, already committed to recovering their own aircraft, now had to recover *Yorktown*'s planes and protect *Yorktown* from Japanese air attacks. At 1209, most of the SBDs from the *flight to nowhere* had landed on *Hornet* except for Lieutenant Robert Johnson's dive-bombers who landed at Midway. These aircraft were refueled on Midway, and they would return to *Hornet* later that afternoon. Ensign Daniel Sheedy, pilot of one of *Yorktown*'s fighters (from Thach's VF-3 group) crash-landed on *Hornet*'s deck and set off his .50-caliber machine guns, which killed three marines and Lieutenant Royal R. Ingersoll, USN, who was the son of Admiral Royal E. Ingersoll, the Commander of the U.S. Atlantic Fleet. From 1200 to 1329, *Hornet* was kept busy recovering and launching aircraft.

By 1210, the last of *Enterprise*'s SBDs had settled down on its flight deck. Best, who had landed on *Enterprise* at about 1210, rushed up to inform Spruance about *Hiryu* but was intercepted by Captain Miles Browning, Spruance's Chief of Staff. Best told him, "There are three carriers aflame but there's a fourth one up to the north." Best recommended that the planes be "rearmed and sent out right away."[31] Before Browning could answer, McClusky arrived to make his report to Browning and Spruance with blood leaking down his arm and onto the flight deck. He had five bullets in his arm and shoulder and was sent immediately to the sick bay. For reasons that are not clear, both Admiral Spruance and Browning were surprised by the news that one Japanese carrier remained untouched to the north. Browning recommended launching immediately with all available planes to Spruance, but Spruance deferred making the decision because he wanted further confirmation of the location of *Hiryu* before sending out any aircraft. Earlier that morning, Browning had given Spruance good advice in delaying the first attack on the Kido Butai until 0700, narrowing the distance between the two enemy forces so that fuel in the attacking aircraft could be conserved.

Yet, at 1404, Spruance signaled Nimitz that he believed that four Japanese carriers were badly damaged, even though Best told Browning that there were three burning Japanese carriers and that the one Japanese carrier to the north was left untouched. So why did Spruance report to Nimitz "all four CV believed to be badly damaged"?[32] Best's after-battle report clearly stated that only three carriers were burning, so why did Spruance not tell Nimitz that there was a fourth undamaged Japanese carrier still out there? Is it possible that Spruance did not believe Best's report that a fourth undamaged Japanese carrier existed, and therefore he would need confirmation by his search planes to determine whether Best was accurate or not?

Seeing black smoke rising on the horizon in the vicinity of *Yorktown*, Admiral Spruance on board *Enterprise* ordered heavy cruisers *Pensacola* and *Vincennes* and destroyers *Balch* and *Benham* to provide any help they could for the disabled *Yorktown*. Fletcher, who was still in a whaleboat, was not able to exert any control over the battle. Spruance, for his part, still had no idea where *Hiryu* was located or if the Japanese had additional carriers in the area.[33]

The Fate of Akagi, Kaga *and* Soryu

Akagi, *Soryu* and *Kaga* continued to burn and were beginning to experience structural damage due to the intense heat and continuing explosions. A number of hand water pumps were established on the anchor deck on the bow of *Akagi*, but without additional power to man the pumps, the fires aboard the carrier could not be contained. *Soryu*'s fires were now out of control.

The fireproof doors had been destroyed, and even the chemical fire extinguishers were not working. Initially, the engine room was functional, but communication lines between the bridge and crews working in the lower levels of the carrier had been severed. As the fires increased, the men working in the bottom of the carrier were overcome by fire and smoke. Not a single man escaped from *Akagi*'s engine room. Captain Aoki Taijiro, skipper of *Akagi*, continued to remain on board, hoping for the best. *Soryu*, which had lost its main engines ten minutes after sustaining three direct bombs by U.S. dive-bombers, was ablaze, and at 1045, Captain Yanagimoto Ryusaku, Commander of *Soryu*, gave the order to abandon ship, but he himself stayed on board the burning carrier to the end. Captain Okada Jisaku replaced *Kaga*'s skipper, Commander Amagai Takahisa, who had died when a bomb landed directly on *Kaga*'s bridge. The carrier, which had been moving very slowly at two knots, had now come to a complete stop because the crew members of its engine room had been consumed by fire and smoke. When the order was given for the engineers to vacate the engine room, they were trapped below and could not get out. Of a total of 323 engineers, 213 would die in the blaze.[34]

Nautilus, which was lurking, spotted *Kaga* dead in the water. At 1359, the submarine attempted to unleash four torpedoes from 2,700 yards away from *Kaga*. The first torpedo never left the submarine tube. The second and third torpedoes ran erratically and missed *Kaga*. The fourth torpedo struck the starboard side, directly in the middle of the carrier, but the contact exploder was either defective or shattered upon contact, and, as a result, no explosion ensued. The heavy part of the torpedo sank immediately, while the after section bobbed up and down in the water.

Nautilus then crash-dived down to over 300 feet to avoid the Japanese depth charges. For over two hours, destroyer *Hagikaze* dropped over eleven depth charges on the submarine, but most of them were set too shallow. However, two depth charges, which were set to 340 feet, bounced off *Nautilus* without detonating—a fortuitous result for the submarine. After dealing with forty-two depth charges from destroyers *Hagikaze* and *Maikaze*, the U.S. submarine was able to escape from the area.[35]

Brockman claimed that his torpedo did strike *Kaga* and sank the carrier. His opinion has been contradicted by multiple accounts on the Japanese side and by the fact that neither *Kaga* nor any other carrier sank at that time. The first of the three carriers to sink was *Kaga*, but it did not go down until 1925 on June 4.[36]

At 1355, Nagumo received a signal from one of *Haruna*'s scout planes that at 1240 the enemy was observed ninety degrees to port and consisted of five carriers and five heavy cruisers. Nagumo placed a question mark alongside the number five in his war diary.

At 1409, *Chikuma*'s Number 5 scout plane (E13A1), which had been observing *Enterprise*, was attacked by two F4Fs, and their .50-caliber machine guns caused the scout plane to explode in midair. One crew member was able to bail out, but he was never seen again.[37]

At 1420, the Kido Butai was approached by two SBDs, which were part of a ten-plane squadron from VS-5 that were sent by *Yorktown* to observe the results of the morning's SBD (VB-3) attack on the enemy carriers. At 1430, Lieutenant Samuel Adams observed the wakes of the remnants of the Kido Butai. The lieutenant immediately reported his findings back to Fletcher in plain English that a lone carrier was seen some 100 miles from his original point of departure from *Yorktown*. He also commented that the Japanese had divided up into two groups, a carrier force and a surface force. Adams, however, erroneously reported *Hiryu* thirty-eight miles west from where it was actually located. The decision by Nagumo and Yamaguchi to keep the carrier close to Nagumo's surface force rather than have *Hiryu* retreat to the northwest at 1057 made it possible for Adams to have discovered *Hiryu* and subject the carrier to assault by U.S. aircraft later in the day. With the discovery of his forces by the Americans, Nagumo changed the disposition of the task forces by placing *Hiryu* in the center of the formation, flanked on the starboard side by heavy cruisers *Tone* and *Chikuma* and on the port side by battleships *Kirishima* and *Haruna*, with *Nagara* leading the group as it continued to steam northeast and into harm's way.[38]

At 1355, *Yorktown*'s radar (recently repaired) detected ten Japanese torpedo bombers and six fighters closing in on *Yorktown* from a north-northwest direction, over thirty-five miles away. *Yorktown*'s repair crew had worked tirelessly to restore the carrier's boilers, and at 1350, the ship could make twenty knots. The carrier, after makeshift repairs of its flight deck with wooden beams and steel plates, now had the ability to launch its fighters (CAP). It was important that its radar was now repaired from its damage from the earlier attack by Kobayashi dive-bombers.

6. The Turning Point 129

Radar was a key factor in protecting *Yorktown* from enemy air attack because it enabled the Americans to detect the Japanese aircraft over thirty miles away from the carrier and vector out the CAP in that direction. Four of the six airborne F4Fs were already directed out to intercept the incoming Japanese aircraft. *Yorktown* immediately ceased its fueling operations and purged its fuel lines with CO_2. None of the ten fighters spotted on its flight deck had more than twenty-five gallons of fuel in its tanks. Eight of the ten fighters on *Yorktown* were readied for takeoff, as Task Force 16 sent eight of its F4Fs to act as a CAP over *Yorktown*, reserving seven of its fighters to function as a CAP for Task Force 16. At 1428, the Japanese torpedo bombers were fifteen miles away from Task Force 17 and closing.[39]

At 1426, Tomonaga radioed back to *Hiryu* that he was about to attack the American task force. Discovery of the U.S. task force was relatively easy as Tomonaga flew east and ran right into the U.S. fleet. *Yorktown*, they observed, was not on fire and was moving at a speed of about twenty knots. Tomonaga logically thought that this carrier could not be the same one damaged by Kobayashi hours earlier. As the two shotai (consisting of five planes each) approached *Yorktown*, a heavy barrage of antiaircraft fire opened up from its escort vessels. The antiaircraft fire was especially intense because of the addition of heavy cruisers *Pensacola* and *Vincennes* and destroyers *Benham* and *Balch*, which were sent over to Task Force 17 by Spruance a few hours earlier. Tomonaga now divided his squadron further into four sections to dissipate the effectiveness of the

CV-5 (*Yorktown*) hit by three bombs, June 4, 1942 (photo 80-G-312018, courtesy Naval History and Heritage Command).

Yorktown's flight deck, June 4, 1942 (photo 80-G-312021, courtesy Naval History and Heritage Command).

enemy CAP and the antiaircraft fire directed at them. At 1434, Tomonaga's squadron began to make its run. Minutes later, his squadron was intercepted by two fighters from CV-5 that were already airborne. One of the two pilots, Ensign Milton C. Tootle from VF-3 (*Yorktown*), was able to shoot down one of the first shotai's torpedo bombers (kankos), but in the process the pilot was lost to escorting Japanese Zeroes. Tomonaga then ordered observer Hashimoto, leader of the second shotai (the pilot of Hashimoto's plane was Petty Officer First Class Takahashi Toshio), to fly around and attack the carrier from its starboard side, while Tomonaga, leader of the first shotai, attacked the carrier from its port side. Now they were only six miles away from *Yorktown* and nearing the inside of Task Force 17's defense perimeter. Tomonaga realized that the carrier now was presenting its stern to him, which was an unfavorable tactical position for him to attack the ship. He therefore divided the first shotai further into two groups; two aircraft flew off to the left to attack *Yorktown* from its port side, while his wingman and he flew to approach the carrier from its starboard side. The eight F4F fighters, just launched from *Yorktown*, joined *Enterprise*'s CAP fighters which had just arrived on the scene.[40] Lieutenant *Jimmy* Thach, leader of the VF-3 (*Yorktown*) fighters, immediately sought out Tomonaga's aircraft and set his left wing on fire, but before Tomonaga went into

CV-5 (*Yorktown*) radar antennae, June 4, 1942 (photo 80-G-312018-A, courtesy Naval History and Heritage Command).

the sea, he skillfully released his torpedo at *Yorktown*—however, his "fish" missed *Yorktown*. Tomonaga's wingman was also able to drop his torpedo, but he too missed his target. As his torpedo plane (kanko) was flying away from the American fleet and heading back to *Hiryu*, he ran into three F4Fs from CV-6 and was quickly shot down. The two Nakajima B5N2 Type 97 torpedo bombers (kankos) from the first shotai flying around to the port side were also shot down by *Yorktown*'s F4Fs. Although one of the two Japanese torpedo bombers was able to drop its torpedo before the plane exploded in midair near *Yorktown*, the torpedo missed its mark. The plane was hit either by one of the F4Fs' .50-caliber machine-gun fire or possibly by the carrier's antiaircraft flak. Thus, all five aircraft of the first shotai were unable to inflict any damage on *Yorktown*.[41]

As the five kankos (torpedo bombers) led by Hashimoto approached *Yorktown* in a V formation, it began to make its run. Hashimoto's plane missed with its torpedo as it crossed *Yorktown*'s bow and headed southeast. One of the other four remaining

CV-5 (*Yorktown*) listing, June 4, 1942 (photo 80-G-170061, courtesy Naval History and Heritage Command).

torpedo bombers was from *Akagi*, and its observer, Warrant Officer Nishimori Susumu, was unable to release his torpedo because of a malfunction of his torpedo release gear. Thus, only three carrier attack planes were left to strike *Yorktown*.

The remaining three carrier attack planes headed toward the carrier and released their torpedoes. One of the three kankos came close enough to the carrier that the gunner in the aircraft could be seen shaking his fist at U.S. sailors—the Americans returned the gesture.

At 1423, the first torpedo struck the carrier on the port side, fifteen feet below the water line, resulting in the carrier listing six degrees to port. Although nine of her boilers were disabled in the forward generator room, *Yorktown* was still able to maintain some movement. Moments later, a second successful strike was made by a Japanese carrier attack aircraft. The torpedo struck close to where the first torpedo hit, creating a huge sixty-by-thirty-foot hole on the carrier's port side. The entrance of sea water totally knocked out all the boilers, with a resultant loss of all power. The backup generators also failed, and the ship became dark. The carrier became motionless in the water with a twenty-six-degree list. Without power, the fire hoses became useless, and counter-flooding was impossible. At 1455, with conditions as they were, Captain Buckmaster ordered the ship to be abandoned. The sailors proceeded from the carrier in an orderly manner as they descended down ropes into the water. The neighboring destroyers picked up some 2,280 men. Captain Buckmaster was the last one off the carrier, but only after touring the areas that were not flooded to make sure that no one was left behind. With the list now at thirty degrees, the hangar deck was close to the water, so he entered the water and swam away. He was soon rescued by a destroyer and taken to heavy cruiser *Astoria*, Fletcher's new flagship. Of the ten carrier attack planes that assaulted *Yorktown*, only two aircraft were able to hit their target.[42]

Hiryu's second attack on *Yorktown* had paid the price for its success. Not only was Lieutenant Tomonaga and Lieutenant Mori Shigeru, the leader of *Hiryu*'s fighter squadron, killed, but only five of the ten torpedo bombers (all from the second shotai) survived the attack, as did four Zeroes.

Two of the five returning torpedo bombers and three of the Zeroes were so damaged that the aircraft were questionable as to whether the planes would make it back to *Hiryu* or remain operational for further battle. At 1445, Hashimoto radioed back to *Nagara* the results of the attack on *Yorktown*.

At 1540, the surviving Japanese planes from the torpedo attack on *Yorktown* began landing on *Hiryu*. With the arrival of the five torpedo bombers (two severely damaged) and four fighters (three severely damaged), Nagumo only had five dive-bombers, three torpedo bombers and six fighters available for a dusk attack on the Americans. At 1520, *Tone*'s Number 4 plane (search line number 4) reported that the task force it sighted had six cruisers and six destroyers that preceded a lone U.S. carrier (*Enterprise*) by a distance of twenty miles. The description of a U.S. carrier sailing alone is curious and difficult to explain except that possibly the scout plane did not see the total picture. *Chikuma*'s Number 1 (search line number 5) plane, which had been airborne since 0938, had not signaled back any information to Nagumo because it had been shot down by the enemy CAP.[43] Keep in mind that Nagumo did not become aware that the Americans had three carriers in the area until *Soryu*'s high-speed scout bomber (Yokosuka D3Y1) landed on *Hiryu* at 1335. Up to that time, he had no strong conviction that the Americans had more than a single carrier to the northeast of Midway. Whether Nagumo believed the intelligence (that three U.S. carriers were present northeast of Midway) he received at 1300 from Commander Watanabe, who had interrogated Ensign Osmus on *Arashi*, is open to speculation. At 1330, only *Yorktown* was vulnerable to Japanese counterattack, as definitive intelligence on the existence of Task Force 16 was as yet unavailable. With the distance between his carrier force and those of the enemy widening, Nagumo decided

Ensign John "Jack" Crawford, USN (CV-5) (courtesy of Jack Crawford and the International Midway Memorial Foundation).

to cancel his plan for a daytime surface attack with the Americans and ordered the Kido Butai after recovering all of Tomonaga's returning aircraft to retire to the northwest. Nagumo decided he would make a dusk attack on the Americans with his remaining aircraft and then engage the enemy in a night action with his surface ships.

U.S. Plans Second Attack to Sink Hiryu

With news from Lieutenant Samuel Adams (VS-5) that he had spotted *Hiryu* and that the carrier was indeed intact, Spruance now awaited the details of the observation before deciding that one more air attack on the remaining Japanese carrier in the Kido Butai was feasible. The possibility of utilizing the torpedo bombers was out of the question, as the torpedo squadrons from all three carriers had been rendered useless by the Japanese. The air attack would have to be made by dive-bombers—by far the most effective aircraft in the battle. Checking his inventory, Spruance discovered he had eleven dive-bombers from *Enterprise*: four SBDs from Bombing Six and seven SBDs from Scouting Six. There were also fourteen SBDs from VB-3 (*Yorktown*) aboard *Enterprise*, bringing the total available dive-bombers on the carrier to twenty-five aircraft. *Hornet* had thirty-two SBD aircraft, which brought the total number of planes in the second strike force to a total of fifty-seven planes.

At 1445, Spruance received the detailed information he was waiting for from Adams that the enemy was only 110 miles away from *Yorktown*. Spruance immediately requested *Enterprise* and *Hornet* to lift off their available SBDs. *Hornet* was not ready because Mitscher, who had ordered Rodee's VS-8 to be spotted, had just learned that the eleven planes from Ruff Johnson's VB-8 were in the process of returning from Midway and were ready to land on *Hornet*. He therefore reversed his decision to launch the VS-8 SBDs by moving Rodee's aircraft forward so that Johnson's aircraft could land. *Enterprise* began to lift off its planes at 1525. When the twenty-five SBDs were airborne, they climbed to 13,000 feet. Shortly after takeoff, one of the aircraft developed engine trouble and returned to *Enterprise*. The remaining twenty-four planes flew to the target in three squadrons. There were seven VS-6 SBDs from Earl Gallaher's group, four SBDs from Richard Best's VB-6 and fourteen SBDs from Max Leslie's VB-3 group. Leslie did not participate because his plane never made it back to *Yorktown* or to *Enterprise*.

McClusky, who had received multiple bullets to his arm, was unable to fly. Lieutenant Earl Gallaher was made senior man and placed in charge of the group. Gallaher tactically decided, for reasons that are not perfectly clear, to have the ten *Enterprise* planes attack *Hiryu* and the fourteen planes from VB-3 attack the Kido Butai's battleship rather than have all the planes attack the last remaining Japanese carrier—*Hiryu*.[44]

At 1603, *Hornet* finally began to get its SBDs airborne. Sixteen were aloft when two of the aircraft reported engine failure and turned back to *Hornet*. The launching of aircraft came to a halt when the two SBDs landed. Over thirty minutes had been spent in the process, and now it was too late to launch the fourteen remaining SBDs on the flight deck because the first sixteen planes to take off were well on their way. Lieutenant Edgar Stebbins was placed in charge of *Hornet*'s group looking for *Hiryu*.

Yamaguchi had believed that the first and second waves he launched against U.S.

forces had severely damaged two American carriers. Yamaguchi was determined to send off a third wave from *Hiryu* at dusk, even though he had available only four dive-bombers and five torpedo bombers. Lieutenant Hashimoto would be in command of the nine-plane flight. The aircraft were still in the hangar deck and would not be ready for flight until 1730. An attempt was made by Yamaguchi to get the planes to depart earlier, but he deferred when he found that the planes' crews were so tired that they needed stimulant tablets to boost their energy. Yamaguchi also ordered them to have a good meal before they took off. At 1627, thirteen Zeroes circled overhead to provide combat air patrol, which all came from carriers *Soryu*, *Kaga* and *Akagi*. This time the CAP were flying at different altitudes (unlike the low altitudes they were at in the morning) looking for enemy planes. *Hiryu* was now in the center of the task force with the battleships and heavy cruisers on the perimeter providing antiaircraft fire. *Nagara* was in the lead of the task force as the remaining fleet steamed to the northwest.[45]

After flying for about ninety minutes, Gallaher, flying north of the three burning Japanese carriers, spotted the remaining Japanese fleet forty miles away. At 1645, Gallaher brought his strike force of twenty-four planes down from 19,000 feet in anticipation of an attack on *Hiryu*.

He turned the detachment due west so that the assault would come from out of the sun. The thirteen Japanese CAP in the air did not see the Americans until it was too late. This was the second time on that day that the Japanese were caught flat-footed.[46]

At 1701, *Soryu*'s high-speed D4Y1 carrier bomber reconnaissance plane was getting ready to take off from *Hiryu*. The carrier had just made a sharp turn to port at a speed of twenty-four knots.

Chikuma was the first to spot Gallaher's group getting ready to begin its dive on *Hiryu*. Heavy antiaircraft fire from the supporting ships was ineffective because they were located too far away from the dive-bomber attack. The CAP, however, this time were able to destroy two of the twenty-four dive-bombers in their dive-bombing attack on *Hiryu*. The carrier made great evasive turns so that it was a difficult target compared to the other three carriers the Americans attacked earlier. After the first few SBDs missed the carrier, *Yorktown*'s dive-bombers, which were headed toward the battleship *Haruna*, changed their target to *Hiryu*. *Yorktown*'s planes dove in front of Richard Best's *Enterprise* group of four SBDs, causing Best and his SBDs to interrupt their dive and gain altitude. In the process, Japanese Zeroes shot down one of Best's wingmen, Ensign Fred Weber. Best proceeded to begin a second dive on *Hiryu*'s port bow, while Lieutenant Dewitt Shumway's (VB-3) group targeted *Hiryu*'s starboard bow. The first ordnance to strike *Hiryu* was a 1,000-pound bomb, which, delivered by Ensign Richard Jaccard (VS-6), struck the forward elevator. *Enterprise*'s Richard Best, who had delivered the sole bomb on *Akagi* earlier that morning; Lieutenant Norman Kleiss (VS-6), who had a direct bomb hit on *Kaga* that morning; and another unidentified SBD produced four direct hits on *Hiryu*. All of the four 1,000-pound bombs landed forward of the carrier's island, creating a huge crater in her flight deck.[47]

The forward portion of *Hiryu*'s flight deck was blown skyward by the four direct hits and then came down, collapsing upon itself. Severe fires immediately broke out. Nineteen Zeroes, which were stored in the forward hangar deck, exploded on contact.

Although there was less ordnance in the hangar deck at this time compared to the three other Japanese carriers, the impact from the four bombs in igniting the aviation fuel and ordnance in the Zeroes and other aircraft that were present was enough to doom the carrier. Smoke began to enter the engine room ventilators, and the lights went out. *Hiryu*'s engines were unharmed, so Captain Kaku Tomeo ordered the engine room to give him the best possible speed. *Hiryu*'s damage-control crew were quick to respond and were able to use its fire hoses because one of the fire mains was still operational. The carrier steamed ahead at thirty knots in a northwest direction with smoke flowing down the entire length of its flight deck and fires now raging from its bow to its stern. The end of the carrier's life was near.[48]

The other SBDs that took off from *Enterprise* made diving attempts on battleship *Haruna* but were ineffective. At 1720, *Hornet*'s sixteen SBDs arrived and, deciding that bombing *Hiryu* would not produce better results, turned their attention to the heavy cruisers *Tone* and *Chikuma*.

When the SBDs were given an opportunity to inflict some damage to the Kido Butai, they again failed. The record of *Hornet* on June 4, 1942, was that it had all of its torpedo bombers destroyed and its dive-bomber and fighter squadrons depleted—without one hit recorded on any Japanese ship.

Just after Richard Best landed on *Enterprise*, he began to cough up blood. While flying on his mission in the morning, a faulty oxygen bottle expelled caustic soda (sodium hydroxide) into his lungs. Over the next twenty-four hours, his hemoptysis (coughing up blood) continued, and he became acutely ill with a temperature of 103 degrees. He was admitted to the Pearl Harbor Hospital on June 5, 1942, where his chest film revealed an infiltrate in the right upper lobe and increased mottling extending out from the hilus (the triangular location of each lung whereby the pulmonary artery and vein, lymphatics and bronchial tube enter and leave each lung) to the periphery of the lungs. Stomach washings and sputum analysis revealed the tuberculosis organism. He was transferred to Fitzsimons Army General Hospital in Aurora, Colorado, where he received proper treatment for his tuberculosis. Best was hospitalized in Fitzsimons Hospital until September 1943.[49]

Best, sometime in the past, had contracted tuberculosis, which remained in his lungs in an inactive state for years. His accident in the morning with the faulty oxygen bottle permitted the inhaled caustic soda to erode away a tuberculosis granuloma (a benign nodule of chronic inflammatory tissue) which contains an inactive form of the tuberculosis organism. The erosion of the granuloma by the caustic soda transformed the inactive form of the organism into an active form. In addition, the caustic soda caused an aspiration pneumonia. June 4, 1942, was the last day Best would fly for the U.S. Navy.

Best was one of only two pilots who obtained direct hits on two Japanese carriers on June 4, 1942; the other pilot was Lieutenant Norman Kleiss. Kleiss' bombs landed on *Kaga* and *Hiryu*, and Best's bombs struck *Akagi* and *Hiryu*. However, Best's direct hit on *Akagi* (while he had active tuberculosis) was solely responsible for its ultimate demise as it was the only bomb that hit the carrier. The latter fact is critical in evaluating Best's performance on that day, for without his direct hit on *Akagi*, the Japanese would have had the use of two undamaged carriers to challenge the U.S. forces. Best's performance had a significant impact on the tactical disposition of Japanese carriers in the battle that greatly contributed to the U.S. Navy's decisive naval victory at Midway.

At 1742, Lieutenant Colonel Walter Sweeney, USA, arrived over the target with four B-17s after having taken off from Midway. This group was complemented by six B-17s under the command of Major George Blakey, USAAC, which had just flown to Midway from Barking Sands Airfield on the island of Kauai in the Hawaiian Islands. All thirty of the 500-pound bombs dropped by the ten B-17s missed their targets. Thus, the role played by the B-17s in the morning and in late afternoon was negligible. At 1832, all the B-17s had left the area and headed back to Midway.[50]

Fletcher and Spruance's main concern was the condition and disposition of *Yorktown*. By 1639, all of the carrier's survivors had left the ship. *Yorktown*'s lights were out, and the carrier lay motionless. Fletcher was concerned about a Japanese night attack on *Yorktown* as well as on the rest of his fleet. Six of the U.S. destroyers were loaded with survivors negating any possibility that the destroyers could be utilized in a night action. Fletcher made the decision for Task Force 17 to close the distance to Task Force 16, leaving *Yorktown* behind with destroyer *Hughes*. The purpose of *Hughes* was to sink the carrier if *Yorktown* was about to be captured by the enemy.

Fletcher notified Hawaii to send a fleet tug to rescue the carrier. Admiral Fletcher then radioed Spruance that he would conform to the movements of Task Force 16's commander. Spruance decidedly had no intention of fighting a night action with the Japanese. He would wait until 1945, when all his aircraft would have returned, before turning the fleet east until midnight where his forces would be out of harm's way. After midnight, he would turn the task forces to the north for an hour and then west so that he would be in position to protect Midway by dawn. His action in making this decisive decision has been criticized for being too passive. In retrospect, it is clear the U.S. naval forces had fulfilled Nimitz's directive to destroy the Japanese carrier fleet. U.S. forces had overwhelmingly succeeded in this mission, and to give the Japanese an opportunity to reverse their misfortunes of the day would be folly.[51]

At 1800, Admiral Nagumo was confronted by the disposition of the burning carriers *Kaga* and *Soryu*, which were at that time the most likely carriers that were beyond any hope of saving. Prior to Parshall and Tully's *Shattered Sword*, it had been accepted knowledge that both carriers sank of their own accord. However, careful scrutiny of the evidence suggests otherwise. Although there is no written evidence in Nagumo's report stating that the two carriers were scuttled, there is reason to believe that the two carriers were torpedoed by Japanese escorts with *Long Lance* torpedoes. *Soryu*, which was sixty miles to the south of *Hiryu*, was being watched over by destroyers *Isokaze* and *Hamakaze*, while further to the west and south, destroyers *Hagikaze* and *Maikaze* were standing by over *Kaga*. In addition, *Kazagumo*, *Makigumo*, *Yugumo* and another unnamed destroyer were actively assisting *Hiryu*, while destroyers *Nowaki* and *Arashi* were supporting *Akagi* in its efforts to control its fires. Most of these destroyers were nearly eighty miles away and a good three hours steaming time from Nagumo's forces. A total of ten destroyers had been assigned to the four burning Japanese carriers.[52]

The preceding information is important because in a night action, the destroyer with its Type 93 *Long Lance* torpedoes was the mainstay of the Japanese attack. The torpedo had an astonishing twenty-mile range. The remaining eleven destroyers and three cruisers in the Kido Butai had 120 torpedo tubes mounted on their decks. Of the total, eighty-eight were present on the destroyers. Therefore, the ten destroyers assigned to the burning carriers were essential to a night attack. It was also known that the Japanese used the destroyers for scouting the enemy at night because their ships lacked radar. Thus, the need for the destroyers in a night attack would mean that some of the carriers would have to be abandoned. The only way this action could be accomplished was if the two carriers *Soryu* and *Kaga* were torpedoed so that the carriers would not fall into American hands, and in addition, this would make it possible for four more destroyers to become available for a night action. *Hiryu* was still making twenty-eight knots, and it appeared that it might be saved. *Akagi*'s condition was less clear, as there was a chance its engines might be restored. At 1915, Captain Aoki Taijiro, in command of *Akagi*, received news from his chief engineer that the carrier could no longer operate under its own power. At 1920, Aoki gave the order for all hands to abandon ship.

Captain Ariga Kosaku, Commander of Destroyer Division Four, sent a message to *Kaga* and *Soryu*'s destroyer escort commanders asking whether the carriers were in danger of sinking. All the replies came back that the carriers were not operational, but no mention was made that they were in any danger of sinking. All the damage to the carriers, except possibly for *Akagi*, was above the water line. Fires by themselves would not cause a ship to sink, and a carrier could float indefinitely after its fires burned out. Thus, none of the carriers were in danger of sinking in the immediate future. At 1605, Captain Ariga ordered that all hands on board *Kaga* and *Soryu* and the men in the surrounding water be rescued. It is important to state that there was no record in the Nagumo report that the two carriers were to be scuttled. However, both carriers sank within twelve minutes of each other, and great explosions were heard at the site of both carriers. It is reasonable to conclude that Japanese torpedoes sank *Soryu* and *Kaga* just as *Akagi* and *Hiryu* were torpedoed the next day, as documented by Fuchida and Okumiya in *Midway*. *Soryu*, which was still on fire and deemed unsalvageable, would not be towed back to Japan. *Soryu*, which was the first Japanese carrier to sink to the bottom of the ocean, went down stern first at 1913. The carrier suffered the greatest loss of life, with 711 men dying out of a total crew of 1,103 (64 percent). *Kaga*'s fires had diminished somewhat, but the carrier structure above the lower hull was irreversibly destroyed, so *Kaga* too would not be towed back to Japan. At 1925, *Kaga* slipped into the sea stern first and settled down to the bottom of the ocean to a depth of 17,000 feet.[53]

To the north, the last of Japan's CAP had ditched into the sea. None of the fighters were from *Hiryu* but originated from either *Kaga* or *Soryu*. There was now no air cover for the Kido Butai, and its men wondered about the remaining fleet's disposition when daylight came less than ten hours away. At 1910, *Hiryu* was still able to steam ahead at twenty-eight knots, but its fires were still raging and now encroaching on the engine room. The carrier's fate had yet to be determined.[54]

After midnight, Spruance changed course of the U.S. task force from directly east to due west (but not northwest where the Kido Butai was located) and at a reduced speed, so that his fleet did not run into the enemy's surface forces during the night and because he wanted to conserve the carriers' fuel supply.[55]

Nagumo was trying to estimate the size of the U.S. forces that he confronted. He felt that the American forces must contain at least three to four carriers, with two of these carriers damaged. Cruiser Division Eight offered to Nagumo its assessment of U.S. carriers. At 1830, Rear Admiral Abe Hiroaki, commander of the group, felt that U.S. forces were heading due west with a force of four carriers (originally thought by Abe to be five carriers), six cruisers and fifteen destroyers. The assessment was accepted by Nagumo, but he was in no position to take offensive action against such a powerful U.S. fleet, especially with his destroyers still occupied with the Japanese carriers. He decided, as a result, to continue to watch over the burning *Hiryu*, which was still capable of making twenty-eight knots and was steaming to the northwest. However, at 2123, *Hiryu*'s engines ceased to function, and the carrier came to a stop. At 2130, Nagumo signaled Yamamoto that *Hiryu* was no longer capable of movement and relayed to him Abe's assessment that the United States had five carriers (later revised to four carriers) and was traveling due west. Nagumo would continue to protect *Hiryu* and would retire to the northwest at eighteen knots.[56]

At 2120, Yamamoto commanded Vice Admiral Kondo Nobutake, Commander of the Midway Invasion Force, to send two battleships and four cruisers northeast to engage in a night battle with U.S. forces. Yamamoto had heard at 1800 that *Kaga* was lost and, shortly thereafter, that *Hiryu* had been bombed. Admiral Ugaki, Chief of Staff of the Combined Fleet, and Yamamoto were already concerned about Nagumo's handling of the battle (even though it was Yamamoto's operational Midway plan that was responsible for the outcome of the battle). Thus, at 1915, Yamamoto sent the following signal to all units of the Combined Fleet: (1) the enemy is retiring to the east; (2) Combined Fleet units in the area were preparing to pursue the remnants of the enemy fleet and to occupy Midway; (3) the Main Body is scheduled to reach east 175 degrees and north 32 degrees at 0300 on June 5 (just northeast of where the American task force was discovered at 0820 on June 4); and (4) the Mobile Force, Occupation Force and Advance Force will search for and attack the enemy. A few minutes later, Yamamoto ordered submarine I-168 to surface off Midway and fire on Midway's military targets, particularly the atoll's airstrip. Vice Admiral Kurita Takeo, Commander of Cruiser Division Seven, should continue to close on Midway so that it could deliver a heavy bombardment of the atoll. At 1836, Yamamoto and Ugaki were under the impression that the U.S. fleet had retired to the east, based on information they received from *Chikuma*'s Number 2 scouting plane at 1728 that the U.S. carrier force was observed to be moving in that direction. At 1810, the same aircraft reports that the American task force was now heading south. With both of these conflicting reports, at 2130 Nagumo transmitted erroneously to Yamamoto that the U.S. force was moving due west with five (later Rear Admiral Abe's Cruiser Division Eight's intelligence reduced that number to four) U.S. carriers, but this intelligence was dismissed by Yamamoto and Ugaki as fallacious. The fact that Yamamoto and Ugaki had to correct Nagumo's latest intelligence was the last straw for Ugaki.[57]

At 2255, Ugaki relieved Nagumo of his command of the Kido Butai, except for the disposition of *Akagi* and *Hiryu* and their escorts, and placed Vice Admiral Kondo Nobutake, Commander of the Midway Invasion Force (Second Fleet), in charge of the Mobile Force (Kido Butai). At 2320, Yamamoto contacted Kondo directly by radio to bring Yamamoto up to date on the movements of Cruiser Division Eight and the second section of Battleship Division Three. By inference, Yamamoto no longer trusted Nagumo for intelligence.

At 2330, thirty minutes after being relieved of command of the Kido Butai, Nagumo contacted Yamamoto that none of his carriers were operational and took the opportunity to repeat the intelligence he had sent earlier that the enemy had four carriers. June 4, 1942, ended with two of the four Japanese carriers sunk and with the other two carriers non-operational and burning. Nagumo had been relieved of his command of the Kido Butai, and the Japanese were to suffer a decisive setback in the war in the Pacific from which they would never recover.[58]

7

June 5–7, 1942

Friday, June 5, 1942 (U.S. Date):
Hiryu *Sunk*

At a few minutes after midnight on Friday, June 5 (U.S. date), Kondo informed Destroyer Squadron Two, Cruiser Division Five, Cruiser Division Four, and Destroyer Squadron Four to prepare to engage the enemy in a night action at about 0100. He directed Nagumo to approach the enemy from the north. However, Nagumo did not follow the orders of either Kondo or Yamamoto in a night action. Instead, Nagumo continued to have the surviving ships of Kido Butai watch over *Hiryu*. When two explosions rocked *Hiryu* a little while after midnight, he decided that there was no hope to save the carrier, and at 0112, he ordered *Hiryu* abandoned. Then, instead of turning east to engage the enemy, he moved west to close to the Main Body. Many of Nagumo's subordinates were astonished at such an act of insubordination. Thus, in the Midway saga, both sides (recall Waldron's act of defiance) had their acts of insubordination performed by major participants in the battle.[1]

Nagumo Withdraws

Yamamoto and Ugaki began to worry that the remnants of the Kido Butai forces had not yet encountered the enemy and that, if they continued to steam east, their surface forces would be subject to U.S. air attacks when daylight came. They also realized that Vice Admiral Kurita Takeo, commanding Cruiser Division Seven, who had been covering the Transport Group and was steaming northeast, would not reach Midway before sunrise, making these ships vulnerable to U.S. airpower. Thus, at fifteen minutes after midnight, Yamamoto issued the order to cancel the mission of Kurita's cruisers to bombard Midway and directed Nagumo (without *Akagi* and *Hiryu* and their escorts) to retreat to the west and join the Main Body. At 0255, Yamamoto signaled to the Combined Fleet that (1) the Midway occupation was canceled, (2) the Main Body would join the Occupation Force and First Mobile Force and refuel on June 7, (3) the Screening Force would steam to the same position, and (4) the Landing Force would head west and out of harm's way of Midway's airpower.[2]

With Yamamoto finally realizing the significant U.S. naval forces arrayed against him, he ordered the surviving ships of Kido Butai to move west toward the Main Body. This directive vindicated Nagumo's earlier insubordinate decision to move his forces toward Yamamoto's forces.

While the Kido Butai was in the process of regrouping to the northwest of Midway, Kurita's four heavy cruisers, *Kumano*, *Suzuya*, *Mikuma* and *Mogami*, were racing northeast toward Midway at thirty-five knots. The cruisers were equipped with twelve twenty-four-inch torpedo tubes and ten eight-inch guns. The ships were within fifty miles of Midway when they received a signal at 0230 that the mission had been canceled. The message was delayed in reaching *Kumano*, the flagship of the four-cruiser group of Cruiser Division Seven, because the communication had mistakenly been sent to Rear Admiral Abe's Cruiser Division Eight. When they received the message, Captain Tanaka Kikumatsu, Commander of Cruiser Division Seven, had no choice but to turn around and return to the Main Body. He knew that, since they had gotten so close to Midway, his ships would be vulnerable to U.S. air attacks in the morning.[3]

At 0238, submarine *Tambor* was seen by a lookout on cruiser *Kumano*, and the sighting was immediately communicated by signal lamp to the other ships. With the heavy cruisers traveling at high speed, confusion broke out as each ship veered to avoid torpedoes that might be launched by *Tambor*. *Kumano* initially turned due west and then northwest, and in doing so was almost hit by cruiser *Suzuya*, which was directly behind *Kumano*. *Mikuma*, which was next in line as it proceeded due west, almost collided with *Suzayu*. However, this movement to the west by *Mikuma* sent the ship on a path that would place the cruiser on a collision course with *Mogami*, already steaming to the northwest. Before any corrective action could be taken, *Mogami* rammed *Mikuma* directly under the ship's bridge, where its heavy armor belt was located. The accident caused *Mogami*'s bow to be pushed back to its number 1 turret, resulting in the bow being forty feet shorter. *Mogami*, as a result, was unable to operate under its own power. *Mikuma* fared better with all of its damage being above the water line. However, a fuel tank in *Mikuma*'s number 4 boiler room was damaged, resulting in the leakage of oil into the sea in a trail that was sixty-five feet long and twenty feet wide.[4]

Kurita directed *Kumano* and *Suzuya* to leave the area at high speed and instructed Destroyer Division Eight, which was located east of the cruisers, to escort *Mogami* and *Mikuma* (ordered to stay with *Mogami*) back to Japan. *Mogami* was now able to make twelve knots, but the cruisers were less than 100 miles away from Midway. Damage control aboard *Mogami* was one of the better efforts made by the Japanese, and it prevented massive explosions from occurring on *Mogami* from a U.S. air attack: the cruiser's twelve tons of high explosives, 24,000 liters of compressed oxygen and two tons of kerosene torpedoes, as well as any inflammable materials, were thrown overboard. *Mikuma*, on the under hand, was considered to be battle-worthy and decided to retain its Type 93 *Long Lance* torpedoes.[5]

Tambor (SS-198) was unaware of the destruction its detection had caused. At 0215, Lieutenant Commander John W. Murphy, Jr., its skipper, observed four unidentified ships about three miles away. In the dark and at a distance of three miles, it was difficult for Murphy to be sure what types of ships he was observing and whether the vessels were friendly or not. He attempted to follow the ships by taking a course parallel to the cruisers. He continued to have trouble seeing the vessels in the dark and gradually began to lose visual contact with the cruisers at about 0238, because as the cruisers and *Tambor* moved west, the greater speed of the cruisers (twenty-eight knots) over the submarine (twenty-one knots) caused the heavy cruisers (which were, in fact, Japanese) to outdistance the submarine. However, at 0238, the heavy cruisers turned north when Yamamoto canceled the order for the ships to attack Midway. The change in course brought the ships steaming directly toward *Tambor*, and the vessels came into view of the U.S. submarine once again. As dawn ensued, there was now enough light for Murphy to conclusively identify the ships as enemy cruisers. However, a submarine attack by enemy destroyers prevented the intelligence from being sent to Midway. At 0432, the submarine attack was over, and Murphy was now able to report to Midway that the ships were enemy cruisers and that they were heading west at 270 degrees.[6]

Japanese submarine I-168 did not receive the message from Yamamoto that the Midway invasion had been called off. At 0120, Lieutenant Commander Tanabe Yahachi dutifully came to the surface on the east side of Sand Island's lagoon and fired eight rounds of shells from its four-inch deck gun. Midway guns responded within a few minutes, and the island's searchlights were able to outline the submarine against the dark sky. Tanabe submerged immediately. The shells that the submarine fired had fallen harmlessly in the lagoon and did no damage.[7]

On June 5, at 0120, Midway's dive-bombers, which had left at 1915 to destroy the burning Japanese carrier (*Kaga*), were still in the air and had not yet returned from their mission. The Japanese carrier was spotted by a PBY at 1700, and Captain Cyril Simard, USN, commander of Midway Atoll, suggested that its remaining operational dive-bombers immediately take off to attack the carrier. Simard had already replaced Major Lofton Henderson, USMC, squadron commander of VMSB-241 (who had died in action earlier that morning), with Major Benjamin Norris, USMC. The twelve-plane group consisted of six SBD-2s under the command of Captain Marshall Tyler and six SB2Us under the command of Norris. Norris preferred to wait until dark so that they would not have to face the Japanese Zeroes. In addition, Simard ordered eight of the PT boats at Midway to proceed to the same area.

Norris's squadron never found the burning Japanese carrier *Kaga* because it sank at 1925. The weather began to deteriorate as heavy thunderstorms and a low cloud ceiling ensued as Norris decided to turn around and head back to Midway. The twelve planes flew at 10,000 feet, which was under the low cloud ceiling. When the formation was forty miles from Midway, Norris's plane suddenly went into a steep dive and descended down to an altitude of 500 feet where the lights of his plane were lost. The cause of the descent of the aircraft was never determined. In the process of flying back to Midway, some of the squadron got lost in the bad weather, and the last plane did not land on Midway until 0145. The PT boats found no trace of *Kaga*, which was now resting on the bottom of the ocean.[8]

On board *Nagara*, Nagumo was contemplating suicide but was eventually talked out of taking his own life by his chief of staff, Rear Admiral Kusaka Ryunosuke. Nagumo actually never got over the devastating loss at Midway. In 1944, when he was departing for Saipan to command the garrison on the island (a significant demotion for a man who commanded the Kido Butai in its attacks on Pearl Harbor and Midway), he described to his sons the terrible loss at Midway as tears rolled down from his eyes.

Nagumo would never return to Japan, as he committed suicide on Saipan as the island's final defenses broke down.⁹

Akagi *Sinks*

At 0220, the conversation on *Yamato* was centered on determining the fate of *Akagi*, and Vice Admiral Kondo Nobutake, commander of the Midway Invasion Force, contacted Captain Ariga Kosaku, Commander of Destroyer Division Four, to inquire about *Akagi*'s present condition; but with daylight hours away, the threat of U.S. airpower made that question irrelevant. At 0450, Yamamoto ordered *Akagi* to be scuttled by destroyer torpedoes. The four destroyers of Destroyer Division Four lined up with *Arashi* (Ariga's flagship) in the lead, with destroyers *Nowaki*, *Hagikaze* and *Maikaze* following in that order. Each destroyer, as it traveled at a speed of twelve knots past *Akagi* from a distance of about 4,000 feet, fired a single Type 93 *Long Lance* torpedo in succession at the carrier. Two or three of the four torpedoes fired hit *Akagi*'s starboard side, which was fatal to the carrier. At 0520, the carrier began to sink, bow first with its stern lifted in the air, as it slipped beneath the waves. Two hundred sixty-seven men out of an initial crew of 1,620 were lost in *Akagi*'s demise.¹⁰

At 0230, Nagumo sent Yamamoto a more detailed report on the battle events of the day. In the summary, Nagumo still felt that *Hiryu* could be saved, but on board *Hiryu*, Yamaguchi had decided the end was in site for *Hiryu*. At 0250, he ordered the 800 members of the crew to prepare to abandon ship. Yamaguchi accepted blame for the loss of *Hiryu* and *Soryu*, and in a measure to make restitution for his failings, he decided that he would go down with the carrier. A Japanese military ceremony was performed with all hands on deck, and the ship's flags were taken down for the last time. At 0315, the ceremonies ended, and the order to abandon ship was given.

Destroyers *Makigumo* and *Kazagumo* assisted the sailors off the ship. When Yamaguchi waved good-bye to the crew, Captain Kaku Tomeo, Commander of *Hiryu*, declared that he too would stay on board the carrier and share its fate. The admiral's staff also announced that they would like to share Yamaguchi's fate. He immediately rejected the idea. Thus, the idea of a mass suicide was firmly denied by Yamaguchi as he said his final farewell to all of his staff and crew. The last crew member left the carrier at 0430. The details of where on the carrier and in what manner Yamaguchi and Kaku met their end will never be known.¹¹

At 0510, destroyer *Makigumo* set out to launch a torpedo at *Hiryu* as its sister destroyer *Kazagumo* headed west toward Japan. Captain Fujita Isamu, skipper of *Makigumo*, decided that before he would fire his torpedoes at *Hiryu*, he would send Lieutenant Commander Tamura (first name not known) back to *Hiryu* to ascertain whether there were any crew members left on board the carrier. Finding no one, he returned to *Makigumo*. The destroyer then moved in position to fire its first torpedo, which ran under the hull of *Hiryu* and failed to explode. Fujita then ordered the destroyer to increase its range from the carrier to obtain a better firing angle and released a second torpedo. The Type 93 *Long Lance* torpedo hit the carrier on its starboard side near the bow gangway. Fujita decided the carrier would soon sink from that one torpedo and began to depart for Japan. At that moment, a group of men appeared on *Hiryu*'s deck, trying to get the attention of the destroyer. Fujita, intending to leave the area at once, flashed back a coded message on his lamplight, but the survivors on *Hiryu* lacked the ability to decode the signal (the true nature of the communication was never discovered) and therefore remained on *Hiryu*. The carrier went down at 0910 with the loss of 416 crew members and the deaths of Vice Admiral Yamaguchi and Captain Kaku.[12] Thus, *Hiryu* would be the last of the four Japanese carriers to sink to the depths of the ocean.

At 0630, a PBY from Midway sighted the two heavy cruisers (thought to be battleships) 125 miles west of Midway.[13] At 0700, Captain Simard directed Marine Captain Marshall Tyler to lead six SBD-2s and Marine Captain Richard Fleming to command six SB2Us to search and destroy the two Japanese ships. Forty miles away from their target, they discovered *Mikuma*'s oil trail and followed it to their target. At 0805, the twelve planes made their run on *Mogami* and *Mikuma* but failed to get a hit on either heavy cruiser. Fleming was hit as he attacked *Mikuma*, and his plane burst into flames; but just before Fleming died, he released his bomb on *Chikuma* and obtained a near miss on the stern of the cruiser.[14]

At 0830, eight U.S. Army B-17s were the second group of aircraft from Midway to find the cruisers. The first four planes dropped nineteen 500-pound bombs, and the second group of four aircraft released twenty 500-pound bombs on the target, but all of the ordnance missed the two cruisers. The commanders of the *Mogami* and *Mikuma* began to wonder if they might make it back to safety after all.[15]

Shortly after 0700, Spruance received the intelligence of the two Japanese battleships (heavy cruisers) discovered by Midway's PBY west of Midway. He had more than sixty-four dive-bombers operational for a planned mission against the *Mogami* and *Mikuma*, which included thirty-two aircraft from *Enterprise* and thirty-two planes from *Hornet*. He decided to wait and see if *Hiryu* was discovered before launching an attack on the heavy cruisers. His answer came at 0800, when Spruance learned that a seriously damaged carrier was observed to the northwest of Midway Atoll by another PBY from Midway. Forty minutes earlier, a search plane from *Hosho* had found *Hiryu* still afloat with crew members on board. It appeared also to the pilot that *Hiryu* was in no danger of sinking, so Yamamoto ordered destroyer *Tanikaze* to go back to the area and sink *Hiryu*.[16]

Spruance delayed an immediate response to the discovery of *Hiryu* because of conflicting reports in its location which would not get resolved until early afternoon. By that time, the carrier would be 270 miles away, which was beyond the ideal range for the SBDs to fly safely without running out of fuel. Commander Miles Browning, the senior aviator on board wanted to launch at once. He became irritated when his order to lift off was immediately countermanded by Spruance.

Another conflict arose that centered on the weight of the bombs to be carried by the SBDs. Browning felt that by having the U.S. task force get closer to the enemy after the launch, the aircraft would conserve enough fuel to be able to return to the carriers. He also felt that the planes should carry 1,000-pound bombs instead of 500-pound bombs because the former would inflict greater damage. However, this action would place a greater strain on fuel reserves. As a result, the leaders assigned to finding the burning *Hiryu*, Lieutenants DeWitt Shumway and Wallace Short, objected, and both men, who were from *Yorktown*, decided to discuss the matter with McClusky, who was in sick bay. McClusky confirmed that the distance to the Kido Butai was close to 270 miles and that the distance was at the outer range of the SBD's fuel capacity to fly. In addition, he reaffirmed that the weight of the 1,000-pound bombs would place a further strain on fuel reserves. McClusky pressed Browning on the issue and reminded him that in the morning's mission the distance was 170 miles away from the carriers and that the planes ran out of gas. He asked Browning if he had ever taken off from a carrier with a 1,000-pound bomb and with a full load of gasoline. Browning replied in the negative. McClusky recommended that the launch be delayed for one hour to close the distance to the enemy and that only 500-pound bombs be utilized in the mission. As Browning was about to reject the suggestion, Spruance, who was close by, interrupted the conversation by stating, "I will do what you pilots want." Browning then silently left the bridge and returned to his cabin.[17]

Changing the weight of the SBD's bombs took time, but for reasons that are not fully explainable, Spruance did not launch his strike force until 1512. Thirty-two planes lifted off from *Enterprise*: seven SBDs from VS-5 and nine SBDs from VS-6, all under the command of Lieutenant Wallace Short, and ten SBDs from VB-3 and six SBDs from VB-6, which came under the command of Lieutenant DeWitt Shumway. *Hornet* sent aloft only ten SBDs from VB-8 because the remainder of the dive-bombers were not yet ready to launch due to the change in the weight of the bomb load. At 1530, Ring led the eleven-plane formation, all loaded with 500-pound bombs, out to the target. At 1543, the remaining twenty-one SBDs took off under the command of Rodee (fifteen SBDs from VS-8, five SBDs from VB-8 and one SBD from VS-5) and headed for the target. Seven of the SBDs still carried 1,000-pound bombs in direct violation of Spruance's order. A total of sixty-four dive-bombes headed for *Hiryu*.[18]

In *The Battle of Midway*, Craig L. Symonds states that *Hornet* launched first, while Robert J. Cressman et al. report in *A Glorious Page in Our History* that *Enterprise* sent its aircraft to the target first, as *Hornet*'s aircraft did not leave until 1530 due to delays in launching.

At 1800, Ring arrived at the reported location of *Hiryu* but found an empty ocean. The reason for the vacant seas was that shortly after 0800 water began to be visible on the flight deck of *Hiryu*. There remained about forty crew members still on board, and upon observing the Japanese scout plane at 0720, they gained hope and launched a thirty-two foot cutter into the water. Shortly thereafter, *Hiryu* sank between 0907 and 0915. The last moments of Vice Admiral Yamaguchi and Captain Kaku are not known. Ironically, the surviving crew members in the cutter were at sea for two weeks before they were spotted by a U.S. PBY and rescued by submarine tender *Ballard*. Admiral Spruance did not know for certain that *Hiryu* had sunk until June 19, 1942.[19]

Ring continued to fly west after not finding *Hiryu*, and at 0620, he came upon a light cruiser (destroyer *Tanikaze*) but bypassed the ship hoping to still locate *Hiryu*. He flew for over 300 miles (his second *flight to nowhere*) but found no sign of the Japanese carrier. Ring then radioed Shumway and Short as to the location of the light cruiser (destroyer *Tanikaze*) he saw on his way out to find *Hiryu*. As a result, all sixty-four SBDs headed for *Tanikaze*.

At 1808, Ring's group of eleven dive-bombers attacked *Tanikaze*, but Commander

Katsumi Motoi adroitly evaded the attempts of the SBDs to make a direct hit on the destroyer. At 1834, Shumway's group of planes reached the reported ship below and dove down on the destroyer, but they too were unsuccessful. *Tanikaze* continued to make sharp turns at high speed, presenting a difficult target for the SBD pilots, and as a result the destroyer remained unscathed. *Tanikaze* also brought to bear all its antiaircraft fire on the incoming planes. Ironically, Samuel Adams's plane from VS-5 (the pilot who found *Hiryu* the day before) was hit, and his aircraft descended into the sea. Frustrated pilots who had expended their ordnance headed back to their respective carriers as dusk was setting in.[20]

At 1845, five B-17s from Midway arrived and began dropping fifteen 600-pound bombs and eight 300-pound bombs from 11,000 feet on *Tanikaze*. Two B-17s were lost in the process, both from lack of fuel, while the other three B-17s landed safely on Midway. *Tanikaze* finally was able to realize that *Hiryu* was nowhere in sight and turned west at high speed toward Nagumo and the Main Body forces.[21]

At 1930, the pilots were returning from their search for *Hiryu* to *Enterprise*. The planes were low on gas, and the pilots had never landed in the dark before. Only Lieutenant Samuel Adams's plane (Scouting Five), which was shot down by destroyer *Tanikaze*'s antiaircraft fire, did not return from the original thirty-two SBD dive-bombers sent on the mission. Spruance, realizing the situation and in spite of appreciating the risk of a submarine attack, decided to turn on *Enterprise*'s huge thirty-six-inch searchlights and directed them skyward. The big lights stayed on until 2000, at which time they were turned off and the carrier's sidelights were turned on until 2230. Spruance then learned for the first time that several dive-bombers from *Hornet* had taken off with 1,000-pound bombs, even though Spruance had given the order that all the planes should carry 500-pound bombs. This information was added to a list of concerns he had already had about Mitscher's ability to command a carrier.[22]

At 1941, Spruance received a message that a PBY flying from Midway had been attacked by Japanese carrier fighters. The intelligence revealed that at 1812, Lieutenant Dale Newell of VP-44 had discovered the Main Body of the Japanese fleet. The CAP that attacked the PBY came from the Main Body's escorting carrier *Zuiho*, which had launched its fighters to chase off the patrol plane. By that time, the remaining forces of Nagumo, Kondo's Midway Invasion Force and Yamamoto's Main Body, had all formed into one formation. Meanwhile, destroyers *Asashio* and *Arashio*, which were detached from *Akagi* and the Kido Butai, were now heading west toward *Mogami* and *Mikuma*. The destroyers expected to reach the heavy cruisers by 0500 the next morning.[23]

June 5 ended with the naval forces of Yamamoto, Nagumo and Kondo heading away from Midway and from the U.S. forces. Yamamoto moved his naval forces out of harm's way but had not yet decided that the battle was over, as he would wait and see what June 6 would offer.

Saturday, June 6, 1942

In the early dawn of June 6, Task Force 16 was 350 miles northwest of Midway. At 0500, Spruance decided to launch eighteen SBDs from *Enterprise* to search the area west of his forces. At 0645, one of the SBD pilots covering the search area reported that he spotted one battleship, one cruiser and three destroyers moving at ten knots, but the information in its deciphering was translated as one carrier and five destroyers. It was learned that Japanese ships were only 128 miles southwest of Spruance's forces. To clear up the issue of whether a Japanese carrier was present, Spruance ordered float planes from *Minneapolis* and *New Orleans* to search out and assess the recent intelligence. Just then, Ensign Roy Gee dropped a beanbag from his aircraft onto *Enterprise*'s flight deck with a note stating that there were actually only two cruisers and two destroyers discovered, with no mention of a Japanese carrier being sighted, which were located 133 miles to the southwest.[24]

At 0800, with this intelligence in hand, Spruance ordered *Hornet*'s eleven SBDs of VB-8 under the command of Ruff Johnson and fourteen SBDs (mostly from VS-8) under the command of Walter Rodee to be launched. Eight of the aircraft carried a 500-pound bomb, and seventeen planes carried 1,000-pound bombs. Eight F4Fs escorted the twenty-five planes to the target. The leader of the group was Stanhope Ring, granting him the third opportunity to achieve some positive results. At 0850, while *Hornet*'s aircraft were on their way to the target, it received a message from *Enterprise* that a battleship was erroneously reported as a carrier and that Ring should attack the battleship. Spruance decided to keep back *Enterprise*'s SBDs in case there still was a carrier in the area.[25]

At 0930, flying westward, Johnson spotted the two heavy cruisers *Mogami* and *Mikuma*. Both the fourteen planes from Rodee's Bombing Eight group and Johnson's group of eight planes (VB-8) dove down and attacked the heavy cruisers. Two of Rodee's dive-bombers scored direct hits on *Mogami*'s number 5 turret and near the cruiser's stern. Unlike the Japanese carriers that had ordnance spread throughout the hangar deck floor, *Mogami* had scuttled all of its torpedoes, so no secondary explosions occurred. The bombs of Johnson's eight planes all missed *Mikuma*, although Johnson had a near miss on the cruiser. Ensign Don Adams was able to land a 500-pound bomb on destroyer *Asashio*, which resulted in medium damage to the ship. All in all, the results of the attack by *Hornet*'s twenty-five dive-bombers and eight Wildcat fighters were marginal at best.

Thirty-three planes had attacked a severely damaged *Mogami* and a slightly damaged *Mikuma*, which were escorted by two destroyers, and failed to sink any of the vessels. All the ships continued to steam ahead at twenty-eight knots toward the 700-mile radius of Wake Island, which would provide air-cover protection for the ships. However, they were twenty hours away from reaching their destination, and there were still eight hours of daylight left in the day.[26]

At 1045, Captain Sakiyama Shakao, Commander of *Mikuma*, signaled Yamamoto that *Mogami* had received only slight damage and that three (actually two) SBDs had been shot down due to antiaircraft fire. The presence of U.S. float planes over the cruisers certainly meant to Sakiyama and Captain Soji Akira that more U.S. planes would be coming to attack *Mogami* and *Mikuma*.

At 1100, they changed course to the southwest in an effort to reach the air cover of Wake Island, which was still 710 miles away.

True to Sakiyama and Soji's expectations, at 1045, *Enterprise* began launching its aircraft to attack the two cruisers. The carrier lifted off thirty-one SBDs, comprised of dive-bombers from VB-3, VB-6, VS-5 and VS-6 which were under the command of Lieutenant Short from *Yorktown*. Twelve Wildcat fighters under the command of Lieutenant James Gray would escort the thirty-one dive-bombers and the last three remaining operational TBD torpedo bombers from *Yorktown* to the target. The three torpedo bombers, which were vulnerable due to their slow speed, were under strict orders by Spruance not to engage in combat unless the Japanese cruiser's antiaircraft batteries were first neutralized by the other planes on the mission. The dive-bombers climbed to 22,500 feet, while the TBDs flew at a much lower altitude and headed southwest.[27]

Short was chosen to lead the group of SBDs because Lieutenant Commander Clarence McClusky, Commander, *Enterprise* air group, was in sick bay from wounds sustained on the morning of June 4, and Lieutenant Richard Best was resting below with active tuberculosis.

At 1200, the two heavy cruisers with the two escorting destroyers were steaming at twenty knots and heading west by southwest. At 1211, Short's group spotted the two heavy cruisers but bypassed them to search for the imagined battleship. Meanwhile, Gray's fighters closed in on the heavy cruisers, which prompted a very heavy barrage of antiaircraft fire by the cruisers and preempted any possibility of participation by the U.S. torpedo bombers. Gray became confident as he approached the ships that their size was consistent with a heavy cruiser and concluded that the battleship previously reported did not exist. He radioed Lieutenant Wallace Short to turn around and return to the two very large cruisers. Short was now thirty miles west of the Japanese cruisers, and the ocean was devoid of any additional ships, let alone a battleship. Short decided then to return to the ships he had passed over earlier.[28]

Upon returning, Short found *Mikuma* still in the lead as the heavy cruiser suddenly changed course because *Mogami* was now under attack. Two direct hits on *Mogami* ensued: one bomb landed amidships on the top deck, and the other bomb hit forward of the bridge, resulting in moderate damage. The greater number of aircraft in Short's squadron, however, chose to attack *Mikuma*. The first bomb hit the roof of the Number 3 main turret in front of the bridge and totally destroyed the turret and killed Captain Sakiyama as he placed his head outside the manhole cover on top of the bridge. Two more bombs destroyed the starboard forward engine spaces. Bombs continued to rain down on the stricken cruiser in the aft engine room, which was in the neighborhood of the ship's torpedo tubes. *Mikuma* had been struck by five bombs and sustained at least two near misses. At 1358, the fires on *Mikuma* reached the torpedo storage racks and triggered off explosions from a number of the torpedoes. In addition to the topside damage, the cruiser had sustained severe damage to its underbelly from the bomb hits and the torpedo explosions. Water was now beginning to flow into the ship, causing the cruiser to list. It appeared its demise was now inevitable. At 1420, *Mikuma* appeared to be so damaged that *Mogami* reported to Yamamoto that the ship was going to sink.[29]

Short gathered his planes and realized that none of them had been lost to antiaircraft fire. He then led the planes back to *Enterprise* with the knowledge that his group had fatally damaged one cruiser and severely damaged another. Yamamoto was still not willing to accept defeat at Midway, so at 1340, he ordered Kondo to send the following directive: (1) the Main Force of the Occupation Force (less Battleship Division Three and Destroyer Squadron Two) with Cruiser Division Eight (*Tone* and *Chikuma*) were to seek out and destroy the enemy carrier force and to assist *Mogami* and *Mikuma* in reaching Wake Island, (2) *Zuiho* with its nine operational torpedo bombers and twelve Zeroes (six A6M2 models and six older A5M models) were to prepare for action, and (3) all available seaplanes were to be used for search-and-destroy missions.

Yamamoto, as late as 1340 on June 6, was still hopeful (though unrealistic) of one last engagement with the American task force. Yamamoto's Main Body and Kondo's forces were fortunate that they were not detected by U.S. aircraft on that day, for their discovery would most likely have resulted in the loss of additional ships for the Japanese navy.[30]

Stanhope Ring was replaced by Walter Rodee as the leader of *Hornet*'s second strike because Ring's radio was not functioning. There was another plane available, but Mitscher decided not to use it. The serious lack of effectiveness of *Hornet*'s planes under Ring's leadership in the battle thus far was most likely the basis for Mitscher's decision. At 1330, twelve SBDs from VS-8 led by Rodee and twelve SBDs from VB-8 under Lieutenant Alfred Tucker took off and headed for the target. All the planes were armed with 1,000-pound bombs. Shortly after launching, one of the SBDs had a problem with the aircraft and had to return to the carrier. At 1345, the remaining twenty-three planes flew toward the damaged Japanese heavy cruisers.[31] At 1400, *Mikuma*'s midships were completely engulfed in flames, and the ship was beginning to settle in the water. Explosions were still going off, and the escorting destroyers could offer little assistance. Crew members were abandoning the ship by jumping into the sea and creating makeshift rafts from debris in the water. At 1445, the third attack of the day occurred, when the twenty-three planes from *Hornet* arrived over the cruisers. At 1500, Rodee and Tucker's dive-bombers dove down on the cruisers and destroyers. *Mogami* experienced another direct bomb hit on its seaplane deck, and all the undamaged hatches around the area were sealed for damage control. In spite of the bomb hit, *Mogami* was able to maintain its engine power. At 1525, *Mogami* reported that it was heading due west at twenty knots, a remarkable feat considering its heavy damage. *Mikuma* sustained another direct bomb hit, and the cruiser settled deeper into the water. Destroyer *Arashio* received a direct bomb hit near its Number 3 gun turret. Thirty-seven men were killed, and its Commander, Nobuki Ogawa, was wounded. Its steering mechanism was damaged by the bomb hit. The destroyer resorted to manual steering for navigation, and its crew members were able to extinguish the fires. Its sister destroyer *Asashio* was strafed by U.S. aircraft, killing twenty-two men. Both destroyers, however, would make it back home.[32]

As *Mogami*, *Asashio* and *Arashio* departed from the area, *Mikuma*'s fate had become obvious. It stayed afloat for four additional hours and then began to list to port as the burning inferno continued. U.S. aviators returning from the attack could not agree on whether they had attacked a battleship or not. Spruance still wanted to know the accuracy of the identification of the ship attacked so that he could make a decision on whether another strike was necessary. At 1553, the Japanese cruisers were still only ninety miles away, so Spruance sent two SBDs to photograph the ship to settle the issue. At 1715, the two dive-bombers found *Mikuma* alone as *Mogami* had left the area. Two and one-half hours later, *Mikuma* rolled over on its port side and sank. Seven hundred officers and a crew of 888 men were lost in *Mikuma*'s fate.[33]

Japanese Submarine I-168 Torpedoes Yorktown

Captain Elliot Buckmaster, Commander of *Yorktown*, was able to call upon a number of volunteers to board the carrier with him to help him quell a few fires that were still burning and to attempt to decrease *Yorktown*'s list by counter-flooding its starboard tanks and by throwing the portside guns and aircraft parts on that side of the hangar deck overboard. As a result, he was able to decrease the list on the carrier from twenty-six degrees to twenty-two degrees. Destroyer *Hammann*, which was close by on the carrier's starboard side, provided power and support to the ship. At 1308, *Vireo*, a minesweeper, which had been ordered up to the Midway area from French Frigate Shoals by Nimitz, took the carrier in tow but was only able to make three knots. The reason for the slow speed was that *Yorktown* was low in the water, and its rudder was not able to move, which caused the carrier to constantly drift off course. As a result, the carrier was not able to distance itself far enough to the east to get out of range of Japanese submarines. There were five other U.S. destroyers *Hughes*, *Gwin*, *Monaghan*, *Balch* and *Benham* guarding the carrier.[34]

In the daylight hours of June 5, progress was continuing to be made on board the carrier as the skipper of the submarine I-168, Lieutenant Commander Tanabe Yahachi, kept his submarine submerged, stalking the carrier until the opportunity occurred at which he could execute an attack. At night, he surfaced and cruised at a speed of sixteen knots. The excellent Japanese night glasses allowed him to follow *Yorktown* until his submarine was spotted, and then he retreated but still stayed on the surface. At 0410, on June 6, a submarine lookout observed the American carrier to the east, silhouetted against the rising sun, while his ship was hidden by the western darkness. At 0600, on June 6, Tanabe submerged his submarine and headed toward the stricken carrier. The six destroyers had difficulty hearing the propellers of I-168 with sonar because of the terrible acoustics existing on that day. As a result, Tanabe was able to get into position to fire his torpedoes without being detected by the destroyers. Tanabe was also aware that the surface waters were still and thus his periscope could be seen. To reduce this risk, he only raised his periscope once every thirty minutes and then for only five seconds. He would then navigate by dead reckoning and with the use of his sound gear only.[35]

At ten miles away, he started his run against the carrier which took about four hours, utilizing periodic periscope observations along the way. When he was about one mile from *Yorktown*, he reached the inner circle of the destroyer's line of defense and knew that he could no longer use his periscope until his final attack. He could hear the sounds given off by the destroyers' sonar, which were still unable to detect any indication of the Japanese submarine in the area. This was due to a strong thermal layer which prevented the sound waves of the destroyers' sonar from detecting the submarine. When Tanabe instinctively decided to raise his periscope, he found that the submarine was a mere 1,500 feet away from *Yorktown*.[36]

Tanabe was forced to turn around and readjust his position so that he was about 4,500 feet away from the carrier. Realizing that he would have only one chance to succeed in the attack, he restricted the angle of firing his torpedoes to two degrees and would release his four Type 89 torpedoes in a tight pattern. At about 1331, he fired two of his fish, and seconds later, the second pair of torpedoes was aimed at *Yorktown*.

Tanabe then dove his submarine down to a depth of 300 feet. Less than a minute later, he heard the sound of three explosions and knew he had been successful.

The four torpedoes were seen on the surface as they approached the carrier, but there was no way to stop them. *Yorktown* was barely moving and was the perfect target for the torpedo attack. Destroyer *Hammann* was snuggled against *Yorktown*'s starboard side. The first torpedo struck *Yorktown* near the bow, killing eighty-four of the personnel on the carrier. The second torpedo hit *Hammann* amidships in the Number 2 fire room and split the vessel in two. Its crew leaped into the water, but after the ship's stern hit the water, its depth charges began to go off. The severe explosions in the water killed many of the *Hammann* crew. The third torpedo detonated on contact at frames 84 and 85 on *Yorktown*'s starboard side. The fourth torpedo missed the carrier. The two torpedo hits and the explosions of the depth charges near the carrier was more than *Yorktown* could bear. The ship's list actually improved to seventeen degrees because of the counter-flooding of the carrier from the torpedo hits on the starboard side (Tomonaga's torpedo planes had previously hit *Yorktown* on its port side). However, the ship was now visibly lower in the water. *Vireo* pulled up close to the carrier to rescue the men on board and in the water and then distanced itself from the carrier.[37]

Destroyers *Gwin*, *Monaghan* and *Hughes* went into action and began dropping depth charges on the submarine which lasted for over two hours. I-168's batteries were now almost depleted and, due to the deterioration of its battery casing wax, it leaked sulfuric acid. The combination of sulfuric acid with the seawater of the bilge resulted in the release of chlorine gas into the hull of the submarine. Its air supply was marginal, and its diving planes were not functioning well. At this point, I-168 had to surface to survive. At 1640, Tanabe took the submarine to surface, and as he climbed out from the conning tower hatch, he observed that the destroyers were now withdrawing. *Yorktown* was not seen, so he assumed that the carrier had sunk. In the process of withdrawing from the area, the submarine's engine exhaust produced a smoke screen, alerting the destroyers, which then fired salvos of shells, all of which missed the submarine. At the same time, the smoke provided a screen which made the submarine a difficult target for the destroyer's guns. With its air flasks recharged and its ventilation improved, Tanabe submerged the submarine and headed for Kure in Japan. A remarkable attack given the circumstances.[38]

There is a difference of opinion between Parshall and Tully's *Shattered Sword* and Symonds's *Battle of Midway* on which torpedo from I-168 struck *Hammann*. The former authors reported that the first torpedo struck Hammann, while Symonds states it was the second torpedo.

The continuing air attacks by U.S. forces on *Mogami* and *Mikuma* and the then-available Japanese intelligence at hand led Yamamoto to believe that the Americans had at least five or six carriers involved in the battle. He concluded that the Americans would plan, after their attempts to sink the two heavy cruisers, to seek out Vice Admiral Kondo's Invasion Force on June 7. Thus, he ordered the Main Body to close in on Kondo's forces. His hope was that the aircraft from *Zuiho* (twenty-one planes) and *Hosho* (eight planes) would be able to do some damage to the American carriers. With his destroyers running very low on fuel, at 1500, Yamamoto would have to first refuel the destroyers and then head south at eighteen knots to join Kondo.

On the night of June 6, Spruance decided that his forces had steamed more than 400 miles to the west and as close to Wake Island's Japanese land bombers as he wanted. His fleet was also very low on fuel, and refueling the ships was becoming an imperative. Thus, at 1907, he ordered U.S. forces to head southeast back to Pearl Harbor and cease any further air operations against the Japanese fleet.[39]

Sunday, June 7, 1942 (U.S. Date)

On the morning of June 7, *Yorktown* had begun to list significantly to port. At 0443, the carrier rolled over on its port side revealing the holes caused by Tanabe's two torpedoes. The stern of the carrier then began to descend, lifting the carrier's bow above the water before the ship sank in over 16,000 feet of water and then settled upright at a twenty-five-degree list to starboard on the ocean floor (as described upon his discovery of *Yorktown* by Dr. Robert Ballard on May 19, 1998). Out of the approximately 2,400 men aboard *Yorktown*, 2,270 were rescued from the water and the carrier.[40]

The Japanese realized on the morning of June 7 that no further U.S. air attacks would be forthcoming and that the United States had departed from Midway and returned to Pearl Harbor. Search planes from Kondo's ships found no evidence of the American fleet, and even longer-range aircraft from Wake Island found an empty sea. The idea of a counteroffensive by Japanese surface forces was cleverly avoided by Spruance, and now the only decision the Japanese could make was to head back to Japan. Japan could only console itself by the fact that *Yorktown* had been sunk; the remote and insignificant islands of Attu and Kiska had been successfully occupied by Japanese forces; and *Mogami*, *Asashio* and *Arashio* would make it back to Japan. In the end, the United States had won a decisive naval battle, one from which Japan would never recover and again be able to take the offensive in the war in the Pacific, all occurring just six months after Japan's devastating attack on Pearl Harbor.

8

Analysis of the Defeat

There are many reasons for Japan's devastating defeat at Midway, but by far the most significant factor was the target itself—the Midway Islands. By deciding to include the Midway Atoll in its Midway operational plan, Japan doomed itself to the possibility of total defeat in the battle because it gave the Kido Butai two competing missions: the destruction of the U.S. carrier force and the takeover of Midway Atoll. This dual purpose of the mission prevented the Japanese carriers from having the freedom and flexibility of naval movement at sea, an imperative if one is to be victorious in sea battles. It was exactly this nautical fixation on Midway that prevented flexibility of movement of the Kido Butai and provided an opportunity for the United States to target the Japanese carriers at their most vulnerable moment—with all their planes fueled and armed and still in the hangar decks.

There were critical consequences to this nautical fixation on Midway Atoll that contributed significantly to Japan's defeat. U.S. intelligence determined by deciphering the Japanese naval code the exact location and direction that the Kido Butai would be steaming on the morning of June 4, 1942. U.S. cryptologists knew that Japanese forces would attack Midway from the northwest at a bearing of 315 degrees and would eventually close to within fifty miles of Midway. They also knew that at about 0700, the Japanese would attack the atoll's ground and air defenses and return to their carriers at 0815. If the islands of Midway had not been included in the Midway operation plan, U.S. intelligence would clearly have been less valuable. This conclusion is drawn because the United States could not have launched their aircraft at a specified time and distance to catch the Japanese carriers when they were most vulnerable with all their aircraft on board. If the Kido Butai had not focused on Midway as a target, their approach to Midway could have come from any direction, and their presence could only have been discovered by the PBY search planes from Midway or scouting aircraft from *Yorktown*.

The value of Japanese flexibility of naval movement, even with U.S. intelligence foreknowledge of the mission, is amply illustrated in the events that occurred during the Battle of the Coral Sea, where U.S. intelligence alerted Nimitz that the Japanese were bringing two large carriers (*Shokaku* and *Zuikaku*) into the Coral Sea to support the invasion of Port Moresby. When the American aircraft attacked Tulagi Island, the presence of American carriers in the area became known to the Japanese, and the invasion of Port Moresby was temporarily postponed. With this action, Yamamoto freed the carriers from a fixed course of naval movement and allowed *Shokaku* and *Zuikaku* to move at will.

Once the Japanese launched their attack on Midway, it would be impossible for Japan to attack the U.S. carrier force first. The reason for this conclusion is based on the fact that *Enterprise* and *Hornet* had launched their aircraft at 0700, and the Japanese did not discover an American carrier until 0820. It is also true that on June 4, between the hours of 0445 and 1330, Nagumo knew the location of only one U.S. carrier—*Yorktown*, which launched its aircraft at 0838. Nagumo did not become aware of the other two U.S. carriers until after *Soryu*'s high-speed Yokosuka D4Y1 carrier bomber reported the information to Yamaguchi at 1330.

It was the ability of the Americans to strike first that led to the loss of all four Japanese carriers at Midway. This deduction is consistent with the result of Captain Wayne Hughes, Jr.'s mathematical probabilities in carrier-to-carrier warfare as explained in his book *Fleet Tactics*. In the text, he reasons that if the ratio of carriers was 4:3 (actually 4:4 if Midway is considered an unsinkable carrier) in favor of the Japanese and if the U.S. carriers attacked first, Japan would lose three carriers to the loss of only one American carrier from a Japanese counterattack. These mathematical calculations produced by Captain Hughes are based on the premise that an entire air group from one carrier has the potential to sink only one enemy carrier on its mission (the contrary concept in carrier warfare was believed in 1942, whereby the thinking was that one squadron of dive-bombers [thirty-six] and one squadron torpedo bombers [eighteen] had the ability to sink more than one enemy carrier with a coordinated strike). Thus, the enemy that strikes *first* is clearly the determining factor in predicting which opponent is victorious in the battle as events revealed in the actual Battle of Midway. If the Japanese were not focused on Midway as a target, their approach to Midway could have come from any direction and their presence would have had to be discovered by the PBY search planes from Midway or scouting aircraft from *Yorktown*.

Switching the ordnance of the carrier attack planes on *Akagi* and *Kaga* from land-based bombs to torpedoes prevented their being launched against the U.S. carrier fleet when the first wave of Japanese planes was returning from Midway at 0830. Also, time constraints led to the ordnance on *Akagi* and *Kaga* being haphazardly placed near the aircraft and in open places rather than being stowed away in protected storage. Aircraft were fully fueled in the hangar decks on all carriers, but the Japanese dive-bombers were not armed until they reached the flight deck. This scenario would create a highly explosive situation should a bomb strike either of the two hangar decks, resulting in the Japanese carriers becoming very vulnerable to a U.S. air attack.

Much has been said about the fact that if *Shukaku* and *Zuikaku* or *Ryujo* and *Junyo* had been present in the battle, it would have been difficult for Japan to lose the Battle of Midway. Parshall and Tully, in their book *Shattered Sword*, postulate that "the fundamental truth remains that had CarDiv 5 (*Shokaku* and *Zuikaku*) been present at Midway, it is difficult to see how the Americans could have won, despite their intelligence and demonstrable luck." This statement has been regarded as conventional wisdom regarding the addition of these two carriers, including by this author.

The following is not to discredit the value of Japan having two more carriers, but given the circumstances as they occurred in the battle, another possibility exists. Upon closer analysis, the addition of two more carriers by Japan may not have unequivocally guaranteed a Japanese victory. On the surface, six Japanese carriers versus three U.S. carriers would appear to place the advantage clearly to the Japanese. But this conclusion is based on the assumption of a carrier-to-carrier sea engagement and not on one in which one of the opponents has a dual objective—the capture of Midway and the destruction of the U.S. carrier fleet. Once Japan launched the first wave of planes from all four carriers to attack Midway, the Kido Butai became vulnerable to the U.S. attacking first. As a result of the U.S. striking first, even if Japan had two additional carriers, the mathematical calculations, as ascertained by Captain Hughes in *Fleet Tactics* (ratio 6:4, assuming Midway is an unsinkable carrier), would be that three carriers would be lost by Japan and one carrier would be lost to the Americans in Japan's counterattack. However, at Midway, one critical factor makes the case to exclude this battle from Hughes's calculations: the dual purpose of the Midway operational plan. In Hughes's *Fleet Tactics*, his calculations were applied to four sea battles: the Coral Sea, Midway, the Santa Cruz Islands and the Philippine Sea. In three of the battles the conflicts were mainly of singular purpose: carrier-to-carrier warfare. However, at Midway there was duplicity of purpose, which could exclude the battle from his calculations.

In the actual Battle of Midway, three Japanese carriers were burning by 1330, and the Japanese only knew the location of *Yorktown* and were not aware of the other two U.S. carriers. Thus, only one U.S. carrier could have been attacked at that time. By 1335, Japan did learn the location of all three U.S. carriers, and if two additional Japanese carriers were present, the carrier-to-carrier ratio at this time would have been 3:3 (*Yorktown* damaged at this time) if we still include Midway Atoll as an unsinkable carrier. The outcome of the battle in these circumstances would have depended on which opponent made the first strike, leaving the final outcome of the battle uncertain as to its results. One must keep in mind that Japan could not afford to lose any of its carriers in the Battle of Midway, and at 1335 on June 4, Japan had already lost three significant carriers.

If Yamamoto had included *Zuikaku* and *Shokaku* (assuming the carriers were not assigned to the Coral Sea operation) in his attack on Midway, he most likely would not have altered his operational plan in any way, other than including the two carriers in the Kido Butai and not having the two carriers operate independently. This conclusion is reached because of the rigidity in Japanese planning and its inability to adapt to changing circumstances as they occurred; therefore, the preceding statistical analysis stands on its own merits.

The foregoing describes a number of the crucial flaws in the Japanese Midway operational plan. Another significant flaw was Japan's lack of commitment to a vigorous reconnaissance plan (only seven aircraft were used in the search for the American task force). These flaws led to the loss of any opportunity for Japan to strike at the American carrier fleet first. Striking first was irrevocably linked to the number of aircraft Japan devoted to finding the U.S. carrier fleet. In addition, and most importantly, is the fact that the search aircraft needed to be launched earlier than 0445 so that discovery of the U.S. fleet would reach Nagumo before the first wave of Japanese planes lifted off for Midway. Even so, the first strike by Japanese aircraft would have needed to reach the U.S. task force before 0700 when the United States was first launching its aircraft from *Enterprise* and *Hornet*. Early detection and an aggressive approach to scouting should have become an imperative if the Japanese were to have any opportunity to completely destroy all three U.S. carriers. If Yamamoto had not been wedded to occupying Midway and had instead limited his mission to the destruction of the American fleet, the outcome at Midway would most likely have been either—at best—a total victory for Japan (if Japan struck first) or—at worst—an even exchange in the loss of carriers for both opponents. This opportunity would have presented itself in the battle because the advantage of flexibility of naval movement would have negated the advantage that pre-battle U.S. intelligence offered at Midway—as it did in the Battle of the Coral Sea.

The following portion of the discussion is related to the tactical decision made by Nagumo at 0832 when he decided not to immediately launch all his available aircraft against the American fleet. The decision is analyzed from a new perspective; that is, during the entire morning of the battle, only *Yorktown* was vulnerable to Japanese attack. This conclusion is evident because *Tone*'s Number 4 plane lost sight of the first carrier he saw after being chased away by an *Enterprise* F4F fighter. The pilot of the Japanese scout plane then resumed his navigational course and reported back at 0820 seeing a U.S. carrier (*Yorktown*) that he presumed to be the same carrier that he had seen earlier. When *Chikuma*'s Number 5 scout plane replaced the *Tone*'s Number 4 scout plane, it flew to the last reported sighting by *Tone*'s plane and came upon *Yorktown*, not *Enterprise*. Thus, the Japanese knew only *Yorktown*'s location at this time and had no awareness of Task Force 16's presence in the area, until *Soryu*'s D4Y1 landed aboard *Hiryu* at 1335.

Between 0800 and 1330, Nagumo only knew for certain that the U.S. had one carrier in the area. Therefore, if Nagumo had taken the opportunity to launch all his available aircraft at 0830, his only target would have been *Yorktown* before U.S. forces attacked the Kido Butai between 0920 and 1022 on the morning of June 4.

The tactical dilemma that Nagumo faced could have been alleviated if all the aircraft in the first wave of the strike on Midway had been launched from just two carriers. This would leave the other two carriers to operate independently and be available to lift off a considerable strike force immediately if U.S. carriers were discovered in the area. However, Japanese officers, including Yamaguchi, opposed the concept of independent carrier operations involving both Carrier Division One and Carrier Division Two. Keep in mind that even if this tactical plan had been adopted, only *Yorktown* would have been at risk of sinking. The timeline for the foregoing is as follows: At 0820, *Tone*'s Number 4 plane reported sighting the U.S. carrier *Enterprise* (later *Yorktown*), but Nagumo decided not to act on this intelligence. Instead, he delayed the launchings and lost his chance to attack *Enterprise* (actually *Yorktown*).

This would be a lost opportunity to counterattack Task Force 17 because U.S. aircraft were already heading toward the Kido Butai. Even if the other scout aircraft (*Chikuma*'s Number 1 plane) had discovered *Yorktown* on its outbound leg between 0615 and 0630, it would have given Nagumo only forty-five minutes (a marginal opportunity at best) to launch all his available aircraft to attack *Yorktown* at that time.

It is important to point out that in *Midway*, Fuchida states that Nagumo should have implemented a two-phase search pattern. In this case, the first plane to take off would depart in the dark and the second plane at dawn. Fuchida suggests that this plan would have resulted in the discovery the U.S. task force at an earlier time. The difficulty with this proclamation is that this method of search did not exist in the Japanese naval doctrine in June 1942, and the rigidity of Japanese thinking prevented the possibility of a two-phase search from even being considered.

Japan's fixation on attacking Midway precluded any real opportunity for them to strike the American fleet first. Even if they had attempted to strike first, only *Yorktown* would have been vulnerable, for the location of *Enterprise* and *Hornet* were not known by the Japanese until 1335. To attack *Yorktown*, the Japanese would have needed to spot their aircraft by 0630 but half of their total striking force was over Midway at that time. Thus, at best, a strike against *Yorktown* at that time would have been made by half of the Kido Butai's available planes.

However, Japan's search aircraft did not locate an American carrier until 0820, precluding any possibility of Japan ever striking the U.S. fleet first. Japan's fixation on Midway and its failure to locate an American carrier much earlier in the morning condemned Japan to the disastrous results in the battle that followed.

In summary, Nagumo never had an opportunity to strike the U.S. task forces first and lost an opportunity to make a counterattack on *Yorktown* at 0830. The location of Task Force 16 was not known to Nagumo until 1330. By that time, *Enterprise* and *Hornet* could have been anywhere. It is true that *Soryu*'s Yokosuka D4Y1, a fast single-engine bomber, did discover all three U.S. carriers at 1110, but the pilot was unable to transmit the information due to radio trouble. The plane landed on *Hiryu* shortly after 1335, but by that time the information would not aid the Japanese, as *Hiryu* would soon be severely damaged, and would ultimately sink.

A counterattack by the Kido Butai against *Yorktown* could have been launched at 0830. The Japanese had thirty carrier attack planes, thirty-four dive-bombers, and about twelve to twenty fighters (a total of seventy-six to eighty-four aircraft to counterattack the U.S. task force).

Therefore, Nagumo passed on an early opportunity to counterattack Task Force 17. As a result, the striking force Nagumo had available after the United States attacked at 1022 was half (forty aircraft) of the force he had available at 0830.

The critical point here is that whether Nagumo sent a counterstrike against the U.S. carrier fleet at 0830, 1055 or 1330, the results would have been the same; that is, only *Yorktown* would have been attacked and ultimately lost, which is exactly what happened with the counterattacks of 1055 and 1330 and the sinking of the carrier by I-168. Task Force 16 was not vulnerable to a counterattack because the Japanese did not know for certain where Task Force 16 was until 1335. Thus, given the operational plan by Yamamoto, the best the Japanese could hope for would be the sinking of one U.S. carrier—*Yorktown*. This is a fact not well appreciated by historians.

The foregoing is an analysis of the crucial factors that were responsible for the defeat of Japan at Midway. The deeper question is why these errors of judgment occurred. Before analyzing the root cause of these misjudgments, I will first summarize Japan's miscalculations. Japan's failure to recognize that *concentration of force* is a prerequisite for victory in battle is a case in point.

Certainly, at Pearl Harbor, Yamamoto appreciated the role that concentration of force plays in obtaining victory at sea when he insisted on using six carriers in the operation. Yamamoto again applied the principle of concentration of force in the Indian Ocean campaign that followed, when he used five Japanese carriers in that operation. Yet Yamamoto lost sight of this critical principle at Coral Sea and Midway when he never forcefully complained to the Combined Fleet that the allocation of *Zuikaku* and *Shokaku* to the Coral Sea operation or *Ryujo* and *Junyo* to the Aleutian campaign would dilute his carrier force at Midway. Inclusion of these carriers, as has previously been cited, would have at least allowed the Japanese the opportunity of attacking *Enterprise* and *Hornet* after 1335, even though they still would have lost at least three carriers at Midway.

He also dispersed his powerful surface forces in his operational plan for Midway. The powerful surface force lay 300 miles to the west of Nagumo's Kido Butai. This distance was beyond the range where the surface force could support the Mobile Force, should it need assistance. Thus, when it came to a face-to-face confrontation with American carriers at Coral Sea and Midway the concept of concentration of force was abandoned by Yamamoto. The desertion of this concept would deprive the Kido Butai of the additional carriers it needed, as well as the surface forces' extensive defensive firepower at a time when it would be needed most—during the actual Battle of Midway.

There are also other errors of judgment made by Yamamoto and the Naval General Headquarters in its operational planning. Japan formulated its operational plans on what the enemy would probably do rather than what they were capable of doing. Thus, including Midway in the operational plan would not cause any difficulties for the Japanese because the American carriers would probably not be present in the area. However, this flaw in their military planning had even deeper roots than the foregoing indicates. This conclusion is amply illustrated by their dismissal of the results of the Midway war games. In the Japanese war games, the umpire proposed that two Japanese carriers were sunk by land-based Midway bombers, but he was overruled by Admiral Ugaki, who then reintroduced both carriers back into the war games as not having been sunk. This action by Ugaki demonstrates a dreamlike quality in Japanese thought processes that were a perfect recipe for defeat when facing the realities of actual military combat. Another example was the lack of consideration by Yamamoto and the Nagumo staff in its Midway operational plan to deal with the presence of an American fleet on its right flank at Midway. When this critical lapse was questioned at the war games, no one there could give a credible answer. The question, however, did prompt an ill-advised tactical plan whereby Nagumo would maintain half his aircraft on board his four carriers during the Midway raid, just in case the Americans were in the area, rather than eliminate the Midway Atoll from his operational plan. The decision made at the war games did not free Nagumo from the dual purpose in his mission at Midway, which was the major factor in Japan's overwhelming defeat at Midway.

Yamamoto clearly was not influenced by the intelligence he had in hand that should have raised the suspicion that a U.S. carrier fleet might be off Midway. Even the failure of Operation K did not cause him to cancel his attack on Midway and give orders that the Kido Butai should seek out and destroy the American fleet. Yamamoto also failed to insist that the three Japanese submarine cordons between Hawaii and Midway be in place by June 1. Neither did he demand that he be notified if his order was not able to be executed on time. His indifference to these important matters was another example of the dreamlike state that existed in Japanese thinking prior to the Battle of Midway.

The root of Japan's military failures at Midway can be traced back to fatal flaws that existed in the Japanese character and certainly in Yamamoto and the Naval General Staff, which were not well appreciated before Midway because the war in the Pacific was going well for Japan.

However, once adversity presented itself, the leaders of Japan regressed back into their dreamlike state, which exposed the flaws in their thinking. Japan had developed a culture whereby individual initiative and flexibility of action were not valued assets in its people. Instead, rigidity of purpose and adherence to an operational plan with no changes in thinking, despite changing circumstances or what reason dictated, should be the mode of thought. As long as the Japanese mission was successful and going as planned (as in the early part of the war), the flaw was not exposed. But once adversity set in, as in the Doolittle Raid, reason did not exist and a dreamlike state prevailed over Japanese thought. Once Yamamoto, Nagumo, the Combined Fleet and the Naval General Headquarters had their Midway operational plan, there would be no changes in its execution, despite what the circumstances dictated.

Other reasons that contributed to the Imperial Japanese Navy's defeat at Midway were (1) Yamamoto's insistence on keeping the Main Force 300 miles to the west of the Kido Butai rather than be included in the Mobile Force, which precluded him from having direct control of the battle at Midway; (2) the lack of radar in any of the ships of the Kido Butai at Midway prevented the Japanese from detecting incoming U.S. planes when they were miles from the Kido Butai; (3) the use of a single radio frequency and of inferior-quality and limited-range radios in the CAP aircraft prevented the planes from being vectored out to the incoming dive-bombers at the crucial moment of 1022; and (4) overemphasis by Japan on the offensive side of its military assets with minimal attention being paid to the defensive side of the battle equation is amply demonstrated by the suboptimal defensive firepower that Japan's surface warships would have provided if they were part of the Kido Butai at the time of the battle.

A factor not previously discussed in detail by historians for the defeat at Midway was the target itself. It is important to discuss an alternate choice of location for Japan to confront the U.S. Navy and destroy the U.S. fleet. This is an important discussion because it means that Japan had a choice between defeat at Midway and victory in the Coral Sea and unwittingly made the wrong choice. The reason for stating that Japan was destined to be defeated at Midway was clearly the result of its flawed Midway operational plan (as previously discussed) and the United States' excellent decision making, courage and good fortune.

Japan could have enticed the entire U.S. carrier fleet to engage the Kido Butai in the Coral Sea by threatening the sea-lanes to Australia by its invasion of Port Moresby. This conclusion is supported by the fact that *Lexington* and *Yorktown* steamed to the Coral Sea on the basis of U.S. intelligence which indicated that a Japanese invasion (with as many as four Japanese carriers) of Port Moresby on May 1, 1942, was eminent. In addition, Nimitz indicated his willingness to risk all four American carriers to protect Australia from being isolated when he ordered *Enterprise* and *Hornet*, after the Doolittle Raid on April 18 (Japanese date), to speed toward the Coral Sea to reinforce American carrier strength in the area. Therefore, a much wiser decision for Yamamoto would have been to force a confrontation with the United States in the South Pacific, which would have included *Zuikaku* and *Shokaku*, and possibly even *Ryujo* and *Junyo*. This action would have given Japan six and possibly eight carriers to oppose America's four carriers, a ratio of 6:4 or 8:4, with a clear advantage to the Japanese. Again, and most importantly, Yamamoto would have had to act as he did in the actual Battle of the Coral Sea, that is, to postpone the Townsville air raid (an Allied air base in Northeast Australia) and allow his six to eight carriers freedom of movement in the Coral Sea.

Japan needed to force a naval engagement between itself and the United States to achieve the very success that Japan was seeking to accomplish at Midway. The advantages that would have accrued for Japan at Coral Sea would be: (1) the use of at least six carriers in the operation; (2) a significant lessening of the importance of pre-battle U.S. intelligence, because the Kido Butai at the Coral Sea would not be focused on a fixed target—Midway; (3) freedom of movement of the Japanese fleet that would make it more difficult to be discovered by U.S. scouting aircraft, especially since the thirty-two PBY-5 and PBY-5A scouting aircraft from Midway would be absent; (4) the Japanese air base at Rabaul in New Britain, which could provide air cover for the Japanese task force was just 500–600 miles away from the Louisiade Archipelago, compared to the air base at Japanese-occupied Wake Island, which was 1,182 miles from Midway; and (5) Coral Sea was moderately further away from Japan (3,155 miles) as compared to the distance from Japan to Midway (2,553 miles). However, the distance from Pearl Harbor to the Coral Sea was 4,287 miles, which was a vastly greater distance for the United States to transverse as compared to the distance from Pearl Harbor to Midway (1,140 miles), making reinforcement of the air bases in Australia and eastern New Guinea difficult if not impossible.

Critically important is that if Japan had flexibility of movement for its carriers in the Coral Sea, the basic flaw in its operational plan at Midway would have been eliminated. Ironically, in the Battle of the Coral Sea, it was Fletcher who was initially restricted in his movements at sea by staying in range of Port Moresby so that he could protect the Allied air base.

In conclusion, Yamamoto could have also achieved his goal of confronting all four U.S. carriers in the Coral Sea as well as off the waters of Midway. In addition, he would have had superior carrier forces, which would not have been restricted in their movement by a fixation on Midway.

America's role in its victory at Midway was multifaceted and consisted of the following factors:

1. U.S. intelligence played one of the most critical roles because it allowed the Americans the opportunity to strike the Japanese first and when they were most vulnerable—with all of their aircraft fueled and armed in the hangar decks (except for the dive-bombers, which were fully fueled but not armed with bombs until they reached the flight deck). That said, it is important to point out that battles at sea are more unpredictable than battles on land. John Keegan commented in *The Price of Admiralty* that a sea battle may have many unexpected turns of events whereby the battle plan does not play out in

reality as it does on paper. There are more uncertainties that occur in sea battles that in those battles that are fought on land.[1]

Therefore, the advantage that the United States had with its intelligence about the upcoming battle did not provide absolute certainty that America would decisively defeat the Japanese. Execution of its operational plan was required by the United States, and that there be no changes in the movements of the Japanese fleet was mandatory for an American victory. Many times, as previously stated, the battle plan on paper does not conform to what actually happens in a battle at sea. This fact was well demonstrated in the Battle of Midway as the conflict unfolded: (1) *Hornet*'s dive-bombers never found the Japanese fleet; (2) only half of *Yorktown*'s dive-bombers participated in the attack on the Kido Butai on the morning of June 4; (3) *Enterprise*'s dive-bombers only found the Kido Butai through good fortune, courage and determination; and (4) the Mobile Force changed course to the northeast at 0918 before *Enterprise*'s and *Yorktown*'s dive-bombers could reach them.

2. Parshall and Tully in their book *Shattered Sword* challenge the concept that Midway was an "incredible victory" for the United States because they believe the U.S. Navy did not face an overwhelming superior Japanese naval force. Although this is true on an operational level, it is not true at a tactically functional level. If one analyzes the battle on a functional basis, it becomes evident that all three carrier torpedo bomber groups and the incoming aircraft from Midway were ineffective in their attempt to damage or destroy the Japanese carriers. *Enterprise* was the only carrier that succeeded in contributing its full complement of dive-bombers to the mission of attacking the Kido Butai. *Yorktown* provided only half of its dive-bombers to strike the Japanese carrier fleet (the other half of the dive-bombers were held back for scouting), and *Hornet*'s dive-bombers and fighters never found the Kido Butai at all. These functional statistics place the carrier odds in the Battle of Midway at 4:1.5 in favor of the Japanese. These odds are slightly better for Japan than if *Shokaku* and *Zuikaku* were present (2:1) at the beginning of the battle. This fact clearly points out the value of attacking your enemy's carriers first, with all of its aircraft armed and fueled in the hangar decks, regardless of the carrier odds. It also demonstrates that the American success at Midway was undeniably an incredible victory.

3. Luck is said to be the cause when a series of unplanned or unlikely circumstances combine to produce a favorable outcome. The following critical moments in the Battle of Midway were a series of independent circumstances in which those involved had no idea that carrying out their missions would result in such a favorable outcome. For example, as Lieutenant Commander William H. Brockman, Jr., Commander of the submarine *Nautilus*, was carrying out his mission to attack the Kido Butai, the submarine was detected by an observer in the Japanese fleet, which resulted in destroyer *Arashi* being ordered to leave the fleet to drop depth charges on the submarine. If *Nautilus* had not been aggressively pursuing the Japanese fleet, *Arashi*'s wake would

8. Analysis of the Defeat

never have been seen by McClusky's aircraft as the destroyer headed back to the Kido Butai. Otherwise, *Enterprise*'s aircraft most likely would have missed the Japanese fleet entirely, especially since its planes were low on fuel.

The role that luck played in this episode is undeniable and was a critical factor not only in *Enterprise*'s dive-bombers finding the Kido Butai but in *Enterprise*'s aircraft arriving at the same time as *Yorktown*'s dive-bombers. These circumstances enabled both *Enterprise*'s and *Yorktown*'s aircraft the ability to execute an uncoordinated coordinated attack on the Kido Butai between 1015 and 1030. Without the foregoing occurrences, *Yorktown* would have attacked the Kido Butai alone, which most likely would have resulted only in *Soryu* being fatally damaged. Japan would still have had three remaining carriers, and at best, if *Enterprise* had found the Kido Butai, its aircraft would have made the attack alone.

The second critical instance of luck was on the other end of the uncoordinated coordinated attack, whereby *Yorktown*'s planes arrived on the scene of the battle exactly when *Enterprise*'s aircraft reached the Kido Butai. This unplanned event was a result of two factors: (1) Fletcher's excellent execution in launching his aircraft in a timely and coordinated fashion and (2) because of the excellent navigational skills of *Yorktown*'s pilots which allowed *Yorktown*'s aircraft to get to the target in only one hour and fifteen minutes from takeoff. Thus, luck once again clearly played a major role in Japan's overwhelming defeat at Midway.

4. Courage, determination and bravery all played a role in the U.S. victory at Midway. The courage of all three torpedo squadrons from *Hornet*, *Enterprise* and *Yorktown* to attack the Kido Butai without fighter support can only be described as heroic. Each crew member of the torpedo bomber crew knew they would almost certainly die in the process of the attack, and yet they carried out their mission. The TBD aircraft was slow and extremely vulnerable to destruction by the Japanese Zero. Thirty-seven of the forty-one aircraft did not return safely—or not at all—to their carriers. The torpedo attacks by the Americans gained the admiration of the Japanese at the time of the attacks and impressed upon them that America was no easy foe. All three torpedo attacks disrupted the Japanese counterattack against the Americans. In addition, *Yorktown*'s torpedo bombers brought the Japanese Zeroes down to sea level, allowing the U.S. dive-bombers from *Enterprise* and *Yorktown* to attack the Kido Butai unmolested, free to bomb the Japanese carriers at will.

Another example of great courage was the decision made by Lieutenant Commander Wade McClusky to continue on his search for the Kido Butai even though they were reaching the point of no return on their fuel gauges. The thirty-one planes had flown on a course of 240 degrees and out to a distance of 151 miles. At 0920, they reached the area where they should have intercepted the Japanese fleet but instead found empty ocean. The planes flew on as one of the planes' gas gauge reached empty. McClusky still flew stubbornly on. At 0955, McClusky knew that if he did not find the Japanese carriers in the next five minutes, the dive-bombers would have to return to

Enterprise. All of the planes' pilots and crews were tense when they suddenly spotted the wake of a ship in the distance. One of the SBDs ran out of gas and crashed into the sea. It was under these heroic circumstances that *Enterprise*'s dive-bombers found the Kido Butai and began their attack.

5. The names of some of the outstanding leaders that contributed to the American victory at Midway include the following:

Lieutenant Commander Joseph Rochefort, USN
Head of Communications Intelligence Unit at Pearl Harbor (Hypo)

Joseph Rochefort was at one time among the unsung heroes of the Battle of Midway. His leadership was responsible for deciphering enough of the JN-25B naval code to determine that Midway was the target of the Japanese assault. Decoding Japanese naval intelligence was the first step in gaining intelligence; the second step was the interpretation of that intelligence. OP-20-G under Captain John Redman in Washington, D.C., was adamant that the Japanese target was going to be in the South Pacific. It was Rochefort's belief in his interpretation of the intelligence that led to his setting up an intelligence ruse that was broadcast over the airways in the clear that Midway was out of water. The Japanese cited AF (Midway) in their intelligence communications as the centerpiece of their impending invasion. When the Japanese accepted the bait by broadcasting that AF (Midway) was out of water, it confirmed that Midway was the primary Japanese target.

However, there is more to the story than the foregoing. Rochefort stood firm in his conclusion that Midway was the target and did not defer to the opinion held by his chief, John Redman, that the attack would come somewhere in the South Pacific. There was intense political pressure on Rochefort to defer to Redman because of the friction that existed between Hypo and OP-20-G over who should have control over interpreting the JN-25B naval code. As a result, Redman was determined to remove Rochefort as head of Station Hypo at all costs. Redman undermined the efforts of Rochefort by proclaiming to Hypo cryptanalyst Jack Holtwick that "Station Hypo missed the boat," requiring Station Negat to bail them out.[2] True to his word, Redman was finally successful in removing Rochefort as head of Hypo by gaining the support of Vice Admiral Fredrick Horne, Vice Chief of Naval Operations. On October 22, 1942, Joe Rochefort received orders that ultimately led to his removal as head of Station Hypo. He was to go to San Francisco to report to Rear Admiral John W. Greenslade of the Western Sea Frontier and the Twelfth Naval District. Greenslade wanted him to develop an intelligence center on the West Coast. Rochefort did not feel it was necessary since the Japanese were now on the defensive, but he did not argue.[3]

Rochefort retired from active duty in the Navy on March 2, 1953, and died on July 20, 1976, at the age of seventy-six. Rochefort's superiors opposed him receiving the Distinguished Service Medal (DSM), even though six other individuals in radio intelligence were awarded the DSM. It took forty-four years and the political efforts of Rear Admiral Donald Showers, USN (Ret.), to correct this injustice. Finally, On May 30, 1986, President Ronald Reagan awarded the DSM to Joseph Rochefort, ten years after his death, at a White House ceremony.[4]

Admiral Chester W. Nimitz, USN
Commander in Chief, Pacific Fleet

(A) Nimitz's tactical directive that placed three U.S. carriers to the northeast of Midway fulfilled the concept of concentration of force and allowed the carriers to operate in concert with one another.

(B) His order to Task Force 16 and 17 that they should operate on the principle of calculated risk, which he defined as "the avoidance of exposure of your force to attack by superior enemy forces without a good prospect of inflicting, as the result of such exposure, greater damage to the enemy was critical."[5] This principle allowed Midway's commanders flexibility of decision, and unlike the Japanese commanders, they were not wedded to only one course of action.

(C) His order on May 28 was crucial when he called upon a civilian crew to assist the U.S. Navy in repairing *Yorktown*, a feat accomplished within seventy-two hours so that the carrier could be present at Midway. The absence of *Yorktown* at Midway for the United States would have had a catastrophic effect on the outcome of the battle. A 4:2 superiority of Japanese carriers to U.S. carriers would clearly have given the Japanese the advantage in the outcome. (In reality, the ratio would have been 4:1 in favor of the Japanese as *Hornet*'s dive-bombers and fighters never found the Kido Butai, and its torpedo bombers elicited no damage to the Japanese carriers.)

Rear Admiral Frank Jack Fletcher, USN
Commander of Carrier Striking Force

(A) Fletcher's leadership in turning over the command of the battle to Spruance, when he turned north to search for any Japanese carriers that might be lurking on their right flank.

(B) His excellent execution at 0900 on June 4, in launching *Yorktown*'s aircraft in an orderly manner, gave *Yorktown*'s planes the opportunity to arrive exactly on the scene when *Enterprise*'s dive-bombers found the Kido Butai. This coincidence resulted in an uncoordinated coordinated attack on the Japanese fleet with all of *Yorktown*'s complement of torpedo planes, dive-bombers and fighters participating.

Rear Admiral Raymond A. Spruance, USN
Commander of Task Force 16

(A) Spruance made a vital decision on the morning of June 4 to close the distance to within 150 miles of the Kido Butai before launching Task Force 16's aircraft so fuel could be conserved for their safe return to the carriers. In addition, Spruance continued to steam southwest by west to further decrease the distance that his pilots would have to fly to return to Task Force 16.

(B) Spruance's decision on the eve of June 4 not to head northwest and risk an engagement with the powerful Japanese surface forces. Instead, he steamed east, then south and finally west at a reduced speed on the eve of June 4. These changes in directions and slower speed not only avoided the enemy but also conserved fuel.

6. Japanese courage notwithstanding, the determination and bravery of America's Navy and Marine pilots on Midway and by the Marine forces defending Midway was a contributing factor in the U.S. success at Midway. This courage and determination was best exemplified by the following: (1) the absence of fighter support for the planes launched from Midway in their attacks on the Kido Butai; (2) the interception by Midway's twenty-four U.S. Marine aircraft against the incoming 108 Japanese aircraft attacking Midway resulted in all but two U.S. fighters being destroyed or operational after the attack; (3) the determination and accuracy exhibited by the men operating the antiaircraft guns on Midway, which resulted in the destruction of over 50 percent of *Hiryu*'s seventeen torpedo bombers that attacked Midway Island. This occurrence limited the availability of *Hiryu*'s torpedo bombers in attacking *Yorktown* later that day. Instead of seventeen kankos from *Hiryu* making the mission against *Yorktown* at 1330 on June 4, only ten torpedo bombers were included in the attack (nine torpedo bombers from *Hiryu* and one torpedo bomber from *Akagi*).

7. The United States' employment of ten SBD dive-bombers from *Yorktown* in its search for a possible Japanese fleet on its flank. In comparison, the Japanese used mostly float planes from its battleships and cruisers and utilized a low number of aircraft (seven) to search for the U.S. fleet. On the defensive side of the equation, the U.S. carriers had radar on all three of its carriers for detecting incoming enemy planes, while none of the Japanese carriers had radar.

8. With no experience on both sides prior to the Battle of the Coral Sea in carrier-to-carrier warfare, the United States was able to appreciate that the carrier had replaced the battleship as the prime instrument of naval success in sea battles. Though there was debate in the U.S. Navy on this issue, as to which ship was most important in battle at sea, the forces that favored the carrier won the debate. The carrier concept was adopted but was aided by the fact that all of the U.S. battleships were too slow to keep up with the carriers, and in addition, most of the battleships were damaged or destroyed at Pearl Harbor. From a tactical standpoint, the U.S. Navy had little choice but to accept the change in their tactical decision that would emphasize the carrier over the battleship in future naval engagements with the enemy.

Japan ultimately would not be able to challenge America's military power and assets in the war in the Pacific. Japan had lost four carriers at Midway, and the United States had lost one carrier.

Following the battle and going into 1944, Japan commissioned seven fleet carriers. In comparison, the United States commissioned fourteen fleet carriers, nine light carriers and sixty-six escort carriers. In addition, the number of Japanese aircraft deployed during this period of time was 1,000 aircraft, while America had over 3,000 planes in its arsenal.[6]

8. Analysis of the Defeat

One significant factor that is not well-enough emphasized was Japan's limited ability to replace its pilots lost in battle, so that even if Japan had been able to match America's capacity to construct aircraft carriers, Japan would not have had the pilots to fly its aircraft. Japan had between 1,000 and 1,500 men trained to pilot its aircraft. It could produce only 100 new pilots a year. The loss of at least ninety pilots at Midway meant that an entire annual graduating class was lost.[7] The United States on the other hand produced at least 250 new pilots a year, many of whom entered combat after having only one to five hours' flying time.

In the end, Japan inflicted defeat on itself by its own irrational operational plan for Midway, which was taken advantage of by the United States in its utilization of gathered intelligence, courage, and determination, and by having luck on its side. The American victory at Midway turned the tide of the war in the Pacific in favor of the United States, and Japan was never again able to take the offensive in the war.

During the Battle of Midway, Japan lost four carriers, *Akagi*, *Kaga*, *Soryu* and *Hiryu*, and one heavy cruiser, *Mikuma*. The United States lost one carrier, *Yorktown*, and one destroyer, *Hammann*.

Two hundred forty-eight Japanese aircraft were lost, which included twenty-one Zeroes that the four carriers were ferrying to Midway. The Americans lost 147 aircraft. About three thousand Japanese men were killed in action as compared to 307 Americans. In addition, forty-nine marines were killed and fifty-three were wounded on Midway.

On August 7, 1942, less than two months after the Battle of Midway, U.S. Marine and Naval forces took the offensive by invading a then little-known island in the Solomon Islands called Guadalcanal. The long road to Japan had begun, and now there was no turning back.

9

The Significance of the Battle

When a war is fought on a global level, the outcome of war in one area of battle may have significant influence over the outcome of battle in another area of the world. The decisive American victory at the Battle of Midway in June 1942 had profound effects on World War II in its entirety, having both short- and long-term global consequences. The well-documented short-term consequence of the battle was that it emphatically ended a series of consecutive Japanese offensive successes in the Pacific and resulted in the inability of Japan to regain the offensive in the war in the Pacific. Much less appreciated is the long-term consequence of the decisive victory at Midway, permitting both America and Great Britain to focus the majority of their military resources on defeating Germany rather than diluting their military assets by shifting forces to reinforce the Pacific.

In the aftermath of the Japanese attack on Pearl Harbor on December 7, 1941, and of Germany's and Italy's declaration of war against the United States four days later, America was faced with a choice between focusing its military action either in the Atlantic or in the Pacific. The United States was far from being fully prepared for war in 1941, and it did not have the capability to fight a two-ocean war. Efforts in one theater of operation would limit efforts in the other; attempts to devote most of its military assets in the Atlantic would limit what forces would be allocated to the war effort in the Pacific. Weighing the alternatives, America and Great Britain committed to having to forfeit any attempts to recapture Wake Island or Guam or to defend the Philippine Islands from Japanese conquest.

There were several reasons for this strategic decision implemented jointly by the United States and Great Britain which gave preference to winning the war in Europe rather than stemming the tide in the Far East. First, Great Britain was the only country remaining in Europe that was free of German domination, and as such, it represented the last bastion of democracy in western Europe; second, Britain was the only country in Europe that the United States could count on as a military base; third, German submarine attacks on U.S. Merchant Marine vessels were raging, and the Allies were losing the battle; and fourth, British colonies in southeast Asia, namely Hong Kong, Singapore and the Malaysian peninsula, had fallen into Japanese hands by mid–February 1942, and neither the United States nor Britain was in any military position to recapture these possessions.

Over the past twenty years, recognition that the Battle of Midway was the turning point of the war in the Pacific has greatly improved, in large measure due to the efforts of the International Midway Memorial Foundation. However, as late as 2005, Parshall and Tully in their book *Shattered Sword* challenge this proposition by stating that Midway was not a decisive battle in an absolute sense because the outcome of the war in the Pacific was never in doubt. They conclude that even if all four Japanese carriers returned from Midway intact, the best case scenario would be that the strategic benefit would last only until mid–1943, when the United States commissioned the first of many new Essex-class fleet carriers which were larger, carried more aircraft and were better armed defensively in the number of antiaircraft guns than had previously existed in the service.

While the latter statement is true, Parshall and Tully did not take into account that victory in any war is never assured, regardless of what either side has in military resources. The variables in winning or losing wars are many, but they certainly include the maintenance of public support at home for a war effort. The U.S. victory at Midway in June 1942, after which Japan would never again take the offensive in the war in the Pacific, only increased the desire of the American people to have more U.S. military resources utilized in defeating Japan. After all, Japan had preemptively attacked Pearl Harbor (the immediate impetus for our entry into World War II), and although Germany had declared war on America, prior to the attack on Pearl Harbor, many people in America felt the war in Europe was a European affair and that we should stay out of the conflict.

There were two political perspectives that were inherent in America's public opinion of the global war following the attack on Pearl Harbor on December 7, 1941. The first political viewpoint was that the majority of Americans did not favor the war in Europe at that time. When Roosevelt asked Congress to declare war on Japan on December 8, 1941, he adroitly avoided declaring war on Germany due to the lack of American support for the war in Europe. In actuality, Germany declared war on the United States on December 11, 1941, and only then did the United States declare war on Germany. The second political viewpoint was that Japan's surprise attack on Pearl Harbor on December 7, 1941, mobilized public sentiment to fully support the war in the Pacific; however, public opinion was much less willing to support the strategy of a "Europe First" policy. As a result, when the public learned about the U.S. strategic decision to focus primarily on the war in Europe and relegate the war in the Pacific to second place, the public disapproved of this policy and clearly favored a policy that placed the war in the Pacific as America's primary military mission. One of the few public opinion polls conducted during World War II revealed in February 1943 that 82 percent of Americans identified Japan as the United States' main adversary, and 34 percent chose Germany. Thus, in spite of America's overwhelming victory at Midway on June 4, 1942, public pressure intensified on the military to transfer resources from Europe to the Pacific to accelerate the rate at which the United States was waging war against the Japanese.

On October 3, 1942, General Brehan Somerwell, USA, made an announcement on Movietone News that the United States was still losing the war in Europe and in the Pacific and warned the public about becoming complacent regarding the war effort. In spite of Somerwell's speech, the public still desired that America devote most of its attention to the Pacific and not Europe. By late 1943, it was becoming more difficult for the United States to maintain its strategic Europe First policy (begun in December 1941) while relegating the war in the Pacific to second place. Public opinion would not allow this policy to continue, and the political and military powers were very aware of this sentiment. The U.S. populace were not pleased with the manner in which the war in the Pacific was being fought.[1] The American public wanted the war in the Pacific—not Europe—to be the primary focus of military action. After all, Pearl Harbor was preemptively attacked by the Japanese.

In an effort to maintain the status quo in America's strategic planning in the global war, the U.S. military leadership hastened its efforts to implement the plan for the Normandy invasion so that the United States would be able to devote more attention to Japan. On December 7, 1943, the U.S. government made another effort to influence public opinion by revealing for the first time in the Movietone newsreels shown in theaters the deaths and causalities sustained by the U.S. Marines in the battle for Tarawa and continued the newsreel policy in subsequent Pacific war battles. A review of Movietone newsreels made during 1942 to late 1943 reveals that none of the newsreels showed any deaths or causalities sustained by Americans in the war in the Pacific or in Europe.

The argument can be made that this action was intended to ignite public resolve for continuing the war as it was being fought in the Pacific in mid–1943. Eventually these efforts to sway public opinion did succeed in influencing the public to support America's Europe First policy and for the U.S. military to continue to relegate the war in the Pacific to second place.

The foregoing vividly demonstrates that even with a decisive U.S. victory at Midway, public opinion still favored that less attention be paid to the European conflict and that the United States focus primarily on the war in the Pacific. After the Japanese attack on Pearl Harbor, U.S. public opinion obviously favored that the first priority in the global war be in the Pacific. Ironically, if America had lost decisively at Midway, the opposition to relegating the Pacific to second place in the global conflict would have been dramatically more vocal. Following the devastating Japanese Pearl Harbor attack, a U.S. defeat at Midway would have enraged the public even more, especially since they knew that the Europe First policy was in effect. The swell of public opinion for sending military resources from Europe to the Pacific would have been overwhelming, and the Europe First policy would have been abandoned or modified. Therefore, the victory at Midway was a decisive victory in an absolute sense (and not a relative one as opined by Parshall and Tully), because it influenced the outcome of war in the Pacific and in Europe.

The latter statement is reinforced by former Secretary of Defense James R. Schlesinger's speech at the 2003 Washington, D.C., Midway Night Dinner where he made the case that the victory at Midway paved the way for victory in Europe by allowing Roosevelt to maintain his Europe First policy. Schlesinger pointed out that the invasion of North Africa, Sicily, Italy and Normandy either might never have taken place or would have been greatly delayed in their implementation.

He concluded that without these invasions, the Soviet Union might not have survived, or if it had and the Soviet forces had succeeded in their march westward, the face of post-war western Europe would have been dramatically changed. He concluded, as does this author, that the victory at Midway was clearly the turning point not only in the Pacific but in Europe as well.

It is worth quoting Prime Minister Winston Churchill from his book *Hinge of Fate*, in which he stated in the aftermath of the Battle of Midway that "this memorable American victory was of cardinal importance, not only to the United States but to the whole Allied cause…. At one stroke, the dominant position of Japan in the Pacific was reversed"[2]—a testimony to the far-reaching efforts that the victory at Midway had on the global war.

The military situation for the Allies in the summer of 1942 was precarious at best. Germany was winning the battle in the Atlantic, and in June 1942, its submarines had sunk 823,656 tons of Allied shipping, which was the worst ally loss for the year up to that time; in addition, the German army was at the doorsteps of Stalingrad and the Caucasus oil fields in southeast Russia; and the military outcome of war in Africa was in doubt as Tobruk had just fallen into German hands. More importantly, Germany was well ahead of the United States in the development of its rocket and jet technology, but not in radar. Although this research was in the early stages of its development, the Germans were rapidly closing in on realizing the full potential of the science, which would present to them potent and superior military weapons with which the Allies could not compete—namely, jet aircraft and intercontinental missiles. Time was therefore of the essence, and a delay in the war for one or two years would most likely have provided Germany with air superiority over the skies in Europe and in its ability to reach Great Britain, and possibly the United States, with intercontinental ballistic missiles. It was true that America had the advantage in atomic bomb research over Germany and Japan, but both Axis countries were actively pursuing this avenue of research as well. However, they were slow in making any significant progress. Neither country has been conclusively shown to have detonated a nuclear device during the war, although there have been unsubstantiated reports they may have done so.

The one critical military area that hung in the balance in Europe was the battle of Stalingrad, because the Germans were on the outskirts of the city in June 1942. Eight months later, German forces surrendered to the Russians on February 2, 1943. The Prime Minister of Britain, Winston Churchill, reflecting on the outcome, stated that the victory by the Russians was a significant factor in changing the course of the war against the Axis powers. Churchill described the outcome thus: "the hinge of fate has turned."[3] Reading both the German and Japanese decrypted intelligence, Churchill realized that the Axis plan was to proceed through the Caucasus Mountains, which were south of Stalingrad, and arrive at the borders of Turkey, Iraq and Iran.[4]

The success of this military objective would provide Germany with access to the Persian Gulf and would result in the following: (1) it would likely cause neutral Turkey to join the Axis powers; (2) a major Allied supply route to Russia from Basra on the Persian Gulf through Tehran would be disrupted; (3) it would place the oil fields of the Middle East in danger of being captured; (4) it would provide Germany with another alternative route to supply Field Marshall Erwin Rommel, leader of the German African Corps in North Africa, rather than utilizing the Mediterranean Sea route, which was subject to constant attack by British aircraft and in which Germany was losing merchant ships at an alarming rate; (5) north Afghanistan and India would be isolated; and (6) the Germans, having invaded the Caucasus oil fields, could turn west through Iraq and attack Egypt, control the Suez Canal and link up with Rommel in northern Africa.

The turning of the tide by the Russians at Stalingrad was in part made possible by the transporting of Russian troops from Russia's eastern front on the Manchurian border to the western front at Stalingrad. On September 1, 1942, the Japanese minister in Germany reported to German officials that Russia had transported over 50,000–60,000 troops from the Far East to the western front.[5] On the other hand, the train traveling from the western front to the east was devoid of any troops. While it is true that Japan had no desire to go to war with Russia (since Japan was severely defeated by the Soviets in the battle of Nomonhan in 1939), Russia had no inclination to begin a conflict with Japan; nevertheless, had the Japanese been victorious at Midway, the Japanese Army might have been emboldened to mass its troops on the Manchurian border and thus threaten the Russian position. This was true because Japan had already learned through its ability to decipher Russian coded messages that Russia had intentions to dominate that area of the world.

Either Russia would have decided not to transfer any troops to the western front, which would have weakened its military position at Stalingrad, or it would have allowed the potential Japanese invasion into eastern Siberia to occur. The former alternative most likely would have been implemented by Russia. The consequences of this German victory would have delayed an Allied invasion of North Africa in November 1942 and the invasion of Normandy in June 1944 by at least two years. This delay would have given Germany the time it needed to develop its jet plane technology and intercontinental ballistic program, which could have altered the outcome of the war in Europe or at a minimum prolonged the war for years.

On the Pacific side of the war, if Japan had been victorious at Midway and destroyed all three U.S. carriers, the Americans would only have had three carriers left in its arsenal in June 1942: *Saratoga* (CV-3), *Ranger* (CV-4) and *Wasp* (CV-7). If *Ranger* and *Wasp* were transferred from the Atlantic to the Pacific, this action would leave the Atlantic devoid of any U.S. carriers. The Japanese, on the other hand, would have had six fleet carriers (*Akagi, Kaga, Soryu, Hiryu, Zuikaku* and *Shokaku*), two medium carriers (*Junyo* and *Ryujo*) and two very small carriers (*Hosho* and *Zuiho*). The ratio of 10:3 would have given Japan a decisive advantage should there have been a subsequent confrontation between the two navies. In addition, Midway would have been in the hands of the Japanese, Australia would have been isolated, and the Japanese would have had the freedom to reinforce the islands it had taken and expand its defense perimeter of the home islands of Japan.

If Japan had the foresight following its victory at Midway, it could have realized that it had two critical missions to accomplish: the destruction of the three remaining U.S. carriers (*Saratoga, Wasp* and *Ranger*) and the completion of its unfinished business at Pearl Harbor, where it critically failed to destroy the fuel tanks, dry docks and repair facilities during its attack there on December 7, 1941. America's loss of its oil tanks, dry docks and repair facilities in Pearl Harbor would force the entire U.S. fleet to withdraw to the West Coast. Parshall and Tully stated in their book *Shattered Sword* that Japan would never have invaded Hawaii because it would lack the aircraft that would provide the necessary air cover that would be needed to ensure the success of the invasion. This statement may very well be true, but Japan would not have needed to invade Hawaii if it destroyed the logistical support for Pearl Harbor's U.S. fleet in the Pacific.

On December 7, 1941, the fuel tanks at Pearl Harbor were above ground and located at the eastern end of Pearl Harbor near the submarine base (upper tanks) and between Hickam Field and Pearl Harbor (lower tanks). Neither the fuel tanks, the dry docks nor the repair facilities were targeted in the Japanese attack on Pearl Harbor. The failure to destroy the dry docks and repair facilities permitted *Yorktown* later to be repaired almost six months later, which allowed *Yorktown* to play a significant role in Japan's defeat at Midway. Its absence would have given the United States only two carriers for that confrontation, meaning that the United States would have most likely forfeited Midway to the Japanese.

It was an egregious tactical error that the Japanese planners of the Pearl Harbor attack neglected to include the destruction of the oil and gas storage tanks at Pearl Harbor, which were the U.S. Navy's most vulnerable resources. Lack of fuel at Pearl Harbor would have caused the U.S. fleet to retreat back to the West Coast. The tanks were aboveground and lacked bombproof covers. A few bombs or strafing by Japanese fighters would have set off massive explosions and resulted in the destruction of all the fuel storage tanks.[6]

It is true that the process of relocating the fuel tanks below ground began in December 1940 and continued until September 1943. This was called the Red Hill Storage Tank Project. However, in the summer of 1942, the construction was still in progress.

The fuel tanks at Pearl Harbor held 4.5 million barrels of oil. The loss of this reserve would have been catastrophic for the U.S. fleet, and with only 12,000 tons of fuel at Brisbane and 8,000 tons of fuel each at Sydney and Melbourne, Australia, fuel reserves in that area of the Pacific were precarious at best. Thus, the U.S. Navy's fleet would be forced to relocate to the West Coast of the United States.[7]

The United States had only two oil tankers in Pearl Harbor on December 7 and three tankers at sea. The other six tankers were located on the West Coast, four of which could refuel ships at sea. The total capacity of the Pacific Fleet oilers was 760,000 barrels of oil, but in the first nine days after December 7, the U.S. fleet in the Pacific consumed about 750,000 barrels of oil, leaving only 10,000 barrels left in reserve. With the oil and gas facilities destroyed at Pearl Harbor, the U.S. fleet would not have had enough fuel to operate out of Pearl Harbor.

In the summer of 1942, *Saratoga*, *Ranger* and *Wasp* would need to be destroyed before Japan could contemplate an attack on Pearl Harbor's fuel storage tanks, dry docks and repair facilities.

The loss of America's remaining carriers, coupled with the U.S. fleet retreating back to the West Coast, would have granted profound military and psychological advantages to the Japanese.

Under these circumstances, the question arises, if the remaining three U.S. carriers did not challenge the Japanese striking force approaching Pearl Harbor (an unlikely U.S. decision) and the Japanese effectively destroyed the fuel tankers, dry docks and repair facilities, could the three carriers effectively operate from the West Coast? The nautical range of *Saratoga*, *Ranger* and *Wasp* was about 12,000 nautical miles at fifteen knots. However, 15 percent of that range was lost on antisubmarine maneuvering, and the carrier's range would be further reduced by high-speed runs while in battle, launching and landing aircraft, and search missions.

Therefore, oil tankers would play a significant role in the fleet's range from its home port. To keep the U.S. fleet at sea for long periods of time would require much more than the eleven oil tankers available; the total number needed would have been much closer to seventy-five oil tankers. Thus, it would have been difficult, though not impossible, for the U.S. fleet to operate from the West Coast, as its range would have been determined by the limitations placed on it by the lack of oil tankers.

The arrival of the first Essex-class carrier to the U.S. fleet in the Pacific would not occur until mid–1943. If the three remaining U.S. carriers (*Saratoga*, *Wasp* and *Ranger*) were destroyed in America's defense of Hawaii or alternately sunk in engaging the Japanese carrier forces from the West Coast, the net result would be the same: the Japanese Navy would have had free rein in the Pacific until at least the middle of 1943. If all these events occurred as described, it would have been a long road for the United States to travel in order for it to achieve an absolute unconditional surrender by the Japanese in the war in the Pacific, as well as by Germany in the Atlantic.

If Japan had been victorious at Midway, Japan's primary mission would have been to destroy the remaining three U.S. carriers. An attack on Pearl Harbor would certainly force the U.S. to defend the naval facility by having its three carriers ready to confront the Japanese. The inclusion by Japan of at least eight carriers in the Japanese striking force would be an imperative. With America's loss of its remaining carriers, Japan would then have an opportunity to destroy Pearl Harbor's fuel tanks, repair facilities and docks. The attack on Pearl Harbor would not be easy, as Hawaii now had 275 combat aircraft available for its defense, and the effect of its antiaircraft guns would be fully realized because of the radar protecting the island of Oahu.

Therefore, an attack on Pearl Harbor in the summer of 1942 would not be without risk, but this undertaking would be the only way Japan could prolong the war and hope for a negotiated peace.

Keep in mind that even with America's development of the atomic bomb, it still needed a base from which the B-29 could deliver the weapon. (Russia would not let the United States use its bases in Siberia, so we still needed a Pacific island close enough to Japan to deliver the atomic bomb.)

Nimitz stated after the Pearl Harbor attack on December 7, 1941, that "if Japan had destroyed the U.S.' fuel tanks at Pearl Harbor, the war would have been prolonged for at least two years."

Prolongation of the conflict could have resulted in the loss of will by the American people to continue the fight against Japan, as was the case in 1943 (described previously). Under this scenario, with the U.S. Navy back on the West Coast, the perceived vulnerability of California to Japanese attack might have politically forced President Roosevelt to shift the United States' multiple military resources from the Atlantic to the Pacific, weakening the Allies' military efforts against the Axis. Certainly, a Japanese victory at Midway and a German victory at Stalingrad would have significantly altered the global course of the war in favor of the Axis powers, with the outcome of the world war in doubt particularly in Europe.

9. The Significance of the Battle

The Battle of Midway has been included by military historian John Keegan as among the great sea battles in world history. He states in *The Price of Admiralty* that "Midway was indeed an 'incredible victory,' as great a reversal of strategic fortune as the naval world has ever seen, before or since, and a startling vindication of the belief of naval aviation pioneers in the carrier and its aircraft as the weapon of future maritime dominance."

The Battle of Midway is comparable to a number of the great sea battles of world history. The Battles of Salamis in 480 BC, the Spanish Armada in 1588, Trafalgar in 1805 and Jutland in 1916 are included among this special list.

Salamis, 480 BC

The Greek success against the Persians in the sea battle of Salamis assured that western Europe would politically develop under democratic principles rather than Persian (Oriental) dictatorship.

Greece was also able to experiment with individual liberty, which paved the way for Pericles's Golden Age of Greece.

Armada, 1588

The English victory over the Spanish Armada in the straits of the English Channel ensured that northwestern Europe would culturally be shaped by the principles of Protestantism. Spain lost its spheres of influence in early America and assured that English would be maintained as the major language spoken in the colonies.

Trafalgar, 1805

Britain's decisive defeat of the French and Spanish naval forces at Trafalgar assured that England, not France, controlled the hegemony in the world. It would maintain this position by its control of the seas and commercial maritime trade of the world. The victory ensured the eventual downfall of Napoleon by his failure to invade England.

Jutland, 1916

The British victory at Jutland assured that Germany would not be able to import the raw materials needed to maintain its war effort. This occurrence and the entrance of the United States into the war in 1917 sealed the fate of Germany and resulted in its unconditional surrender on November 11, 1918. In conclusion, the Battle of Midway's profound effects on the outcome of both the European and Pacific theaters of World War II clearly establish the battle as one of the most decisive naval battles in world history.

Appendix I
United States Vessels and Aircraft

U.S. Carriers

Langley (CV-1)

Langley was the first carrier built by the United States. The carrier was constructed from a converted collier (coal tender), *Jupiter*, in 1922. The ship was named after Samuel Pierpont Langley, an American aviator pioneer. *Langley* served as the first training ship for American aviators to learn how to take off and land on a moving ship. Its size and speed limited its value in wartime conditions. The carrier displaced 11,500 tons of water and had a battle speed of fifteen knots with limited range. The deck was 542 feet long and accommodated fifty-five aircraft. *Langley*'s construction resulted in the birth of naval aviation; however, the basic principles of carrier warfare such as fighter support, aerial bombing and torpedo attacks were still in their infancy.

Thus, in the 1920s, the battleship was still considered to be the tactical offensive weapon of the U.S. Navy.[1]

Lexington (CV-2)

Lexington was pressed into service in 1928 and was one of the first true U.S. Navy fleet carriers.

The carrier was very fast, but given the fact that it was the longest ship in the world (888 feet), it took time to change the course of the carrier, a characteristic not favorable to avoiding torpedo and bombing attacks. Its huge smokestack was located on its starboard side just behind the separate island. In 1940, a CXAM air search radar was installed on the forward part of the carrier's stack. The range of the carrier was 10,000 nautical miles, with a maximum speed of 34.8 knots. Defensively, the carrier had four twin eight-inch 55mm antiaircraft guns, five 1.1-inch quadruple machine-cannon guns, twenty-eight .50-caliber machine guns and twelve single five-inch antiaircraft guns. Its pre-war crew was 2,122, and the carrier could hold up to ninety aircraft.[2]

Saratoga (CV-3)

Saratoga, although listed as a CV-3 carrier, was commissioned on November 16, 1927, one month earlier than *Lexington*. She was constructed from a battle cruiser and was the first fast carrier in U.S. Navy history. Visually, the carrier was identical to *Lexington*, so a black vertical stripe was painted on its funnel to distinguish the carrier from *Lexington*. The identifying stripe led the carrier to be nicknamed *Stripe-Stacked Sara*. The carrier was named after the

Battle of Saratoga, which took place in Saratoga Springs, New York, in 1777 and was the turning point of the Revolutionary War. The carrier displaced 36,000 tons of water and had a battle speed of 34.9 knots with a range of 10,000 nautical miles. The ship's deck length was 888 feet and had the capacity to accommodate ninety-one aircraft. Its armament and crew were similar to Lexington.[3]

Ranger (CV-4)

By 1934, the *Ranger* was constructed within the confines of the 1921 Washington Naval Agreement. *Ranger* was the first U.S. Navy carrier built from the keel up as an aircraft carrier.

The carrier was commissioned on June 4, 1934. *Ranger* was named to commemorate the five U.S. warships that had previously borne its name, *Ranger* meaning one that ranges to enforce the law. It displaced 14,756 tons of water and had a battle speed of 29.25 knots with a range of 10,000 nautical miles. Its flight deck was 730 feet in length, and the carrier held eighty-six aircraft. Its armament was composed of eight five-inch/.25-caliber antiaircraft guns, and its crew numbered 1,435 men.[4]

Yorktown (CV-5)

Yorktown was the first of three carriers of the Yorktown class produced by the U.S. Navy. It was commissioned on September 30, 1937. The carrier had a four-inch side-armor belt over its machinery spaces and over its magazine and gasoline storage tanks. The flight deck, which was composed of light steel, offered little protection against bombing attacks. *Yorktown* was 810 feet long with a range of 11,200 nautical miles and a maximum speed of thirty-three knots. The carrier was equipped with CXAM radar in 1940. Defensively, *Yorktown* had eight five-inch/.38-caliber guns, twenty-four .50-caliber machine guns, four 1.1-inch quadruple machine-cannon guns, twenty-four 20mm Oerlikon single-mount antiaircraft guns and eight new five-inch/.38-caliber dual-purpose guns.[5] The carrier had a crew of 1,800 men.

Enterprise (CV-6)

In 1938, *Enterprise* was commissioned on May 12. It was the twin sister of *Yorktown*. Its nickname was *The Big E*. The carrier was the seventh ship to be named *Enterprise* in a series of historic ships given that name, dating back to the early days of America. *Enterprise* displaced 19,800 tons of water and had a battle speed of 32.5 knots with a range of 12,000 nautical miles. Its deck span was 825 feet, and the carrier had a capacity to hold ninety aircraft. Its armament consisted of eight five-inch/.38-caliber antiaircraft guns, and its crew numbered 1,800 men. RCA CXAM was placed on *Enterprise* in 1940.[6]

Wasp (CV-7)

Wasp was commissioned in 1940. It displaced 14,000 tons of water and had a battle speed of 29.5 knots with a range of 12,000 nautical miles. Its flight deck was 688 feet long, and the carrier could accommodate eighty-plus aircraft. It was armed with eight five-inch/.38-caliber antiaircraft guns. Its crew consisted of 1,890 men.[7]

Hornet (CV-8)

Hornet was the Navy's seventh ship named *Hornet*. It was third in a series of Yorktown-class aircraft carriers and was launched from Newport News Shipbuilding of Newport News, Virginia, on December 14, 1940. The carrier was commissioned on October 20, 1941. *Hornet* displaced 25,500 tons of water with a full load and had a battle speed of 33.6 knots with a range of 12,500 nautical miles. Its deck length was 824 feet 9 inches, and the carrier could carry up to ninety aircraft. It had eight five-inch guns. Its crew consisted of 1,800 men. It was the first carrier to be equipped with a specialized space in the island structure to vector out fighters from the information it obtained from its radar. The CXAM radar placed on the carrier came from the battleship *California*, which was sunk at Pearl Harbor.[8]

U.S. Technology

Radar was broken down into search radar and fire-control radar. SC radar was a primitive version of the third type of modification for search radar. *S* stands for search and *C* for the model number. CXAM was a more sophisticated type of radar and was the first official U.S. naval radar.

CXAM stands for a fusion of prior XAF and CXZ technologies. CXAM-1 was a further modification of search radar (CXAM).

U.S. Submarines

Nautilus (SS-168)

Nautilus was a Narwhal-class submarine (designed to hunt down enemy commercial ships, either with its five-inch deck-mounted gun or its six torpedo tubes). The submarine was the fifth ship of the U.S. Navy to be named *Nautilus*. It was laid down on August 2, 1927, and commissioned on July 1, 1930. *Nautilus* was powered by two direct-drive ten-cylinder four-cycle 2,350-horsepower diesel engines and two electric motors. The submarine displaced 2,730 tons of water and had a battle speed of fourteen knots on the surface with a range of 9,300 nautical miles at 10 knots and 25,000 nautical miles at 5.7 knots. Its length was 371 feet, and it could dive down to a depth of 300 feet. *Nautilus* carried six twenty-one-inch torpedo tubes (four forward and two aft), with a total of twenty-four to twenty-eight torpedoes on board.[9]

U.S. Patrol Boats

Patrol boats (PT) were developed in the early twentieth century as an inexpensive way to destroy a battleship. Their mission in World War II was modified to confront destroyers. Actually, destroyers themselves were constructed as a defense against the PT boat and were named accordingly. Elco won the contract to build most of the Navy's PT boats. The boats manufactured were either eighty or seventy-seven feet in length. Contrary to public opinion, the boats were not made of plywood but were constructed of two diagonally layered, one-inch-thick mahogany planks, impregnated with canvas. The crew consisted of three officers and fourteen men.[10]

The boats were powered by three Packard twelve-cylinder gasoline-fueled 3A-2500 V-12 liquid-cooled engines. Each engine had 1,500 horsepower, which generated a speed of forty-one knots. Fuel consumption was enormous, and so the boat carried 3,000 gallons of 100 octane aviation gasoline. Early boats had one 20mm Oerlikon cannon mounted on the stern and two twin M2 .50-caliber machine guns mounted in open rotating turrets toward the rear. The boat was equipped with two to four twenty-one-inch torpedo tubes that could launch multiple Mark 8 torpedoes, each torpedo weighing about one ton. Later the boats were outfitted with a Raytheon SO-type radar for night action.

U.S. Carrier-Based Aircraft

TBD-1 Devastator Torpedo Bomber

In 1937 the Douglas Aircraft Company delivered the TBD-1 Devastator torpedo bomber to the U.S. Navy. At that time, it was the most advanced aircraft flying for the U.S. Navy. The plane was the first all-metal aircraft as well as the first widely used carrier-based monoplane. The glass canopy occupied almost half of the aircraft. The three-man crew consisted of the pilot up front, the bombardier in the middle seat, and the rear gunner/radio operator in the rear seat. The plane was armed with either .30- or .50-caliber machine guns firing forward and a .30-caliber machine gun for the rear gunner. The plane was powered by a 900-horsepower Pratt and Whitney R-1830–64 Twin Wasp radial engine. Its maximum speed was 206 miles per hour with a range of 435 miles with the Mark 13 torpedo and 716 miles with a 1,000-pound bomb.[11]

Douglas Dauntless Dive-Bomber

The Douglas SBD-3 Dauntless was a naval dive-bomber that was introduced to the U.S. Navy in 1941. The plane had a crew of two: a pilot and a rear gunner/radioman. The aircraft had self-sealing fuel tanks and was powered by a Wright R-1820–52 radial 1,350-horsepower engine. Its maximum speed was 255 miles per hour, and it had a range of 773 miles. The SBD-3 had a total of four machine guns: two .50-caliber forward-firing machine guns in the engine cowling and two flexible-mounted machine guns in the rear. The aircraft carried a bomb load of 605 pounds under its wings for scouting and 1,600 pounds under its fuselage for naval action.[12]

Grumman F4F-4 Wildcat Fighter

The Grumman F4F-4 Wildcat fighter, developed from the F4F-1 biplane design, was recast as a single-wing XF4F. The Marines on Midway had the F4F-3 fighter in their contingency of fighters, and the carriers had the newer version—the F4F-4. The crew consisted of a pilot. The F4F-4 was powered by a Pratt and Whitney R-1830–86 double-row radial engine with a maximum speed of 320 miles per hour. Its range was 910 miles. One additional feature was that its wings could fold. The F4F-4 was heavier but not as fast as the F4F-3. The plane was armed with six .50-caliber Browning machine guns in its wings, and it could carry two 100-pound bombs.[13]

U.S. Land-Based Aircraft on Midway

TBF-1 Avenger Torpedo Bomber

The TBF-1 Avenger torpedo bomber was the TBD-1 torpedo bomber's replacement. It had a pilot, turret gunner and radioman/bombardier/ventral gunner. Its maximum speed was 275 miles per hour while flying at 11,200 feet, and it had a range of 1,000 nautical miles. The aircraft had one 30mm machine gun in its nose, one 50mm machine gun in the rear cockpit and a 30mm machine gun in its ventral tunnel. The plane carried either a single Mark 13 torpedo and four 500-pound bombs or one 1,500-pound bomb. Although each torpedo bomber carried a crew of three, the TBF Avenger torpedo bomber was forty-five knots faster than the TBD. The TBF was provided with one .50-caliber machine gun and two .30-caliber machine guns, while the TBD had two to three .30-caliber machine guns. The TBF could carry up to a 2,000-pound bomb load, while the TBD was able to handle only a 1,000-pound load. The Devastator was also heavier, with an empty weight of 10,555 pounds, while the TBF weighed only 5,600 pounds.[14]

SBD-2 Dauntless Dive-Bomber

The SBD-2 Dauntless dive-bomber had a crew of two, a pilot and a gunner/radioman. Its maximum speed was 255 miles per hour, and the aircraft had a range of 773 miles. The plane had two 50mm machine guns in its cowling and one flex-mounted rear-facing 30mm machine gun. It could carry a 500- or a 1,000-pound bomb on its centerline track and one 100-pound bomb under each wing.

Overall the plane was similar to the next generation of dive-bombers—the SBD-3.[15]

SB2U Vindicator Dive-Bomber

In April 1936, the Vought Aircraft Company delivered the first SB2U-2 (Vindicator) dive-bomber to the U.S. Navy. The aircraft was modern in that it was the first monoplane dive-bomber produced for carrier use and had retractable landing gear; however, its flying surface was still made of fabric. The plane had a two-man crew: a pilot in the forward seat and a tail gunner in the rear seat, both sitting under a long glass canopy. The plane was armed with one .30-caliber machine gun in the ventral tunnel under the tail and a twin 50mm machine gun on the tail turret.[16]

Brewster F2A Buffalo Fighter

In 1939, the Brewster Aircraft Company delivered the Buffalo to the U.S. Navy, the first carrier-based monoplane fighter. Although it was made of all-metal construction, its flying surfaces were still covered with fabric. It was designed as a one-seat monoplane, with wing flaps, retractable landing gear, mid-set wings and a streamlined framed canopy. It was powered by an 850-horsepower Wright R1820–40 Cyclone engine with a top speed of 321 miles per hour and a range of 965 miles. The aircraft had four .50-caliber machine guns mounted to its wings and a .50-caliber machine gun mounted in its upper cowling (the metallic cover for the engine), which fired through the propeller arc. The plane was capable of carrying two 100-pound bombs.[17]

B-26 Marauder Bomber

The B-26 twin-engine Marauder bomber had a maximum speed of 287 miles per hour and a range of 1,150 miles. It carried a bomb load of 4,000 pounds or a 21.7-inch-diameter torpedo. The aircraft had one flexible 50mm-caliber machine gun and four fixed 50mm machine guns in its nose, a twin 50mm gun mounted in the dorsal turret, two waist 50mm machine guns, a single 50mm-caliber hand-fired machine gun in the ventral tunnel under the tail and a twin 50mm machine gun on the tail turret. Its crew consisted of a pilot, a co-pilot, a bombardier in the nose and a radio operator and navigator located behind the pilots.[18]

B-17 Flying Fortress

In 1938, the U.S. Army received the B-17 Flying Fortress four-engine bomber from the Boeing Aircraft Company. The length of the B-17 was 73.8 feet and normally required a crew of ten.

The later model—the B-17E Flying Fortress—was powered by four 1,200-horsepower Wright R-1850–65 Cyclone engines. Its maximum speed was 318 miles per hour with a range of 3,300 miles. The aircraft was armed with ten .50-caliber machine guns and one .3-inch caliber machine gun. The plane could carry a 4,000-pound bomb load and had a ceiling of 36,000 feet.[19]

Appendix I

PBY Catalina Patrol Bomber

In October 1936, Consolidated Aircraft delivered the first U.S. Navy PBY Catalina. *PB* stands for "patrol bomber," and *Y* is the code letter for the manufacturer Consolidated Aircraft. The PBY was originally designed to function as a patrol bomber, an aircraft with a long operational range whose mission was to locate and attack ships at sea. The aircraft was nicknamed Dumbo by the aircrew when they were searching for pilots and their crews lost at sea and called CAT when they were on a combat mission. The plane was distinguished by the presence of two side blisters forward of its tail. The original design of the PBY-5 permitted the plane to take off and return only on land.

An upgrade in design led to the PBY-5A, which allowed the plane to operate as an amphibious aircraft. The most noticeable design difference between the two aircraft was that the PBY-5A had a retractable tricycle landing gear, which permitted the aircraft to take off and land both on water and land. The PBY was powered by two 1,200 horsepower Pratt and Whitney R-1830–92 Twin Wasp radial engines with a maximum speed of 196 miles per hour and a range of 2,520 miles. The plane required an eight-man crew. The aircraft was armed with three .30-caliber machine guns (two in the nose turret and one in the ventral hatch near the tail) and one .50-caliber machine gun in each waist blister, and the plane could carry a bomb, torpedo or depth charge load of 4,000 pounds respectively.[20]

Appendix II
Japanese Vessels and Aircraft

Japanese Carriers

Akagi (Red Castle)

The Japanese carrier *Akagi* was also initially laid down as a battle cruiser. Following the same reasoning for the conversion of *Kaga*, *Akagi* was converted from the battle cruiser *Akagi* to an aircraft carrier and commissioned on March 27, 1927. The battle cruiser and carrier were both named after Mount Akagi, a dormant volcano. The carrier was the flagship of Admiral Nagumo Chuichi, who was overall Commander of the First Carrier Striking Force (First Fleet) and Commander of Carrier Division One (*Akagi* and *Kaga*). The carrier was converted from a battle cruiser, and its construction was completed in 1927. It was modernized in 1938 by converting the carrier from a three-flight deck construction to a single-flight deck and by building a small port-side island. *Akagi* initially had two hangar decks and one flight deck with the same purpose as the *Kaga*: to land planes on the flight deck and launch aircraft form the hangar decks. This concept proved unsuccessful, and between October 1935 and August 1938 this carrier also underwent major reconstruction. The hangar decks were moved forward and were no longer designed for launches. The flight deck was lengthened to 857 feet, with its island superstructure added to the port side. The carrier, which displaced 34,364 tons of water, had a battle speed of thirty-one knots with a range of 8,200 nautical miles at fourteen knots.[1] *Akagi*'s armament consisted of ten eight-inch/.50-caliber guns, six of which were placed in single-gun casements along its quarters and four were installed in twin turrets forward of the carrier's flight deck. It also had twelve 4.7-inch/.45-caliber high-angle guns and twenty-two 25mm antiaircraft machine guns. The carrier could hold up to ninety-one aircraft (with sixty aircraft operational), and its crew totaled 1,630 men.

Kaga (Heavenly Castle)

Japan was subject to the same restrictions of the 1921 Washington Naval Treaty as the United States. When Japan signed the treaty in 1922, she was permitted to convert two battle cruisers to aircraft carriers. *Kaga*, the oldest of the four Japanese carriers later present at Midway, was initially laid down in the 1918 building program as a Nagato-type (ten sixteen-inch guns) battleship and launched at Kobe, Japan, on November 17, 1921. Now, with the treaty signed, the battleship was destined to be destroyed. However, when the 1923 earthquake severely damaged one of the two existing battle-cruiser hulls (*Amagi*) available for conversion into an aircraft carrier, the remaining hull (*Kaga*) was not scrapped. The carrier, as was its forerunner the battleship, was named after a Japanese province. *Kaga* was the oldest of the four Japanese carriers, and its construction began in 1923 and ended with its being commissioned in 1929. *Kaga* was originally designed with a triple flight deck, but was redesigned in

1935 to a single flight deck. The carrier displaced 33,693 tons of water (loaded). Its length was increased to about 782 feet 6 inches, and its speed was increased to 28.5 knots with a range of 8,000 nautical miles at sixteen knots. The carrier's small island structure was located on the starboard side. The carrier's armament consisted of ten eight-inch/.50-caliber guns, twelve 4.7-inch guns and twenty-two 25mm antiaircraft guns. The carrier could accommodate up to ninety-one aircraft (with seventy-two aircraft operational), and its crew consisted of 1,340 men.[2]

Soryu (*Blue* or *Green Dragon*)

The carrier was commissioned after Japan withdrew from the Washington Naval Conference at the end of 1936. However, since she was laid down in 1934, the carrier was subject to the limits of size and tonnage imposed by the treaty. *Soryu* was the second Japanese carrier built from the keel up as a flat-deck aircraft carrier, the small carrier *Hosho* being the first. *Soryu* in Japanese means a blue or green dragon and was named after a flying creature. The carrier was commissioned on December 29, 1937. Its island superstructure was forward on the starboard side. *Soryu* displaced 18,800 tons of water with a full load. Its flight length was 746 feet 5 inches, and it had a range of 7,750 nautical miles at eighteen knots with a maximum speed of 34.5 knots. Its armament consisted of twelve five-inch guns and twenty-eight 25mm antiaircraft guns. Its plane capacity was sixty-eight aircraft (with fifty-seven planes operational). Its crew totaled 1,103 men.[3]

Hiryu (*Flying Dragon*)

Hiryu was the flagship of Rear Admiral Yamaguchi Tamon, Commander of Carrier Division Two (*Soryu* and *Hiryu*). Its design was a slight improvement over *Soryu* with a better turning radius, a deeper draft and a fuller beam. Its island was on its port side. The carrier was commissioned in 1939. *Hiryu* displaced 20,250 tons of water with a full load and had a flight deck of 745 feet 11 inches. Its range was 10,330 nautical miles at eighteen knots with a maximum speed of 34.5 knots. Its armaments consisted of twelve five-inch guns and thirty-three 25mm antiaircraft guns. *Hiryu* could hold up to seventy-three aircraft (with fifty-nine planes operational), and its crew totaled 1,103 men.[4]

Shokaku and *Zuikaku*

The strength of the Japanese operation against Port Moresby was the two carriers from the Shokaku class which made up Carrier Division Five of the Kido Butai. These carriers exceeded the design of U.S. carriers until the arrival the Essex class in 1943. *Shokaku* (*Flying Crane*) was commissioned in August 8, 1941, just prior to the Pearl Harbor attack on December 7, 1941. It was 845 feet in length. Its range was 9,700 nautical miles with a maximum speed of thirty-four knots. A small island that was forward existed on the starboard side. It had a crew of 1,800 men. The carrier had sixteen five-inch antiaircraft guns and twelve 12.25mm (.9 inch) Type 96 triple-mount antiaircraft guns. *Shokaku* could hold seventy-two operational aircraft with room for twelve reserve aircraft.

The *Zuikaku* (*Fortunate Crane*) was commissioned on September 25, 1941. Having been built from the same Shokaku-class design, its specifications were identical to those of *Shokaku*.

Shoho (*Auspicious Phoenix*)

The third carrier involved in the MO Operation was *Shoho* (*Auspicious Phoenix*). The carrier was recommissioned as a light carrier, being converted from a submarine tender on

December 22, 1941. It was 712 feet in length. *Shoho*'s range was 9,260 miles with a maximum speed of twenty-eight knots. Its crew consisted of 785 men. It had little defensive armament, with only four Type 89 twin five-inch mounts and eight short-range antiaircraft guns. *Shoho* could hold thirty aircraft, but the carrier held the only eighteen planes available (eight Zero fighters, four Type 96 fighters and six 97 attack aircraft) on May 7 due to a shortage of aircraft. It is significant that all the aircraft on all three carriers were at least 25 percent below the carriers' full capacity due to Japan's inability to manufacture the needed aircraft to supply the carriers. This clearly demonstrated Japan's weakness in maintaining the maximum aircraft level on all of its carriers so early in the war.

Japanese Technology

None of the four Japanese carriers (*Akagi*, *Kaga*, *Soryu* and *Hiryu*) at Midway had radar on board.

Japanese Carrier Aircraft

Nakajima B5N2 Type 97 (Kate) Torpedo Bomber

Introduced in 1939, the Nakajima B5N2 Type 97 (Kate) was a Japanese carrier-borne torpedo bomber, and at the time it was introduced, the aircraft was much faster and more capable than the U.S. TBD Devastator torpedo bomber. The plane was used primarily as a carrier-based aircraft and occasionally as a land-based bomber. The aircraft was nicknamed Kate by the Americans.

Its first flight occurred in January 1937 and was ordered into production as a Type 97 carrier attack bomber (kanko). The B5N2 had a crew of three: a pilot, a navigator/bombardier and a radio operator/gunner. The plane was powered by a fourteen-cylinder air-cooled radial 1,000-horsepower engine driving a three-blade propeller. Its maximum speed was 235 miles per hour with a range of 1,075 nautical miles. The plane had the ability to climb 1,283 feet per minute.

The aircraft was 33 feet 9 inches in length and also included retractable landing gear. The aircraft's armament consisted of one rear-firing 7.7mm Type 92 machine gun and one 1,764-pound torpedo or a 1,764-pound bomb load. Defensive armament was purposefully lacking so as to maintain its speed and high performance.[5]

Aichi D3A1 Type 99 (Val) Dive-Bomber

The production of the Aichi D3A1 Type 99 (Val) dive-bomber (kanbaku) began in 1939 and was designed to be a primary carrier aircraft by the Aichi Aircraft Company in Japan. The plane replaced the existing D1A bi-winged aircraft then in service. The fuselage looked very similar to the Zero, although the plane was built much stronger so that it could withstand the stress of dive-bombing. The prototype's first flight was in January 1938. The plane had a crew of two: the pilot and the gunner. The aircraft was powered by a fourteen-cylinder air-cooled radial 1,070-horsepower engine driving a three-blade propeller. Its maximum speed was 240 miles per hour, with a range of 795 nautical miles. The plane could climb at a rate of 1,640 feet per minute. Its length was 33 feet 5 inches, and its design included fixed landing gear for simplicity, since there was little additional drag on the plane with its relatively slow flying speed. The aircraft armament consisted of two forward-firing 7.7mm Type 92 machine guns and one rear-aimed 7.7mm Type 92 machine gun. The dive-bomber carried one 550-pound bomb or two 130-pound bombs.[6]

Mitsubishi A6M2 Type 0 (Zero) Fighter

On April 1, 1939, the Mitsubishi A6M2 Type 0 (Zero), a lightweight carrier-conceived fighter, had its first flight. The A in the plane's designation signified it was a fighter, the 6 represented that it was the sixth model built by Mitsubishi (M). When the aircraft was introduced, the Zero was the best carrier-based fighter (kansen) in the world. The plane was built of a top-secret aluminum T-7178 that was lighter and stronger than previous aluminum, but more brittle. To maintain its light weight, no protective armor was utilized for the pilot, engine or other critical points of the aircraft, nor did the plane have self-sealing fuel tanks. The Allies called the aircraft a Zero because of the 0 in its Type. The A6M2 Type 0 (Zero) Model 21 was a single-engine single-seat carrier-borne and land-based fighter aircraft that was powered by a fourteen-cylinder air-cooled radial 940-horsepower engine driving a three-blade propeller. Its maximum speed was 332 miles per hour, with a range of 1,010 nautical miles. The plane had an ability to climb 3,100 feet per minute. The aircraft was 29 feet 8 inches in length and included the modern design of retractable landing rear. Its armament consisted of two 7.7mm Type 97 machine guns in the engine cowling and two 20mm Type 99 cannon in its wings. It carried a bomb load of two 132-pound bombs and a 330-liter fuel drop tank. Each plane included a complete radio set and a radio direction finder for long-range navigation.[7]

Nakajima E8N2 Type 95 Scout Seaplane

The Nakajima E8N2 Type 95 was a Japanese ship-borne catapult-launched reconnaissance seaplane introduced in 1935. The plane was assigned to all capital ships (battleships and cruisers).

It was a single engine, two-seat bi-winged plane with a central float and underwing outriggers to support the aircraft. The U.S. code name for the aircraft was Dave. The seaplane was powered by a nine-cylinder air-cooled radial engine driving a two-blade propeller. The plane's crew consisted of the pilot and the rear gunner. Its maximum speed was 186 miles per hour with a range of 485 nautical miles. The plane could climb at a rate of 1,515 feet per minute. The aircraft was 28 feet 10 inches in length with a span of 36 feet. Its armament consisted of one fixed forward-firing 7.7mm machine gun and one rear-firing 7.7mm machine gun. The seaplane carried two 132-pound bombs.[8]

Mitsubishi Aichi E13A Seaplane

The Mitsubishi Aichi E13A aircraft (Jake) was a single-wing and single-engine twin float reconnaissance seaplane made of all metal construction with fabric-covered control surfaces which was launched from a cruiser or a battleship. It was armed with a rear-firing 7.7mm Type 92 machine gun and carried one 551-pound or four 132-pound bombs. Its maximum speed was 234 miles per hour, and the plane could climb at a rate of 1,515 feet per minute. Its range was 1,128 nautical miles.[9]

Japanese Submarines

On July 31, 1934, a Japanese submarine was completed at Kure dockyard. The submarine was I-168, a Kaidai-class submarine (KD6 Type). Lacking expertise in submarine design, Japan first looked at the British design, but engine defects in that design led her to turn to Germany for guidance. The Japanese government had five of the latest German-design submarines in her possession, given to Japan in reparation for her role as an ally in World War I. Impressed, Japan sent naval officers to Germany for consultation and at the same time contracted with German naval constructors and technicians to come to Japan. The Japanese Navy also hired other European technicians to aid in the design of the periscope and range finders. Eventually the Japanese Navy designed its own blueprint, designated the Kaidai-class submarine design, based on World War I–era German submarines. All Kaidai-class submarines originally had two-digit hull numbers. In 1942 many active units of this class had a 1 prefixed to their designation, so I-68 having its first run became I-168. The submarine displaced 1,970 tons of water and had a battle speed of twenty-three knots, the fastest surface speed of any submarine built in the world at that time. Her range was 14,000 nautical miles at ten knots. She was 343 feet in length and could reach a depth of 250 feet. The submarine was powered by two 9,000-horsepower engines and two 1,800-horsepower electric motors. The submarine was well armed with one 3.9-inch deck gun, one .50-caliber machine gun and six torpedo tubes (four at the bow and two at the stern) with fourteen torpedoes aboard. The crew consisted of seventy officers and men.[10]

Chapter Notes

Chapter 1

1. Carroll V. Glines, *The Doolittle Raid* (Atglen, PA: Schiffer Military/Aviation History, 1991), 66.
2. *Ibid.*, 150–153.
3. Mitsuo Fuchida and Masatake Okumiya, *Midway* (New York: Ballantine, 1955), 55.
4. *Ibid.*, 56–57.
5. *Ibid.*, 60.
6. *Ibid.*, 62–63.
7. *Ibid.*, 64–65.
8. *Ibid.*, 72–73.

Chapter 2

1. Rear Admiral Edwin T. Layton, USN (Ret.), Captain Roger Pineau, USNR (Ret.) and John Costello, *And I Was There* (New York: William Morrow and Company, 1985) p.381–382.
2. *Ibid.*, 383, 394.
3. *Ibid.*, 390–391.
4. Mark Stille, *The Coral Sea 1942* (Oxford: Osprey Publishing, 2009), 41.
5. *Ibid.*, 46.
6. *Ibid.*, 41.
7. *Ibid.*, 51.
8. *Ibid.*, 52.
9. *Ibid.*, 53.
10. *Ibid.*, 55.
11. *Ibid.*, 57.
12. *Ibid.*, 60.
13. Samuel Eliot Morison, *Coral Sea, Midway and Submarine Actions* (Boston, MA: Little, Brown, 1988), 42.
14. Stille, *The Coral Sea 1942*, 61.
15. *Ibid.*, 65.
16. *Ibid.*, 68.
17. *Ibid.*, 73.
18. *Ibid.*, 72.
19. *Ibid.*, 81.
20. *Ibid.*, 68.
21. *Ibid.*, 85.
22. *Ibid.*, 86.
23. *Ibid.*, 86–87.
24. *Ibid.*, 87.
25. Fuchida and Okumiya, *Midway*, 91.
26. Jonathan Parshall and Anthony Tully, *Shattered Sword* (Washington, D.C.: Potomac Books, 2005), 63.
27. *Ibid.*, 62.

Chapter 3

1. John B. Lundstrom, *The First Team* (Annapolis, MD: U.S. Naval Institute Press, 1984), 282.
2. *Ibid.*, 284.
3. *Ibid.*, 285.
4. *Ibid.*, 290.
5. *Ibid.*, 291–292.
6. *Ibid.*, 296.
7. Elliot Carlson, *Joe Rochefort's War* (Annapolis, MD: U.S. Naval Institute Press, 2011), 294.
8. *Ibid.*, 295.
9. *Ibid.*, 300.
10. *Ibid.*, 301.
11. *Ibid.*, 302.
12. *Ibid.*, 305.
13. *Ibid.*
14. *Ibid.*, 307.
15. *Ibid.*, 308–309.
16. *Ibid.*, 313–314.
17. Lundstrom, *The First Team*, 297.
18. Carlson, *Joe Rochefort's War*, 326–328.
19. *Ibid.*, 319–322.
20. *Ibid.*, 322.
21. *Ibid.*, 325.
22. *Ibid.*, 324.
23. *Ibid.*, 332, 335.
24. *Ibid.*, 335.
25. *Ibid.*
26. *Ibid.*, 335.
27. *Ibid.*, 336.
28. *Ibid.*, 340–341.
29. *Ibid.*, 341–342.
30. *Ibid.*, 342–344.
31. *Ibid.*, 345–346.
32. *Ibid.*, 350.

33. National Archives and Records Administration, Official Military File of William F. Halsey, Jr.
34. *Ibid.*
35. John Wukovits, *Admiral "Bull" Halsey: The Life and Wars of the Navy's Most Controversial Commander* (New York: Palgrave Macmillan 2010), 83.
36. National Archives and Records Administration, Official Military File of William F. Halsey, Jr.
37. *New York Times*, obituary, November 25, 1983.
38. National Archives and Records Administration, Official Military File of William F. Halsey, Jr.
39. Carlson, *Joe Rochefort's War*, 352.
40. *Ibid.*, 353–354.
41. Lundstrom, *The First Team*, 330.
42. Parshall and Tully, *Shattered Sword*, 37.
43. Fuchida and Okumiya, *Midway*, 214–222.

Chapter 4

1. Robert Cressman et al., *A Glorious Page in Our History* (Missoula, MT: Pictorial Histories, 1990), 31.
2. *Ibid.*, 32–33.
3. *Ibid.*, 35.
4. Lundstrom, *The First Team*, 428–431.
5. Mike McLaughlin, "The Miracle at Midway," *Amvets* (Summer 2001), 1–3.
6. Morison, *Coral Sea*, 92.
7. *Ibid.*, 91.
8. Parshall and Tully, *Shattered Sword*, 37.
9. *Ibid.*, 45.
10. Cressman et al., *A Glorious Page*, 40.
11. *Ibid.*, 44.
12. Peter Chen, "Aircraft Carriers: USS *Enterprise*," WW II Database (2004).
13. Cressman et al., *A Glorious Page*, 47.
14. Parshall and Tully, *Shattered Sword*, 96, 489.
15. Cressman et al., *A Glorious Page*, 40.
16. Parshall and Tully, *Shattered Sword*, 97.
17. *Ibid.*, 98.
18. *Ibid.*
19. Captain Wayne P. Hughes, Jr., USN (Ret.), *Fleet Tactics* (Annapolis, MD: U.S. Naval Institute Press, 1986), 94.
20. *Ibid.*
21. Parshall and Tully, *Shattered Sword*, 136.
22. *Ibid.*, 138–143.
23. *Ibid.*, 143.
24. *Ibid.*, 96.
25. Fuchida and Okumiya, *Midway*, 203.
26. *Ibid.*, 111–112.
27. *Ibid.*, 116–117.
28. Parshall and Tully, *Shattered Sword*, 101.
29. Fuchida and Okumiya, *Midway*, 108–116.
30. *Ibid.*, 111.
31. Admiral Ugaki, Matome, *Fading Victory* (Pittsburgh: University of Pittsburgh Press, 1991) p. 118.
32. Mark Stille, *The Coral Sea 1942* (Oxford: Osprey Publishing, 2009) p. 41.
33. Ugaki, *Fading Victory*, 117–118.

Chapter 5

1. Fuchida and Okumiya *Midway*, 125.
2. *Ibid.*, 126.
3. *Ibid.*, 127.
4. Morison, *Coral Sea*, 173.
5. *Ibid.*, 167–168.
6. *Ibid.*, 170–171.
7. Cressman et al., *A Glorious Page*, 52–54.
8. *Ibid.*, 56.
9. *Ibid.*, 54–55.
10. Fuchida and Okumiya, *Midway*, 128.
11. Cressman et al., *A Glorious Page*, 57.
12. Lundstrom, *The First Team*, 329.
13. Fuchida and Okumiya, *Midway*, 130.
14. *Ibid.*
15. Letter from Petty Office First Class Maruyama Taisuke.
16. *Ibid.*
17. Fuchida and Okumiya, *Midway* 135.
18. Parshall and Tully, *Shattered Sword*, 37.
19. *Ibid.*, 147.
20. *Ibid.*, 148.
21. Lundstrom, *The First Team*, 338.
22. Fuchida and Okumiya, *Midway*, 169.
23. *Ibid.*, 136–137.
24. Cressman et al., *A Glorious Page*, 59.
25. *Ibid.*
26. Lundstrom, *The First Team*, 332.
27. Cressman et al., *A Glorious Page*, 62.
28. *Ibid.*, 61.
29. *Ibid.*
30. *Ibid.*, 62.
31. Letter from Petty Officer First Class Maruyama Taisuke.
32. Parshall and Tully, *Shattered Sword*, 200.
33. *Ibid.*, 201.
34. *Ibid.*, 200, 517.
35. *Ibid.*, 202.
36. *Ibid.*, 204.
37. Cressman et al., *A Glorious Page*, 84.
38. *Ibid.*, 84–86.
39. *Ibid.*, 86.
40. *Ibid.*, 86–87.
41. Cressman et al., *A Glorious Page*, 86.
42. *Ibid.*, 72.
43. Parshall and Tully, *Shattered Sword*, 159.
44. *Ibid.*, 198.
45. Craig L. Symonds, *The Battle of Midway* (New York: Oxford University Press), 291.
46. Parshall and Tully, *Shattered Sword*, 164.
47. *Ibid.*, 175.
48. *Ibid.*, 164, 166.
49. *Ibid.*, 164–165.
50. *Ibid.*, 186.
51. *Ibid.*, 198.

52. *Ibid.*, 199.
53. *Ibid.*, 205.
54. Symonds, *The Battle of Midway*, 282–283.
55. *Ibid.*, 267.
56. Cressman et al., *A Glorious Page*, 84.
57. Symonds, *The Battle of Midway*, 253.
58. *Ibid.*
59. *Ibid.*, 260.
60. *Ibid.*, 258.
61. *Ibid.*, 261.
62. *Ibid.*, 268.
63. *Ibid.*, 263.
64. *Ibid.*
65. *Ibid.*, 264.
66. *Ibid.*, 262–263.
67. *Ibid.*, 268.
68. *Ibid.*, 276.
69. *Ibid.*, 270–272.
70. Lundstrom, *The First Team*, 335.
71. Symonds, *The Battle of Midway*, 278.
72. *Ibid.*
73. *Ibid.*, 275–276.
74. *Ibid.*, 280.
75. *Ibid.*, 285.
76. *Ibid.*, 297.
77. *Ibid.*
78. *Ibid.*, 294.
79. *Ibid.*, 320.
80. Cressman et al., *A Glorious Page*, 122.

Chapter 6

1. Symonds, *The Battle of Midway*, 298.
2. *Ibid.*, 298–301.
3. Parshall and Tully, *Shattered Sword*, 186–188.
4. Stille, *The Coral Sea 1942*, 72–73.
5. Parshall and Tully, *Shattered Sword*, 232.
6. *Ibid.*, 234–235.
7. Cressman et al., *A Glorious Page*, 104.
8. Parshall and Tully, *Shattered Sword*, 251.
9. *Ibid.*, 254.
10. *Ibid.*, 256.
11. *Ibid.*, 260.
12. *Ibid.*, 261.
13. *Ibid.*, 261–262.
14. *Ibid.*, 262–263.
15. *Ibid.*, 264–265.
16. *Ibid.*, 267.
17. *Ibid.*, 269–270.
18. *Ibid.*, 275.
19. *Ibid.*, 276–279.
20. Symonds, *The Battle of Midway*, 312–313.
21. *Ibid.*, 313.
22. Parshall and Tully, *Shattered Sword*, 283.
23. *Ibid.*, 298.
24. *Ibid.*
25. Fuchida and Okumiya, *Midway*, 155.
26. Parshall and Tully, *Shattered Sword*, 284–285.
27. Symonds, *The Battle of Midway*, 320.
28. Parshall and Tully, *Shattered Sword*, 485–486.
29. *Ibid.*, 292.
30. Fuchida and Okumiya, *Midway*, 168–169.
31. Symonds, *The Battle of Midway*, 329.
32. *Ibid.*
33. *Ibid.*, 323.
34. Parshall and Tully, *Shattered Sword*, 299–300.
35. *Ibid.*, 302–303.
36. Fuchida and Okumiya, *Midway*, 166.
37. Parshall and Tully, *Shattered Sword*, 306–308.
38. *Ibid.*, 308.
39. *Ibid.*, 312.
40. Cressman et al., *A Glorious Page*, 128.
41. Parshall and Tully, *Shattered Sword*, 314–315.
42. Symonds, *The Battle of Midway*, 324–326.
43. Parshall and Tully, *Shattered Sword*, 311.
44. Symonds, *The Battle of Midway*, 329–330.
45. Parshall and Tully, *Shattered Sword*, 323.
46. Symonds, *The Battle of Midway*, 323.
47. *Ibid.*, 333.
48. Parshall and Tully, *Shattered Sword*, 326–328.
49. Personal interview with Lieutenant Commander Richard Best, USN (Ret.).
50. *Ibid.*, 329.
51. Parshall and Tully, *Shattered Sword*, 330–331.
52. *Ibid.*, 331–333.
53. *Ibid.*, 336–339.
54. *Ibid.*, 339.
55. Symonds, *Battle of Midway*, 347.
56. Parshall and Tully, *Shattered Sword*, 341.
57. *Ibid.*, 340.
58. *Ibid.*, 341–342.

Chapter 7

1. Parshall and Tully, *Shattered Sword*, 343.
2. *Ibid.*, 345.
3. *Ibid.*
4. *Ibid.*, 346.
5. *Ibid.*, 348.
6. Symonds, *The Battle of Midway*, 340.
7. *Ibid.*, 348.
8. Cressman et al., *A Glorious Page*, 141.
9. Parshall and Tully, *Shattered Sword*, 352.
10. *Ibid.*, 353.
11. *Ibid.*, 349–350.
12. *Ibid.*, 351–352.
13. Symonds, *The Battle of Midway*, 342.
14. Cressman et al., *A Glorious Page*, 143–144.
15. *Ibid.*
16. Symonds, *The Battle of Midway*, 342–343.
17. *Ibid.*, 344–345.
18. Cressman et al., *A Glorious Page*, 149.

19. Parshall and Tully, *Shattered Sword*, 359.
20. *Ibid.*, 365.
21. *Ibid.*, 366.
22. Symonds, *The Battle of Midway*, 347.
23. *Ibid.*
24. Parshall and Tully, *Shattered Sword*, 367.
25. *Ibid.*
26. Symonds, *The Battle of Midway*, 352.
27. *Ibid.*
28. *Ibid.*, 353.
29. Parshall and Tully, *Shattered Sword*, 370.
30. *Ibid.*, 372.
31. Cressman et al., *A Glorious Page*, 156; Symonds, *The Battle of Midway*, 354.
32. Parshall and Tully, *Shattered Sword*, 378.
33. *Ibid.*, 380.
34. Symonds, *The Battle of Midway*, 348–349.
35. Parshall and Tully, *Shattered Sword*, 373.
36. *Ibid.*, 373–374.
37. *Ibid.*, 374; Symonds, *The Battle of Midway*, 350.
38. Parshall and Tully, *Shattered Sword*, 375.
39. *Ibid.*, 381–382.,
40. Robert D. Ballard, *Return to Midway* (Washington, D.C.: Madison Press Books, 1999), 124.

Chapter 8

1. John Keegan, *The Price of Admiralty* (New York: Penguin, 1988), 20.
2. Carlson, *Joe Rochefort's War*, 424.
3. *Ibid.*, 418.
4. *Ibid.*, 442.
5. Cressman et al., *A Glorious Page*, 39.
6. Keegan, *The Price of Admiralty*, 248.
7. *Ibid.*, 246.

Chapter 9

1. Maurice Matloff, *The War Department* (U.S. Army in World War II, 2013), 307–308.
2. Winston Churchill, *The Hinge of Fate* (London: Penguin Classics, 2005), 253.
3. Bruce Lee, *Marching Orders* (New York: Crown, 1995), 46.
4. *Ibid.*, 44.
5. *Ibid.*, 65.
6. Major Patrick H. Donovan, USAF, *Pacific War in and after Pearl Harbor* (Defense Technical Command, 2001).
7. *Ibid.*

Appendix I

1. Norman Polmar, *Aircraft Carriers* (Dulles, VA: Potomac Books, 2008), 466.
2. *Ibid.*
3. *Ibid.*
4. *Ibid.*, 467.
5. *Ibid.*
6. *Ibid.*
7. *Ibid.*, 468.
8. *Ibid.*
9. USS *Nautilus* (SS-168)—Nautilus SSU 571, 2013.
10. *P.T. Boats*, Naval History and Heritage Command, 2013.
11. Kennedy Hickman, *World War II* Douglas *TBD Devastator*, thoughtco.com, 2013.
12. Douglas SBD Dauntless Specifications, U.S. Air Force Museum, 2013.
13. Grumman F4F Wildcat Fighters, Naval History and Heritage Command, 2013.
14. World War II: TBF-1 Avenger Torpedo Bomber, Military History, 2013.
15. *Ibid.*, Douglas SBD-2 Dauntless.
16. SB2U Vindicator, Pacific War Online, 2013.
17. Naval History and Heritage Command, Brewster *Buffalo*, 2013.
18. World War II: Martin B-26 *Marauder*.
19. Boeing B-17E *Flying Fortress*, www.historyofwar.org/articles/weapons_B-17E.html.
20. Emmanuel Gustin, Consolidated PBY Catalina, 2013.

Appendix II

1. Parshall and Tully, *Shattered Sword*, 462–463.
2. *Ibid.*, 466–470.
3. *Ibid.*, 470.
4. *Ibid.*, 471.
5. *Ibid.*, 480–481.
6. *Ibid.*, 482–483.
7. *Ibid.*, 479.
8. *Ibid.*, 485–486.
9. *Ibid.*, 484.
10. Robert Cressman, Japanese Submarine I-168 (Wrecksite.eu, 2013).

Bibliography

Ballard, Robert D. *Return to Midway*. Washington, D.C.: Madison Press Books, 1999.
Bradley, John H., Thomas E. Griess, and Jack W. Dice. *The Second World War: Asia and the Pacific*. West Point, NY: Avery Publishing, 1984.
Carlson, Elliot. *Joe Rochefort's War*. Annapolis, MD: U.S. Naval Institute Press, 2011.
Chang, Iris. *The Rape of Nanking*. New York: Basic Books, 1997.
Churchill, Winston. *The Hinge of Fate*. London: Penguin Classics, 2005.
Cressman, Robert J. *A Magnificent Fight*. Annapolis, MD: U.S. Naval Institute Press, 1995.
Cressman, Robert J., et al. *A Glorious Page in Our History*. Missoula, MT: Pictorial Histories, 1990.
Dull, Paul S. *A Battle History of the Imperial Japanese Navy*. Annapolis, MD: U.S. Naval Institute Press, 1998.
Durant, Will. *The Story of Civilization*. Norwalk, CT: Easton Press, 1935.
Fuchida, Mitsuo, and Masatake Okumiya. *Midway*. New York: Ballantine, 1955.
Glines, Carroll. *The Doolittle Raid*. Atglen, PA: Schiffer Military/Aviation History, 1991.
Hanson, Victor Davis. *What If?* New York: Putnam, 1999.
Haufler, Herme. *Codebreakers*. New York: New American Library, 2003.
Hughes, Wayne P., Jr., USN (Ret.). *Fleet Tactics*. Annapolis, MD: U.S. Naval Institute Press, 1986.
Jansen, Marius. *The Making of Modern Japan*. Cambridge, MA: Belknap Press, 2000.
Jenkins, Robert. *World War 2: Pearl Harbor through Japanese Eyes*. New York: Center for International Training and Education, 2015. Kindle edition.
Keegan, John. *The Price of Admiralty*. New York: Penguin, 1988.
Layton, Rear Admiral Edwin T., Captain Pineau Roger, and John Costello. *And I Was There*. New York: Morrow, 1985.
Lee, Bruce. *Marching Orders*. New York: Crown, 1995.
Lundstrom, John B. *Black Shoe Carrier Admiral*. Annapolis, MD: U.S. Naval Institute Press, 2006.
———. *The First Team*. Annapolis, MD: U.S. Naval Institute Press, 1984.
Martin, James J. *Beyond Pearl Harbor: Essays on Some Historic Consequences of the Crisis in the Pacific in 1941*. Ontario: Planshare Press, 1983.
Moore, Steven L. *Pacific Payback: The Carrier Aviators Who Avenged Pearl Harbor at the Battle of Midway*. New York: Penguin, 2015.
Morison, Samuel Eliot. *Coral Sea, Midway and Submarine Actions*. Boston: Little, Brown, 1985.
Mrazek, Robert J. *A Dawn Like Thunder: The True Story of Torpedo Squadron Eight*. New York: Little, Brown, 2008.
Parshall, Jonathan, and Anthony Tully. *Shattered Sword*. Washington, D.C.: Potomac Press, 2005.
Perry, Commodore M.C. *Narrative of the Expedition to the China Seas and Japan*. Mineola, NY: Dover, 2000.
Pfennigwerth, Ian. *Man of Intelligence: The Life of Captain Eric Nave, Australian Codebreaker*. Dural Delivery Centre, NSW, Australia: Rosenberg Publishers, 2000.
Polmar, Norman. *Aircraft Carriers*. Dulles, VA: Potomac Books, 2008.
Smith, Page. *The History of America*. Norwalk, CT: Easton Press, 1982.
Stille, Mark. *The Coral Sea 1942*. Oxford: Osprey Publishing, 2000.
Stinnett, Robert B. *Day of Deceit*. New York: Free Press, 2000.
Symonds, Craig L. *The Battle of Midway*. New York: Oxford University Press, 2011.
Toland, John. *The Rising Sun*. New York: Modern Library, 2005.

Ugaki, Admiral Matome. *Fading Victory*. Pittsburgh, PA: University of Pittsburg Press, 1991.
United States Navy. *Aerology and Naval Warfare*. CreateSpace, 2012.
Van Der Vat, Dan. *Pearl Harbor*. Toronto: Madison Press Books, 2001.
Walsh, George. *The Battle of Midway: Searching for the Truth*. CreateSpace, 2015.
Wukovits, John. *Admiral "Bull" Halsey: The Life and Wars of the Navy's Most Controversial Commander*. New York: Palgrave Macmillan 2010.

Index

Abe, Rear Admiral Hiroaki (IJN) 119, 139, 142
Adams, Ensign Don (USN) 148
Adams, Lieutenant Samuel (USN) 128, 134, 147
Ady, Lieutenant Howard P. (USN) 48, 79, 80, 121
Aichi D3A1 Type 99 Carrier Bomber (Val) 70, 185
Aichi E13A1 Type 00 reconnaissance float plane (Jake) 74, 186
Akagi (Japanese aircraft carrier) 17, 25, 30, 42, 45, 55, 57, 58, 59, 63, 70, 71, 72, 74, 78, 79
Akebono Maru (Japanese tanker) 70
Amagai, Commander Takahisa (IJN) 127
Amari, Petty Officer First Class Hiroshi (IJN) 74, 76, 91, 93, 96, 105
Aoki, Captain Taijiro (IJN) 117, 118, 127, 138
Arashi (Japanese destroyer) 93, 96, 109, 110, 112, 125, 133, 147
Arashio (Japanese destroyer) 150, 153
Ariga, Captain Kosaku (IJN) 144
Asashio (Japanese destroyer) 147, 150, 153
Attu and Kiska 44, 153

Bagley, Rear Admiral David (USN) 35
Ballard (U.S. seaplane tender) 52, 53
Ballard, Robert 153
Belconnen (U.S. Intelligence Unit in Australia) 117
Best, Lieutenant Richard H. (USN) 88, 109, 115, 117, 127, 135, 136, 149
Blakey, George, Marine Aircraft Group (USAAC) 137
Boeing B-17E Flying Fortress 61, 92, 181
Bottomley, Lieutenant Harold (USN) 117
Brazier, Aviation Radioman Second Class William (USN) 110
Brewster F2A-3 Buffalo fighter 48, 61, 80, 181
Brockman, Lieutenant Commander William H., Jr. (USN) 93, 110
Browning, Captain Miles (USN) 126, 127, 145, 146
Buckmaster, Captain Elliot (USN) 132, 151, 162

Carey, Captain John F. (USMC) 79
Carlson, Elliot 39
Cast (U.S. Intelligence Unit in Corregidor) 32
Chase, Lieutenant William E. (USN) 80
Cheek, Machinist Tom F. (USN) 108, 123
Chikuma (Japanese heavy cruiser) 45, 57, 60, 74, 76, 135, 136, 145, 150; Number 1 plane 78, 90, 91, 93, 94, 124, 133; Number 4 plane 124; Number 5 plane 73, 74, 120, 122, 123, 125, 128
Childers, Lloyd, Aviation Radioman Third Class (USN) 110
Churchill, Prime Minister Winston 171
Collins, Captain William F., Jr. (USAAC) 81, 89
Consolidated PBY-5/5A Catalina 48, 182

Coral Sea, Battle of 12, 14, 16, 17, 18, 24, 25, 28, 33, 154, 156, 159, 160, 161, 166
Corl, Machinist Harry (USN) 110
Crace, Rear Admiral John (USN) 17, 19, 21
Cressman, Robert, et al. 38, 118, 146
Crommelin, Lieutenant Richard (USN) 97

Doolittle Raid 9, 10, 14, 17, 26, 38, 160
Douglas SBD-2/3 Dauntless 48, 61, 70, 81, 92, 180, 181
Douglas TBD-1 Devastator 180

Earnest, Ensign Albert (USN) 188
Egusa, Lieutenant Commander Takeshige (IJN) 78, 84–85, 95, 96, 113, 114, 115, 117, 118, 120, 121, 122, 136, 138, 139, 144, 155, 166, 167, 172, 183
Enterprise (U.S. aircraft carrier) 10, 14, 17, 18, 19, 24, 31, 36, 38, 43, 52, 53, 57, 61, 73, 76, 78, 86, 91, 102, 107, 111, 112, 113, 114, 118, 122, 124, 125, 133, 134, 136, 145, 146, 147, 148, 149, 154, 155, 157, 158, 159, 160, 162, 163, 164, 165, 178
Esders, Radio Electrician William (USN) 110

Fabian, Lieutenant Rudy (USN) 36
Ferrier, Aviation Radioman Third Class Harry (USN) 88
Fieberling, Lieutenant Langdon (USN) 53, 81

Index

Fisher, Ensign Clayton (USN) 101
Fitch, Rear Admiral Audrey (USN) 28
Fleming, Captain Richard (USMC) 145
Fletcher, Rear Admiral Frank Jack (USN) 16, 19, 43, 53, 70, 79, 80, 91, 97, 121, 137, 161, 163, 165
Ford, John 52
French Frigate Shoals 31, 43, 151
Fuchida, Commander Mitsuo (IJN) 53, 63, 79, 94, 118, 124, 157
Fujita, Captain Isamu (IJN) 144, 145
Fukudome, Rear Admiral Shigeru (IJN) 54

Gaido, Aviation Machinist's Mate Second Class Bruno (USN) 122
Gallaher, Lieutenant Wilmer (USN) 88, 108, 113, 116, 134, 135
Gay, Ensign George (USN) 106
Genda, Commander Minoru (IJN) 26, 57, 119
Goto, Rear Admiral Antonio (IJN) 20
Gray, Lieutenant (VF-6) James S. (USN) 97, 100, 107, 149
Gray, Lieutenant Richard (USN) 88
Grumman F4F-3/-4 Wildcat 48, 61, 80, 81, 99, 180
Grumman TBF-1 Avenger 53, 61, 81, 181

Hagikaze (Japanese destroyer) 128, 137
Halsey, Vice Admiral William F., Jr. (USN) 28, 29, 31 32, 36, 38, 39, 40, 41
Hammann (U.S. Destroyer) 43, 110, 151, 152, 167
Hara, Rear Admiral Chuichi (IJN) 19, 20
Haruna (Japanese battleship) 57, 60, 74, 125, 128, 135
Hashimoto, Lieutenant Toshio (IJN) 126, 129, 135
Henderson, Major Lofton (USMC) 48, 81, 93, 143
Hill, Ensign C.R. (USN) 101
Hiryu (Japanese aircraft carrier) 17, 30, 42, 45, 55, 58, 59, 71, 72, 74, 77, 78, 79, 82, 84, 85, 93, 95, 96, 110, 113, 114, 115, 116, 118, 119, 120, 122, 123, 124, 125, 126, 128, 133, 134, 135, 136, 137, 138, 139, 141, 144, 146, 147, 158, 166, 167, 172, 184
Holmes, Lieutenant Wilfred Jasper (USN) 34
Hornet (U.S. aircraft carrier) 10, 12, 14, 17, 18, 19, 24, 31, 36, 43, 52, 53, 57, 61, 73, 76, 78, 81, 86, 91, 96, 97, 98, 100, 101, 102, 108, 111, 124, 125, 134, 136, 145, 146, 147, 148, 150, 154, 155, 157, 158, 159 160, 162, 165, 178
Hosho 58, 152
Hosogaya, Vice Admiral Moshiro (IJN) 44
Hughes, Captain Wayne, Jr. (USN) 58, 155, 156
Hypo (U.S. Intelligence Unit) 30, 31, 34, 36, 37
Hyuga (Japanese battleship) 58, 60

I-168 (Japanese submarine) 53, 143, 151, 187
HMS *Illustrious* (British aircraft carrier) 35
HMS *Indomitable* (British aircraft carrier) 35
Ingersoll, Lieutenant Royal (USN) 126
Inoue, Vice Admiral Shigeyoshi (IJN) 13, 28, 29
Ise (Japanese battleship) 58, 60
Itaya, Lieutenant Commander Shigeru (IJN) 78

Jaccard, Ensign Richard (USN) 135
JN-25B Japanese code 34, 56
Johnson, Lieutenant Commander Robert (USN) 88, 101, 103, 104, 126, 134, 148
Junyo (Japanese light carrier) 26, 44, 51, 58, 66, 67, 120, 155, 159

Kaga (Japanese aircraft carrier) 17, 25, 30, 45, 55, 58, 59, 71, 72, 74, 78, 79, 84, 95, 96, 107, 113, 114, 115, 116, 117, 121, 122, 127, 128, 136, 137, 138, 139, 143, 155, 167, 172, 183
Kaku, Captain Tomeo (IJN) 144, 145, 146
Kakuta, Rear Admiral Kakuji (IJN) 44, 67
Kayahara, Petty Officer Third Class Yoshihiro (IJN) 84
Keegan, John 161
Kelly, Ensign Markland (USN) 101, 104
King, Admiral Earnest J. (USN) 16, 17, 29, 31, 33, 34, 36, 103
Kirishima (Japanese battleship) 60, 79, 93, 110, 125
Kleiss, Lieutenant Norman (USN) 136
Kobayashi, Lieutenant Michio (IJN) 119, 122, 123, 124
Komatsu, Vice Admiral Marquis (IJN) 54, 55
Kondo, Vice Admiral Nobutake (IJN) 13, 26, 30, 46, 120, 125, 139, 141, 144, 147, 149, 150, 152, 153
Kroger, Lieutenant Edwin (USN) 117
Kure's Special Landing Forces 70
Kurita, Vice Admiral Takeo (IJN) 46, 139, 141
Kuroshima, Captain Kameto (IJN) 11, 54, 74
Kusaka, Rear Admiral Ryunosuke (IJN) 63, 64, 118, 143

Layton, Lieutenant Commander Elwin T. (USN) 30, 37, 38
Leslie, Lieutenant Commander Maxwell F. (USN) 97, 108, 115, 117, 134
Lexington (U.S. aircraft carrier) 10, 14, 20, 21, 22, 23, 24, 25, 33, 58, 97, 114, 160, 177
Lindsey, Lieutenant Commander Eugene E. (USN) 88, 97, 106, 107
Lord, Walter 38, 112
Louisiades 18
Lundstrom, John 38
Lyle, Ensign James (USN) 68

Maikaze (Japanese destroyer) 128
Manning, Seaman First Class Jay (USN) 88
Marshall, General George, USA 36
Martin B-26 Marauder 52, 61, 81, 92, 181
Maruyama, Petty Officer First Class Taisuke (IJN) 70
Mason, Commander Redfield (USN) 33

Index

Massey, Lieutenant Commander Lance E. (USN) 97, 108, 110
McClusky, Lieutenant Commander Clarence W. (USN) 88, 100, 107, 108, 109, 112, 113, 126, 134, 146, 149, 163
McCormick, Captain Lynde (USN) 38
McInerney, Ensign John E. (USN) 100, 104
Midway Atoll 19, 26, 73
Mikuma (Japanese heavy cruiser) 142, 145, 147, 148, 149, 150, 152, 167
Mitchell, Lieutenant Commander Samuel G. (USN) 86, 97, 98, 100, 103, 104
Mitsubishi A6M2 Carrier Fighter (Zero) 74, 186
Miyo, Commander Tatsukichi (IJN) 12
Mori, Lieutenant Shigeru (IJN) 84, 133
Morinaga, Warrant Officer Takaoshi (IJN) 115
Murakami, Petty Officer Second Class Toshiko (IJN) 72
Murata, Lieutenant Commander Shigeharu (IJN) 78
Muri, First Lieutenant James P. (USAAC) 89
Murphy, Lieutenant Commander John (USN) 142, 143

Nagano, Admiral Osami (IJN) 14, 44, 51
Nagara (Japanese light cruiser) 60, 79, 120, 124, 125, 143, 144, 185
Nagumo, Vice Admiral Chuichi (IJN) 13, 26, 45, 55, 57, 61, 62, 63, 64, 73, 74, 76, 77, 78, 79, 85, 91, 92, 93, 94, 95, 86, 105, 16, 118, 120, 121, 124, 125, 128, 13, 138, 139, 141, 142, 147, 155, 156, 157, 160, 183
Nakagawa, Warrant Officer Shizo (IJN) 123
Nakajima B5N2 Japanese torpedo bomber 71, 74, 131
Nakajima E8N2 (Japanese reconnaissance float plane) 74, 186
Nautilus (U.S. submarine) 93, 96, 109, 110, 112, 122, 128, 162, 179
Neosho (U.S. oil tanker) 20, 28

Newell, Lieutenant Dale (USN) 147
Nimitz, Admiral Chester W. (USN) 16, 17, 24, 29, 31, 32, 35, 36, 37, 38, 42, 44, 50, 52, 100, 103, 104, 127, 137, 165
Nitto Maru (Japanese cargo ship) 10
Nobuki, Commander Ogawa (IJN) 150
Norris, Captain Benjamin (USMC) 81, 143

Ochi, Petty Officer First Class Masatake (IJN) 84
O'Flaherty, Ensign Frank (USN) 122
Ogawa, Lieutenant Shoichi (IJN) 72
Oishi, Captain Tomatsu (IJN) 62, 64
Okada, Captain Jisaku (IJN) 127
Okumiya, Lieutenant Commander Masatake (IJN) 63, 79 94
Omori, Rear Admiral Sentaro (IJN) 44
OP-20-G (U.S. Navy's World War II signals intelligence and cryptanalysis group) 29, 31, 34, 36, 37
Operation K 30, 32, 54, 55, 63, 159
Osmus, Ensign Wesley F. (USN) 77, 125, 126, 133
Owens, Lieutenant James (USN) 105

Pacific Command Cable 35
Parks, Major Floyd (USMC) 81
Parshall, Jonathan, and Anthony Tully 39, 44, 94, 112, 118, 124, 137, 152, 155, 162, 169, 172
Pederson, Lieutenant Commander Oscar (USN) 97
Perry, Commodore Matthew C. (USN) 9
Point Luck 43, 52
Port Moresby 18, 24, 64, 154, 160
Prange, Gordon 112
PT Boats 52, 84, 179

Ramsey, Captain Logan (USN) 68
Ranger (U.S. aircraft carrier) 172, 173

Redman, Commander John (USN) 16, 34, 164
Redman, Captain Joseph (USN) 34
Reid, Ensign Jewell H. (Jack) (USN) 68
Ring, Lieutenant Commander Stanhope C. (USN) 86, 97, 98, 100, 101, 102, 103, 104, 146, 148, 150
Rochefort, Lieutenant Commander Joseph J. (USN) 16, 17, 30, 31, 32, 34, 37, 164, 165
Rodee, Lieutenant Commander Walter (USN) 86, 101, 102, 103, 104, 134, 148, 150
Ruehlow, Lieutenant Stanley (USN) 101
Ryujo (Japanese light carrier) 26, 44, 51, 58, 66, 120, 155, 159

Sakamoto, Petty Officer First Class Noriyoshi (IJN) 84
Sakiyama, Captain Shakao (IJN) 148, 149
Saratoga (U.S. aircraft carrier) 19, 33, 50, 52, 53, 58, 97, 115, 172, 173, 177
Schlesinger, James 170
Sheedy, Ensign Daniel (USN) 126
Shoho (Japanese aircraft carrier) 18, 19, 20, 58, 184
Shokaku (Japanese aircraft carrier) 16, 17, 18, 19, 20, 21, 22, 23, 24, 25, 26, 27, 33, 51, 52, 58, 60, 64, 114, 115, 154, 155, 156, 159, 161, 162, 172, 184
Short, Lieutenant Wallace (USN) 97, 145, 146, 149
Shumway, Lieutenant Dewitt (USN) 135, 145, 146 147
Simard, Captain Cyril T. (USN) 35, 68, 80, 143, 145
Sims (U.S. destroyer) 20
Sixth Marine Defense Battalion 48
Soji, Captain Akira (IJN) 148
Somerwell, General Brehan, USA 169
Soryu (Japanese aircraft carrier) 17, 30, 42, 45, 55, 58, 71, 72, 73, 74, 76, 79, 84, 93, 95, 96, 110, 113, 115, 117, 119, 121, 122, 127, 136, 137, 138, 144, 163, 167
Soucek, Captain Apollo (USN) 98

Index

Spruance, Rear Admiral Raymond A. (USN) 38, 43, 79, 88, 91, 103, 106, 112, 126, 127, 134, 137, 138, 145, 146, 147, 148, 150, 153, 165, 172, 183
Stafford, Captain Laurence (USN) 34
Stark, Admiral Harold (USN) 35
Stebbins, Lieutenant Edgar (USN) 134
Suganami, Lieutenant Masaji (IJN) 72
Susumu, Warrant Officer Nishimori (IJN) 132
Sweeney, Lieutenant Colonel Walter C. (USAAC) 68, 137
Symonds, Craig 39, 103, 146, 152

Takagi, Rear Admiral Takeo (IJN) 20, 28
Takezaki, Petty Officer First Class Masake (IJN) 76
Tambor (U.S. Submarine) 142, 143
Tanabe, Lieutenant Commander Yahachi (IJN) 53, 143, 151, 152
Tanaka, Captain Kikumatsu (IJN) 142
Tanaka, Rear Admiral Raizo (IJN) 46, 64
Tanakaze (Japanese destroyer) 146, 147
TF-8 50, 67
TF-16 68, 80, 86, 88, 91, 96, 133, 147, 165
TF-17 68, 91, 96
TF-44 17, 18, 19
Thatch, Lieutenant Commander John S. (Jimmy) (USN) 97, 108
Theobold, Rear Admiral Robert (USN) 51, 67

Tomeo, Captain Kaku (IJN) 136
Tomioka, Captain Sadatoshi (IJN) 12
Tomonaga, Lieutenant Joichi (IJN) 72, 81, 85, 93, 94, 95, 125, 16, 129, 131, 134
Tone (Japanese heavy cruiser) 45, 57, 60, 74, 96, 107, 136, 150; Number 1 plane 124; Number 4 plane 73, 91, 92, 94, 120, 133, 157
Tucker Lieutenant, Alfred (USN) 101, 150
Tulagi 18
Tully, Anthony, and Jonathan Parshall 39, 44, 94, 112, 118, 124, 137, 152, 155, 162, 169, 172
Turner, Rear Admiral Richmond (USN) 33
Tyler, Captain Marshall (USN) 145

Ueno, Lieutenant Commander Toshitake (IJN) 54
Ugaki, Rear Admiral Matome (IJN) 11, 25, 64, 65, 74, 139, 141

Vaughan, Dr. Warren W. 40
Vireo (U.S. minesweeper) 151
VMF-221 49, 80, 81
VMSB-241 48, 49, 84
Vought SB2U-3 Vindicator 49, 61, 81, 181
VP-23 48, 52, 79, 80
VP-44 48, 79, 147

Waldron, Lieutenant Commander John (USN) 86, 88, 98, 100, 102, 103, 104, 105, 106, 107, 108
Ware, Lieutenant Charles (USN) 122
Wasp (U.S. aircraft carrier) 58, 172, 173, 178

Watanabe, Commander Yasumasa (IJN) 12, 110, 125, 133
Weber, Ensign Fred (USN) 118, 135
Weisheit, Bowen 104
Wright, Lieutenant Ham (USN) 37

Yamaguchi, Rear Admiral Tamon (IJN) 76, 95, 120, 121, 124, 125, 128, 135, 141, 144, 145, 146, 157
Yamamoto, Admiral Isoroku (IJN) 11, 12, 13, 14, 16, 24, 28, 44, 51, 53, 55, 56, 57, 61, 62, 63, 64, 65, 74, 96, 119, 125, 139, 142, 143, 144, 147, 148, 150, 152, 154, 156, 158, 159, 160, 161
Yamato (Japanese battleship) 37, 45, 62, 144
Yanagimoto, Captain Ryusaka (IJN) 127
Yokosuka D4Y1 Type 13 experimental carrier bomber 73, 74, 76, 77, 95, 120, 126, 133, 135, 155, 158
Yorktown (U.S. aircraft carrier) 12, 14, 18, 20, 22, 23, 28, 36, 43, 49, 50, 52, 58, 61, 62, 70, 73, 74, 76, 77, 78, 85, 90, 91, 93, 95, 96, 97, 108, 111, 112, 113, 114, 117, 118, 122, 123, 125, 128, 129, 131, 132, 133, 135, 146, 157, 158, 160, 162, 163, 165, 166, 173, 177

Zuiho (Japanese light carrier) 30, 46, 58, 125, 147, 149, 150, 151, 152, 153
Zuikaku (Japanese aircraft carrier) 16, 17, 18, 19, 20, 21, 22, 23, 24, 25, 26, 27, 28, 31, 32, 42, 51, 52, 58, 60, 64, 154, 155, 156, 159, 161, 162, 172, 184